FOR REFERENCE

Do Not Take From This Room

U•X•L ENCYCLOPEDIA OF

water science

U·X·L ENCYCLOPEDIA OF

water science

Volume 2
Economics and Uses

K. Lee Lerner and Brenda Wilmoth Lerner, Editors

Lawrence W. Baker, Project Editor

U·X·L

An imprint of Thomson Gale, a part of The Thomson Corporation

THOMSON
GALE

Detroit • New York • San Francisco • San Diego • New Haven, Conn. • Waterville, Maine • London • Munich

U•X•L Encyclopedia of Water Science

K. Lee Lerner and Brenda Wilmoth Lerner, Editors

Project Editor
Lawrence W. Baker

Editorial
Charles B. Montney

Permissions
Denise Buckley, Shalice Shah-Caldwell, Ann Taylor

Imaging and Multimedia
Lezlie Light, Kelly A. Quin, Dan Newell

Product Design
Jennifer Wahi

Composition
Evi Seoud

Manufacturing
Rita Wimberley

LIBRARY OF CONGRESS CATALOGING-IN-PUBLICATION DATA

UXL encyclopedia of water science / K. Lee Lerner and Brenda Wilmoth Lerner, editors ; Lawrence W. Baker, project editor.
    p. cm.
    Includes bibliographical references and index.
    ISBN 0-7876-7617-9 (set : hardcover : alk. paper) — ISBN 0-7876-7673-X (v. 1 : hardcover : alk. paper) — ISBN 0-7876-7674-8 (v. 2 : hardcover : alk. paper) — ISBN 0-7876-7675-6 (v. 3 : hardcover : alk. paper)
    1. Water—Encyclopedias, Juvenile. 2. Hydrology—Encyclopedias, Juvenile. I. Lerner, K. Lee. II. Lerner, Brenda Wilmoth. III. Baker, Lawrence W.

GB662.3.U95 2005
553.7—dc22   2004021651

This title is also available as an e-book.
ISBN 0-7876-9398-7 (set)
Contact your Thomson Gale sales representative for ordering information.

Printed in the United States of America
10 9 8 7 6 5 4 3 2

Contents

Reader's Guide

Water is important and special because it takes part in almost all of the processes that form and shape the Earth. Water is also essential to life. Without water, life—in all its many forms—would not be possible. The study of water science helps toward understanding how and why water plays such an important role.

Water also unites and divides us. Water is the subject of numerous treaties, laws, and agreements between nations, states, and communities. However, because water is an increasingly important and scarce resource, there are often complex legal and political issues surrounding the use of water. Many wars and court cases have arisen over who owns a body of water, who has a right to use it, or how water should be divided and used among those who claim it. To assure an adequate supply of water to meet broad needs of humans around the world, the development of scientifically sound strategies for sustainable water development are critical.

In many cases, disputes over water are related to preserving the quality of waters that nourish and protect both human and natural communities. To better understand these issues, one also needs to know the essentials of water science.

Scope and format

U•X•L Encyclopedia of Water Science takes an international perspective in exploring water science and water issues. The encyclopedia features more than one hundred entries in three volumes, with each volume broken into separate chapters:

Volume 1 (Science): Basics of water science; Oceans and saltwater; Fresh water; Estuaries and wetlands; Ice; Water, weather, and climates

Volume 2 (Economics and Uses): Science and technology; Science and research; Economic uses of water; Recreational uses of water; History and culture

Volume 3 (Issues): Environmental issues; Legal and political issues

Within each chapter, entries are arranged alphabetically. Among the topics covered in Volume 1 are the Hydrologic cycle; Kelp and seaweed; Lakes; Wetlands; Glaciers; and Clouds. Volume 2 covers Dams and reservoirs; Marine biology; Petroleum exploration and recovery; Tourism on the oceans; Dangerous waters; and Exploration of the oceans. And Volume 3 includes topics such as Acid rain; Groundwater issues; Oil spills; Sediment contamination; Endangered species laws; and Exclusive economic zones.

Each entry provides definitions for scientific terms and sources for further research. In addition, a general glossary, a research and activities section, and a cumulative index to the set are included in each volume. Numerous sidebars highlight significant facts and describe water-related activities. More than 150 black-and-white photos—as well as a different set of color photo inserts in each volume—help illustrate *U•X•L Encyclopedia of Water Science.*

Acknowledgments

In compiling this edition, the editors have been fortunate in being able to rely upon the expertise and contributions of the following scholars who served as academic advisors, contributing advisors, and writers for *U•X•L Encyclopedia of Water Science:*

Juli Berwald, Ph.D., Geologist (ocean sciences), Chicago, Illinois

Marcy Davis, M.S., Science writer, Austin, Texas

Laurie Duncan, Ph.D., Marine geologist, Austin, Texas

Brian D. Hoyle, Ph.D., Microbiologist, Halifax, Nova Scotia, Canada

Joseph P. Hyder, University of Tennessee College of Law, Knoxville, Tennessee

Adrienne Wilmoth Lerner, University of Tennessee College of Law, Knoxville, Tennessee

Todd Minehardt, Ph.D., Science writer, Austin, Texas

Yavor Shopov, Ph.D., President, Commission on Physical Chemistry and Hydrogeology of Karst, Institute of Statistics, UNESCO, Sofia, Bulgaria

The editors extend special thanks to Carol Nagel and Meggin Condino at Thomson Gale for their invaluable advice and faith in our efforts. Finally, and most importantly, the editors would like to thank U•X•L senior editor Larry Baker. His dedication, skill, and creativity were essential to the production of this book.

Additional thanks go to copyeditor Mya Nelson, proofreader Erin Braun, indexer Sandi Schroeder of Schroeder Indexing Services, and typesetter Datapage Technologies International, Inc., for their fine work.

Dedication

The editors lovingly dedicate this book to the brave men and women of the U.S. Navy and the U.S. Coast Guard.

"The sea, washing the equator and the poles, offers its perilous aid, and the power and empire that follow it.... 'Beware of me,' it says, 'but if you can hold me, I am the key to all the lands.'" —Ralph Waldo Emerson (1803–1882), *The Conduct of Life,* "Wealth"

Comments and suggestions

We welcome your comments on *U•X•L Encyclopedia of Water Science.* Please write: Editors, *U•X•L Encyclopedia of Water Science,* U•X•L, 27500 Drake Rd., Farmington Hills, MI 48331; call toll-free: 1-800-877-4253; fax: 248-699-8097; or send e-mail via http://www.gale.com.

K. Lee Lerner and Brenda Wilmoth Lerner, editors

Words to Know

A

Abiotic: Nonliving part of the environment.

Abyssal plain: Vast, flat areas of the deep-ocean floor.

Abyssopelagic zone: The deep ocean that extends from 13,000 feet (4,000 meters) below the surface to the seafloor.

Acid deposition: The collective term for dry deposition and wet deposition of acids as a result of air pollution.

Acid rain: The result of acidic chemicals reacting in the atmosphere with water and returning to Earth as contaminated rain, fog, or snow.

Aeration: Adding oxygen, nitrogen, and other gasses necessary for respiration into water.

Agar: A mixture of sugars found in some types of seaweed that can form a solid surface used in laboratories to grow bacteria.

Air mass: Large body of air with only small variations of temperature, pressure, and moisture.

Air pressure: Force exerted by the weight of a column of air above a particular location.

Algae: Fresh and salt water plants that can convert the Sun's energy into food; they range in size from microscopic cells to forms that are bigger than a person.

Algal bloom: The rapid and huge increase in numbers of algae that can occur in the presence of a food source such as phosphorus.

Alpine glacier: Mass of moving ice that is confined by mountain valleys.

Ambergris: A highly prized fat found in the intestines of some whales.

Anadromous: Fish that are born in fresh water and then move to marine water as adults.

Annelid: A segmented worm such as an earthworm or a polychaete worm.

Antarctic ice cap: Ice covering the continent of Antarctic and Southern Ocean region around the South Pole.

Anticyclone: An atmospheric system associated with dry, clear weather with winds that spiral out away from a center of high atmospheric pressure.

Aquarist: Person who keeps an aquarium.

Aquatic: Relating to water.

Aqueduct: A channel or conduit, usually resembling a bridge, that carries water on land or over a valley, from a higher point to a lower one.

Aquiclude: Permeable (leaky) layers of rock or soil that confine and pressurize groundwater within aquifers.

Aquifer: An underground rock formation that contains water.

Archaeological context: The natural surroundings, physical location, and cultural origin of archaeological artifacts or sites.

Archimedes principle of buoyancy: An object submerged in a fluid is pushed upward by a buoyant force equal to the weight of the fluid it displaces.

Arctic: Region of the Earth between the North Pole and the Arctic circle.

Arctic Circle: Invisible circle around the North Pole above latitude at 66°33' North.

Arctic ice cap: Ice covering the Arctic Ocean and land areas north of the Arctic Circle in the North Pole.

Arid: Lack of rainfall. An arid climate has an annual rainfall of only 10 inches or less per year.

Artesian flow: Water that rises to the land surface from confined aquifers without pumping.

Arthropod: A member of a group of invertebrates that has jointed appendages and an external skeleton.

Artifact: Any object made or modified by humans.

Atmosphere: A unit to measure pressure; one atmosphere is 14.7 pounds per square inch, which is the standard atmospheric pressure measured at sea level.

Atmospheric (barometric) pressure: Pressure caused by the weight of the atmosphere over a surface or object.

Atoll: Ring-shaped coral island that surrounds a shallow lagoon.

Atom: The smallest unit that has all the chemical and physical characteristics of an element.

Autecology: Ecological study of individual organisms or individual species.

Autonomous underwater vehicle (AUV): Remote-controlled motorized crafts that are designed to study and withstand the pressure of the deep ocean.

Autotroph: Organism that uses inorganic substances to produce energy.

B

Bacterioplankton: Plankton composed of bacteria, often serving as the basis of the aquatic food chain.

Baleen: Bristly plates that hang from the upper jaws of baleen whales; acts like a sieve for the microscopic animals during feeding.

Ballast water: Water that is pumped into the hull of a ship to keep the ship balanced correctly in the water when it is empty.

Barge: Large, usually flat boat used for shipping.

Barometer: An instrument used to measure atmospheric pressure.

Barrage: Artificial obstruction such as a dam constructed in a water channel to increase water depth or divert flow.

Barrier Island: Long, narrow coastal island built up parallel to the mainland.

Basalt: Black iron- and magnesium-rich volcanic rock common in ocean basins.

Base level: The water level at the outlet of a stream, usually sea level; streams cannot erode below this level.

Bathymetry: The three-dimensional shape of the seafloor.

Bathypelagic zone: The layer of the ocean below the mesopelagic zone and above the abyssopelagic zone; generally it extends between 3,250 feet (1,000 meters) and 13,000 feet (4,000 meters) below the surface of the ocean.

Bathyscaphe: A submersible vehicle that is capable of going to the deepest parts of the ocean and withstanding extreme pressure.

Beach: Region of sand or rock that slopes down to the water of a lake or ocean.

Benthic: Animals, plants, and microorganisms that live on the floor of the ocean.

Bioaccumulation: Tendency for substances to increase in concentration in living organisms as they take in contaminated air, water, or food.

Biodiversity: The variety of living organisms and the ecosystems in which they occur.

Bioluminescence: Light that is generated by chemical reactions in bacteria, animals, and plants.

Bioremediation: The use of living organisms such as bacteria to remove pollutants from natural resources, such as water.

Biosphere: All the biological communities (ecosystems) that exist in the world.

Biotic: Living part of the environment.

Black smoker: Underwater seep of volcanic magma that deposits minerals.

Boreal forests: Treed areas of the northern temperate regions of North America, Europe, and Asia that are dominated by evergreen trees like firs, pines, and spruces.

Brackish: Water with a salinity (salt content) between that of freshwater and ocean water.

Braided stream: Streams with many channels that split apart and rejoin.

Brine: Water that contains a high concentration of salt.

Bulk carrier: A ship that carries large quantities of raw material, such as steel, timber, or grain, in large cargo holds.

Buoyancy: Ability of an object to float in a liquid.

Buoyant force: Upward force exerted by a liquid on an object; an object will float if the buoyant force of the liquid is greater than the downward force of gravity.

C

Caldera lake: Lake filling a large circular depression left by a volcanic eruption or collapse.

Canal: Man-made or artificially improved waterway used for travel, shipping, irrigation, or hydropower.

Canoe: Boat pointed at both ends and typically with an open top, or deck.

Carbonate: Rock or loose sediment composed of the mineral calcite or calcium carbonate.

Cargo: Goods that are being transported.

Cargo hold: A section of a ship that is divided from other sections for the transport of a single type of cargo.

Cartilage: Tough but flexible material, found between bones in humans and in the skeletons of sharks and rays.

Cetacean: A member of the group of marine mammals that includes whales, dolphins, and porpoises.

Channel: The water-filled path of the stream, river, or man-made waterway.

Chemical oceanology: Study of the molecules and atoms that are dissolved in the ocean.

Chemistry: The science of the composition, structure, and properties of matter.

Chemosynthesis: The use of chemicals, rather than sunlight, for the production of food.

Cistern: A man-made reservoir for storing water.

Clearcut: The total removal of trees and much of the vegetation from a section of forest.

Climate: Long-term meteorological conditions or average weather.

Climate effect: Temperature and moisture patterns that characterize a large region over tens, hundreds, or even thousands of years.

Climate zone: Areas of the world with a characteristic climate. Climate zones are described as arid, Mediterranean, mountain, polar, temperate, and tropical.

Cnidarian: A member of a group of invertebrates that includes corals, jellyfish, and sea anemones; these organisms have stinging cells to capture prey.

Coastal zone: The shallow part of the ocean extending from the high-tide mark on land to the edge of the continental shelf.

Coastline: The land that lies next to the sea.

Commercially extinct: When an animal becomes too rare to be worth hunting.

Community: All of the organisms that live in a certain locations.

Compound: Substance in which two or more elements are joined together.

Computer model: Description of a system, theory, or phenomenon entered into a computer that includes its known properties and conditions and can be used to predict future conditions and events within the system.

Condensation: The transformation (phase change) of a gas to a liquid.

Conservation: Protection, management, or restoration of natural resources such as soil, forests, wetlands, minerals, and water.

Container ship: A ship that transports cargo in sealed containers that may be unloaded directly onto trains or trucks.

Contaminant: Polluting substance that has harmful effects on biological life and other natural systems.

Contamination: Polluted or containing unwanted substances.

Continental glacier: Very large, dome-shaped mass of glacial ice that completely covers the terrain beneath it; also called ice sheet.

Continental shelf: The edge of a continent that gently slopes in relatively shallow water before dropping off steeply to the great depths of the open ocean.

Convection: Circulation of a gas or liquid driven by heat transfer and gravity.

Convention on International Trade in Endangered Species of Wild Fauna and Flora (CITES): A 1973 treaty that restricts international commerce between participating nations for plant and animal species that are believed to be harmed by trade.

Coral: A rocklike deposit formed of the calcium carbonate skeletons of a group of small sea animals.

Coral reef: Tropical marine feature created by numerous colonies of tiny coral animals; coral reefs contain a great diversity of marine animals.

Coriolis effect: The effect of the Earth's rotation on the atmosphere and oceans that causes deflection to the right in the northern hemisphere, and deflection to the left in the southern hemisphere.

Crest: The highest point of a wave. Also, the highest level of floodwaters during a flood.

Cretaceous period: A division of geologic time from 65 to 144 million years ago; along with the Jurassic and Triassic, this period comprised the Mesozoic Era known as "the age of the dinosaurs."

Crevasse: A large crack or fissure in the surface of a glacier.

Cruise ship: A large ship, once used as the primary means of transporting people across an ocean, that now serves as a vacation destination, while visiting various ports of interest.

Crustacean: A member of a group of arthropods that includes brine shrimp, barnacles, copepods, shrimp, lobsters, crabs, and euphausids.

Curation: Cleaning, preserving, and storing artifacts recovered from archaeological sites for further study.

Current: The circulation of ocean waters that produces a steady flow of water in a prevailing direction.

Cyclic changes: Changes that repeat themselves over time.

Cyclone: Rotating atmospheric system of winds that flow into a low-pressure center. Cyclones rotate counterclockwise in the northern hemisphere and clockwise in the southern hemisphere.

D

Dam: A physical barrier constructed across a river or waterway to control the flow or raise the level of water.

Decibel: Unit that measures the loudness or intensity of sound.

Deep-sea fishing: Form of fishing that requires boating several miles out to sea in order to catch fish that live far from shore, such as marlin, tarpon, and barracuda.

Deforestation: Large-scale removal of trees from a woodland.

Delta: The sedimentary deposit that forms at the mouth of a river. Delta means "triangle" in Greek, and river deltas are usually triangular.

Density: The amount of mass-per-unit volume of a substance. In water, density is primarily determined by the combination of salinity and temperature.

Dentricles: V-shaped structures that make up the rough skin of a shark.

Deposition: Process by which dirt, silt, and sand is moved from its original place by wind or water and deposited elsewhere.

Depositional coastline: A coastline formed from the sediment of carbonates, plants, and animals that have hard mineral shells made of calcium carbonate.

Desalination: Process of removing salt from sea water or water contaminated with salt.

Desert: An area of land that receives less than 10 inches (25.4 centimeters) of precipitation per year.

Desertification: Gradual changes that take place over a region or area of land that ultimately result in the formation of a desert.

Detergent: A chemical used as a cleaning agent because it encourages the formation of an oil-in-water emulsion.

Diatoms: Single-celled phytoplankton that produce a thin shell made of silica (glass).

Dinoflagellates: Single-celled phytoplankton that move by propelling whip-like appendages called flagella.

Dipolar molecule: A molecule that has a positive charge at one end and an equal, but opposite, negative charge at the other end.

Discharge zone: Land area where groundwater flows out of aquifers on to land surface.

Dispersant: A chemical agent that reduces the surface tension of liquid hydrocarbons, encouraging the formation of an oil-in-water emulsion. This reduces the volume of residual oil on shorelines or the water surface after a spill.

Dissolution: When water breaks rocks into dissolved chemicals; a form of erosion.

Distillation: The purification of water by heating.

Distributary: Channel of water that runs through deltas.

Diversion: Changing the direction of a water body such as a stream or river by building canals, dams, or channels.

Divide: High point or ridge that separates drainage basins, and in which water flows down in all directions.

Diving suit: Sealed suit that receives a constant supply of air, usually surface air supplied by hoses; used for early ocean dives.

Doldrums: A zone of dead air and still water, usually at the equator where the trade winds and equatorial currents converge.

Downwelling: Ocean zones where surface water sinks into the deep ocean.

Dowsing: Pseudoscientific practice of using alleged spiritual powers and a "divining rod" to locate underground water.

Drag: A force that resists movement.

Drainage basin: Land area from which surface runoff drains into a stream or lake.

Dredge: Device for scooping or digging rock and sediment from the seafloor.

Dredging: A process where a ship drags a hook or grate along the bottom of a waterway in order to remove the accumulated silt and mud.

Drought: A temporary but extended period of abnormally low rainfall.

Dry deposition: Acidic gases and solid particles containing acids that settle out of the air and land on surfaces.

Dynamic equilibrium: State of balance attained by maintaining equal rates of input and withdrawal from a system.

E

Echinoderm: A member of the group of invertebrates that includes feather stars, sea stars, brittle stars, sea urchins, and sea cucumbers.

Echolocation: The ability of dolphins, bats, and some other animals to detect objects and prey by emitting sound waves that bounce off objects and return to the animal's ears or other sensory organ.

Echosounder: A tool that bounces sound waves off the ocean floor to record water depths or create maps of the ocean floor.

Ecology: Study of the relationships among organisms and between organisms and their environment.

Ecosystem: Community of plants and animals that interact with each other and with their physical environment.

Ecotourism: Tourism that focuses on nature and the environment without harming it.

Ectotherm: An animal that has a body temperature similar to that of its environment.

Effluent: Wastewater that has been treated to remove most impurities.

Electrical current: Flow of electricity.

Electromagnetic spectrum: The range of electrical waves of varying wavelengths that make up light. The visible range is only a small portion of the full spectrum.

Electron: A particle with a negative charge that orbits the nucleus of an atom.

Element: A substance that cannot be divided by ordinary chemical means.

Embayment: Indentation in the shoreline that forms a bay.

Endangered: A species that is in danger of becoming extinct within the foreseeable future throughout all or a significant portion of its natural habitat.

Endangered Species Act: Law passed in 1973 that identifies species that face possible extinction and implements measures to prevent extinction; species may be listed as either endangered or threatened under the act.

Endotherm: An animal that can maintain a relatively constant body temperature regardless of its environment.

Endothermic: Chemical reaction or phase change that absorbs energy.

Environmental impact study: A survey conducted to determine if a landfill project could have negative effects on the environment.

Environmental Protection Agency: Federal agency responsible for enforcing laws designed to protect the environment, including air quality, water quality, wetlands, hazardous wastes, and other environmental matters.

Epilimnion: The surface of a lake that extends as deep as light penetrates.

Epipelagic zone: The surface of the ocean where light penetrates; also called the photic zone.

Equatorial current: A sustained pattern of water flowing westward near the equator.

Erosion: Wearing away of soil, rock, sand, or other material by the action of wind and water.

Erosional coastline: A coastline formed by rising tectonic plates that gradually wears away.

Escherichia coli: Type of bacteria that is found in the intestines of warm-blooded animals including humans; some types can cause illness if ingested.

Estuary: Wide part of a river where it nears the sea; where fresh and salt water mix.

Eutrophic: Waters with a good supply of nutrients.

Eutrophication: Proliferation of plant life, especially algae, that results when excess nutrients are added to lake or pond water, which reduces the oxygen content and often causes the death of animals.

Evaporation: The change of liquid water to water vapor.

Exclusive economic zone: A 200-mile (322-kilometer) area extending from a nation's coastline that permits that nation to extract resources such as oil, gas, and fish and to pass laws to protect those resources.

Exothermic: Chemical reaction or phase change that produces heat.

Export: Raw materials or goods that are shipped, traded, or sold to other nations.

Extinction: The total disappearance of a species; the irreversible loss of a living species.

Eye: Small circular area of relative calm at the center of a cyclone.

F

Ferry: Ship that transports cars and people across bodies of water on a regular schedule.

Filtration: The process by which pollutants are removed from water.

Fishing regulations: Restrictions placed on where, when, and how fish may be caught.

Fixed wave power device: Wave power electrical generator that is attached to the seafloor and/or shore.

Fjord: A long, narrow, deep glacial valley flooded by the sea.

Flash flood: Flood that rises and dissipates rapidly with little or no advance warning, usually as the result of intense rainfall over a relatively small area.

Floating wave power device: Wave power electrical generator that is floating in shallow water.

Floodplain: Flat land adjacent to rivers that are subject to flooding during periods of heavy rainfall.

Food chain: Relationship of organisms in an ecosystem in which each member species feeds on other species.

Food web: The predator and prey relationships between animals and plants.

Free diving: Underwater swimming without the use of a breathing apparatus; also known as skin diving or breath-hold diving.

Frond: A long, feathery leaf, or the blade of a kelp plant or sea plant.

Front: The boundary between two air masses of different temperature and humidity.

G

Generator: Machine that converts mechanical energy to electrical energy.

Geothermal: Heat from Earth; energy obtained from the hot areas under the surface of the Earth.

Glacial erratic: Boulders carried by glaciers and deposited away from their original location.

Glacial flour: Sediments that have been crushed and ground into a fine texture beneath a glacier.

Glacial outwash: Sand and gravel deposited by water melting from a glacier.

Glacial till: Sediments, or the rock, gravel, and sand carried and deposited by a glacier.

Glacier: Large mass of moving ice.

Global warming: Increase in the average temperature of the Earth's surface.

Gorge: A deep, narrow ravine, often with a river or stream running through it.

Graben: Rifts or holes formed when tectonic plates pull away from each other; when filled with water they can form large lakes.

Graded profile: A stream or river with a constant slope (incline).

Graded stream: A stream that has achieved a constant slope (profile) by reaching a balance of erosion and deposition.

Gravity: The natural force of attraction between any two objects that depends upon the mass of the objects and the distance between the objects. Planets, like Earth, draw objects toward their surfaces. Attraction is directly proportional to the product of the masses of the bodies and inversely proportional to the square of the distance between the bodies.

Gray water: Water that has been used for bathing, in the kitchen, or other purposes that do not generate highly-contaminated wastewater.

Greenhouse effect: The process where light from the Sun is reflected off Earth's surfaces and then trapped by clouds to warm Earth's atmosphere and surface.

Greenhouse gases: Gases in Earth atmosphere's that include water vapor and carbon dioxide, methane, nitrous oxides, ozone, halogens (bromine, chlorine, and fluorine), halocarbons, and other trace gases (gases found in very relatively small amounts).

Greenhouse layer: Layer of gases in the atmosphere that lets pass incoming solar rays and traps escaping heat.

Gross tons: A marine term equal to 100 cubic feet (about 10 cubic meters) used to describe the size of a boat, ship, or barge.

Groundwater: Freshwater that resides in rock and soil layers beneath Earth's land surface.

Groyne: A wall-like structure that sticks out into the water from the beach, which is intended to trap material.

Guyot: A flat-topped submarine mountain.

Gyres: Large circular patterns created by surface water currents in the oceans.

H

Habitat: The environment in which a species naturally or normally lives and grows.

Hadal zone: The layer of the ocean in deep trenches and submarine canyons at depths that can extend down to 35,750 feet (11,000 meters).

Halite: A mineral composed of sodium chloride, commonly known as rock salt.

Halocline: Layer of water where the salinity changes rapidly with depth.

Headland: Point that extends into the ocean; usually a high rocky point surrounded by sea cliffs.

Heavy metal: Element such as lead or mercury that tends to be toxic to plant and animal life, even when present in a low concentration.

Heterotroph: Organism that consumes another organism to obtain energy.

Himalaya Mountains: Tall mountain range in central Asia that includes nine of the world's ten highest peaks, including the tallest one, Mt. Everest.

Holdfast: The part of a seaweed that allows the plant to attach to a rock.

Holoplankton: Plankton that spend their entire life cycle floating and drifting among the currents.

Homeostasis: Tendency for a system to resist change.

Hovercraft: Ship that floats over the surface of the water on a cushion of air.

Humidity: Water vapor (moisture) in the air.

Hurricane: An organized storm (tropical cyclone) with sustained winds of 74 miles per hour (119 kilometers per hour) or greater in the Atlantic Ocean, Gulf of Mexico, Caribbean Sea, or eastern Pacific Ocean.

Hydrocarbon: Chemical substance made up of carbon and hydrogen; propane, gasoline, kerosene, diesel fuel, and lubricating oil are common hydrocarbons.

Hydrofoil: Ship that has wing-like foils under the hull of the ship that provide lift that raises the hull of the ship out of the water.

Hydrogeologist: Scientist who studies the properties and distribution of freshwater, especially as it relates to the soil and rock structure of the Earth.

Hydrologic potential: Potential energy in water stored in reservoirs above the elevation of a river downstream.

Hydrologist: Scientist who studies the properties and distribution of Earth's freshwater.

Hydrophilic: Easily dissolvable in water.

Hydrophobic: Not easily dissolvable in water.

Hydrosphere: The whole body of water that exists on or around Earth, including water in the atmosphere, lakes, oceans, rivers, and groundwater.

Hydrothermal deposit: Mineral-containing geologic unit that was formed by hot waters percolating through source rocks.

Hydrothermal vents: Volcanic-powered, hot spring openings in the ocean floor that spew out a fluid that is rich in chemicals and minerals.

Hypolimnion: The deep part of a lake where no light penetrates.

Hypopycnal flow: River water that floats on top of sea water as it flows out to the ocean; it is caused by the fact that river water is less dense than salty sea water.

Hypothermia: Condition in which the body becomes too cold to function properly.

Hypoxia: Condition in which the concentration of oxygen in body tissues is too low for the body to function normally.

I

Ice budget: The total amount of frozen water on Earth.

Ice cap: Ice at the poles; large dome-shaped glaciers that are smaller than ice sheets.

Ice front: The ice at the lowest end of a glacier.

Ice sheet: Very large, dome-shaped mass of glacial ice that covers a large continental area; also called continental glacier.

Ice shelf: A floating platform of ice where an ice sheet flows out over water.

Ice stream: Portion of a glacier or ice sheet that flows faster than the surrounding ice.

Iceberg: Large chunk of ice that breaks off from glaciers and floats in the oceans.

Ichthyology: The scientific study of fish.

Import: Raw materials or goods that are produced in a foreign country and brought into another.

In situ: In place.

Industrial Revolution: Period of rapid industrial growth, usually dated from 1750 to 1900, that resulted in a shift from economies based on agriculture and small businesses to economies based on industry and large corporations.

Influent streams and ponds: Bodies of surface water in recharge zones that contribute groundwater.

Interdistributary: Land or water that is between distributaries in deltas.

Internal combustion engine: An engine that takes the energy in fuel and combusts (burns) it inside the engine to produce motion.

International Maritime Organization (IMO): International agency of the United Nations that is concerned with shipping regulation and safety.

International organization: A group that includes two or more countries and that operates in more than one country.

Intertidal: The zone of the seashore between the high tide point and the low tide point.

Inuit: The native human inhabitants of the Arctic coastal regions of Eastern Asia (Siberia), North America and Greenland; also known as Eskimo, although this term has fallen out of favor.

Invertebrate: An animal without a backbone.

Ion: An electrically charged atom or group of atoms.

Irrigation: Diverting freshwater from lakes and rivers for use in agriculture to provide water for crops.

J

Jet stream: High-speed winds that race around the planet at about five miles above the Earth.

Jetty: Structure built out into the sea, a lake, or a river to protect the harbor or shore against waves or tides.

K

Karst: Landscape with caverns, sinkholes, underground streams, and springs created by erosion of limestone rock layers by groundwater.

Kayak: Boat that is pointed at both ends and has a closed deck except for a small hole where the paddler sits.

Kettle: Round depression left in glacial sediment after melting of a buried block of ice; it forms lakes and ponds when filled with water.

Kettle pond: Small round pond that forms when a melting glacier leaves chunks of ice buried in its deposits.

L

Lagoon: A shallow body of water that is separated from the sea by a reef or narrow island.

Lake overturn: Mixing of lake waters from temperatures causing changes in the water layers' density.

Land bridge: Strip of dry land that connects islands or continents when it is exposed by lowered sea level during glacial periods.

Latitude: Imaginary lines that tell how far north or south a place is from the equator.

Lava: Hot, liquid rock that reaches the Earth's surface through a volcano or opening in Earth's crust.

Leachate: An acidic wastewater that contains contaminants from decomposed materials in a landfill.

Lentic: Relating to waters that are moving, like in rivers and streams.

Levee: A natural or man-made wall along the banks of a stream channel that helps confine floodwaters within the channel.

Limnology: Study of the ecology of continental surface waters including lakes, rivers, wetlands, and estuaries.

Liner: A sheet of plastic or other material that is put on top of clay on the inside of a landfill to prevent material from leaking out of the landfill.

Lithosphere: Rocky outer shell of Earth that is broken into large, rigid pieces called plates.

Littoral zone: Shallow, sunlit zone along lake shores where rooted plants grow.

Lock: One in a series of gates that allows boats or ships to pass through multiple water levels.

Longshore current: Near-shore current that runs parallel to a coastline.

Lotic: Relating to waters that are stationary, like in ponds and lakes.

M

Macroplankton: Plankton large enough to be seen by the naked eye, including larval forms of jellyfish and some species of crustaceans.

Magnetometer: Used in marine archaeology to locate shipwrecks by finding metal objects used in the ship's construction such as nails, brackets, decorative ironwork, or artillery.

Malacostraca: A class of marine invertebrates that includes shrimp, lobsters, crabs, and euphausids.

Mammal: A vertebrate that nurses its young with milk, breathes air, has hair at some point in its life, and is warm-blooded.

Mariculture: Farming of marine animals and aquatic plants in a controlled marine environment.

Marine biology: Study of life in the ocean.

Marine geology: Study of the formation and structure of underwater land and rock formation.

Marine Mammal Protection Act: Law that seeks to increase the population of marine mammal species by prohibiting the hunting, capture, or killing of marine mammals.

Marsh: Wetland dominated by grasses, reeds, and sedges.

Meandering stream: A stream with a channel that follows a twisting path of curves and bends.

Mesopelagic zone: The layer of the ocean below the epipelagic zone and above the bathypelagic zone; generally it extends from about 500 feet (150 meters) to about 3,250 feet (1,000 meters).

Metabolic rate: The rate at which the biochemical processes occur in an organism.

Metal: Substance that is a conductor of electricity and heat.

Meteorology: The science of atmospheric conditions and phenomena.

Mid-ocean ridge: A continuous chain of low, symmetrical volcanoes that extends through all the ocean basins.

Milankovitch cycles: Predictable changes in Earth's average temperature that are caused by changes in Earth's position relative to the Sun.

Mines: Explosive devices that usually explode when an object makes contact with them; sea mines usually float on or just below the surface.

Molecule: A group of atoms arranged to interact in a particular way; the smallest part of a substance that has the qualities of that substance.

Mollusk: A member of a group of invertebrates that includes the snails, clams, oysters, scallops, mussels, squid, and octopuses.

Monsoon: A wind from the southwest that brings heavy rainfall to India and other parts of southern Asia during the summer.

Moraine: A ridge formed by the unsorted gravel, sand, and rock pushed by a glacier and deposited at the outer edge, or front, of the glacier.

Mousse: A water-in-oil emulsion that is formed by turbulence of the surface water after a petroleum spill to the aquatic environment.

Municipality: A village, town, or city with its own local government that provides services for its residents.

N

National Weather Service: Government agency that predicts the weather and warns the public of dangerous weather situations and their consequences, including severe weather and flood warnings.

Native species: A species naturally occurring in an environment.

Natural gas: Naturally occurring hydrocarbon gas.

Natural resources: Economically valuable materials that humans extract from the Earth; water is one of humans' most essential natural resource.

Navigable: Describes a body of water wide and deep enough for boats or ships to travel.

Navigation: The ability to determine the correct position of a ship in the ocean and the direction to sail in order to reach the desired destination.

Navigation channel: Passage in a waterway that is naturally deep or dredged to permit the passage of ships, or a defined, well-marked passage that leads from the docks to open waters; also called ship channel.

Navigation rights: The right of the ships from one nation to pass through certain waters, particularly the territorial waters of another nation.

Neap tide: Lowest tides of the month that occur at the second and fourth quarters of the Moon.

Neutron: A particle found in the nucleus of an atom that has no electric charge.

Non-point source pollution: Water pollution that comes from several unidentified sources, such as contaminated rain, runoff, or groundwater.

Nor'easter: A gale or storm blowing from the northeast, particularly common in New England and eastern Canada.

Nutrient: Chemical such as phosphate and nitrate needed by organisms in order to grow.

O

Ocean currents: The circulation of ocean waters that produce a steady flow of water in a prevailing direction.

Oligotrophic: Describing a body of water in which nutrients are in low supply.

Open-pit mine: Large craters dug into the earth to extract ore that is near the surface.

Ore: Naturally occurring source of minerals.

Organic: Of or relating to or derived from living organisms.

Overfishing: Catching a species of fish faster than it can naturally reproduce resulting in a decline in the overall population of that species.

Ozone layer: Region in the outer atmosphere that absorbs the Sun's harmful ultraviolet radiation.

P

Pangea: A super-continent that existed about two hundred million years ago when all of Earth's continental land masses were joined.

Parts per million (ppm): The number of particles in a solution per million particles of the solution.

Pathogen: Organisms (such as bacteria, protozoa, and viruses) that can cause disease.

Peat: Compressed organic material found in bogs.

Permafrost: Frozen layer of soil beneath the top layer of soil that has remained frozen for two or more years.

Permeability: The ability of fluid to move through a material.

Pesticides: Substances used to kill or harm unwanted plants, insects, or rodents.

Petroleum: A naturally occurring liquid mixture of hydrocarbons that is mined and refined for energy and the manufacturing of chemicals, especially plastics. Also known as crude oil.

Phase change: Transformation of a substance between one phase of matter (solid, liquid, or gas) to another.

Phosphorus: An element used as a food source by a variety of plants and microorganisms.

Photosynthesis: The process where plants use sunlight, water, and carbon dioxide to produce their food.

Physical oceanography: Study of the physical properties of the ocean including temperature, salinity and density, the ability to transmit light and sound, and the flow of currents and tides.

Phytoplankton: Plankton composed of plants and plant-like bacteria, such as algae.

Pinniped: A member of the group of marine mammals that include seals, sea lions, fur seals, and walruses.

Placer deposit: Water-deposited mineral source, such as gold nuggets in streams.

Plankton: Small, often microscopic, organisms that float in the ocean.

Plate tectonics: The theory that Earth's lithospheric plates move over time. It explains geological patterns of earthquakes, mountain chains, volcanoes, and rock types.

Platform: Large buildings, attached to the sea floor or floating, that house workers and machinery needed to drill for oil or gas.

Playa: Flat areas at the bottom of desert basins that occasionally fill with water.

Pleistocene Epoch: Division of geologic time from 10,000 to 2 million years ago; also known as the Ice Age.

Point-source pollution: Water pollution that enters the water body from a particular site.

Point-source wastewater: Wastewater that enters natural waters from defined locations.

Polar: A molecule that has a positively charged part and a negatively charged part.

Polychaeta: The largest class of segmented worms that live in the ocean.

Population: Group of organisms all belonging to the same species that live in a specific location.

Porosity: Amount of empty space within a rock or soil body.

Port: City or town on a harbor where ships dock and cargo is loaded or unloaded.

Potable: Water that is safe to drink.

Precipitation: Transfer of water as rain, snow, sleet, or hail from the atmosphere to the surface of Earth. In chemistry or geochemistry: The process in which ions dissolved in a solution bond to reform a solid.

Proton: A positively charged particle that is located in the nucleus of an atom.

Purification: Process by which pollutants, mud, salt, and other substances are removed from the wastewater.

R

Rainshadow: An area that has decreased precipitation because a barrier mountain range causes prevailing winds to lose their moisture before reaching it.

Recharge zone: Area where water enters groundwater reservoirs by infiltrating through soils, stream beds, and ponds.

Reclamation: Draining submerged or wetter land to form dry, usable land.

Reef: An underwater ridge of rock or coral near the surface of the ocean.

Remote sensing: The use of devices to collect and interpret data; in marine archaeology, remote sensing is used to locate, map, and study underwater sites.

Remotely operated vehicle (ROV): Motorized crafts designed to withstand the increased pressure of the deep ocean.

Reservoir: Natural or man-made lake or body of water, often constructed to control a body of water.

Reservoir rocks: Rocks where petroleum collects.

Residence time: Time an average water molecule spends in one of the reservoirs of the hydrologic cycle.

Respiration: Process in which an organism uses oxygen for its life processes.

Ring of fire: A zone of large volcanoes and earthquakes that surrounds the Pacific Ocean.

Riparian zone: Narrow strip of vegetation that is found bounding the edge of a natural water body such as a stream or river.

River system: A river and its network of headwater streams and tributaries. All the streams that contribute water to the main river.

Runoff: Excess water when the amount of precipitation (water falling to Earth's surface) is greater than the ability of the land to soak up the water.

S

Sailing: Moving across the water in a boat powered by wind energy harnessed by sails.

Saline lake: Saltwater lake that contains high concentrations of dissolved salts.

Salinity: A measure of the salt concentration of seawater.

Sanctuary: A habitat where killing animals or plants is prohibited.

Sanitation: Maintaining clean, hygienic conditions that help prevent disease through the use of clean water and wastewater disposal.

Saprotroph: Organism that decomposes another organism into inorganic substances and in the process obtains energy for itself.

Scuba diving: "Scuba" is the acronym for self-contained underwater breathing apparatus, referring to the air tanks and mouthpieces used by divers.

Sea ice: Frozen seawater floating on the ocean surface.

Seafloor spreading: The process by which a new oceanic seafloor is created by small volcanic eruptions at mid-ocean ridges.

Seamount: An underwater mountain.

Sedge: Grass-like plants.

Sediment: Particles of gravel, sand, and silt.

Seismic waves: Vibrations emitted by earthquakes and large explosions that travel as waves through the Earth.

Semipermeable: Descriptive of a material that allows the passage of some molecules and prevents the passage of others.

Sensor: Device that can detect the waves that have bounced back from the object they contacted.

Sewer system: Network of channels or pipes that carry wastewater to a treatment facility for purification.

Shoreline: A strip of land within a coastal zone that is submerged by high tide; also called shore zone.

Sidescan sonar: Type of sonar that emits sound energy over a wide path, tens or hundreds of miles (kilometers) across, allowing scientists to map large areas of the ocean.

Silt: Sedimentary particles smaller than sand particles, but larger than clay particles.

Sinkhole: A crater that forms when the roof of a cavern collapses; usually found in limestone rock.

Sludge: A semisolid residue, containing microorganisms and their products, from any water treatment process.

Snorkel: A hollow tube attached to a mouthpiece that can jut out above the surface of the ocean to allow a diver to breath.

Snorkeling: Form of diving in which the diver swims at or near the surface of the water using a snorkel to breathe surface air.

Snow line: The lowest elevation where snow stays on the ground or glacier surface without melting.

Solar salt production: A process that yields sea salt by allowing the sun to evaporate saltwater.

Solution: A liquid that contains dissolved substances.

Solution mining: Producing table salt by pumping water underground where it dissolves halite, then returning the solution to the surface where the salt is recovered through evaporation.

Solvent: A substance, most often a liquid, into which other compounds can dissolve.

Sonar: Derived from "SOund NAvigation and Ranging," sonar uses sound waves to locate underwater objects.

Source rocks: Mud layers rich with plant and animal material that become rocks where temperature and pressure transform the plant and animal material into petroleum.

Species: Group of organisms that have a unique set of characteristics, such as body shape and behavior, and are capable of reproducing with each other and producing offspring.

Sponge: One of the least complex multicellular animals; a member of the phylum Porifera.

Spring tide: Highest tides of the month that occur at the new and full Moon.

Stratified: Layered.

Stream: Moving surface fresh water driven towards sea level by gravity.

Stromata: Holes on the surface of leaves that can let water vapor pass out of the plant into the air.

Subarctic: Region just below the Arctic Circle, to the edge of the northern forests in North America, Europe, and Asia.

Subduction: Process by which oceanic seafloor is recycled into Earth's interior at deep ocean trenches.

Submersible: A craft designed to carry a pilot and scientists for underwater study of the deep ocean.

Superfund: A program managed by the Environmental Protection Agency that identifies, investigates, and cleans up the worst hazardous waste sites in the United States.

Surface mixed layer: The surface of the ocean where wind acts as a mixer, dissolving gases such as oxygen into the water.

Surface water: Water that is located on the surface, naturally in the form of streams, rivers, lakes, and other waterways, or in reservoirs, swimming pools, and other containers that have been built.

Sustainability: The use of a natural resource in a manner where it can be maintained and renewed for future generations.

Swamp: Wetland dominated by trees.

Swash: The forward and backward motion of water where waves break upon the shore.

Synecology: Ecological study of groups of organisms and how they work together.

T

Tanker: A ship that transports liquid cargo, usually oil or chemicals.

Tectonic plate: Moving plates of Earth's crust.

Temperate zone: Region characterized by moderate temperatures, rainfall, and weather and overall climate that is neither hot nor cold, wet nor dry.

Tentacles: Long appendages on sea organisms that contain suckers or stinging cells and are used to grasp food and move around.

Terra cotta: Ceramic materials made from baked clay used in Ancient Rome for aqueduct pipes, dishes, and some tools.

Territorial water: Ocean waters governed by a nation; most territorial waters extend for 12 miles (19.3 kilometers) from a nation's coastline.

Thermal spring: Natural spring of water at a temperature of 70°F (21°C) or above; commonly called a hot spring.

Thermocline: The part of the ocean below the epipelagic zone where the temperature changes very quickly with depth.

Threatened: Descriptive of a species that is likely to become endangered in the foreseeable future.

Tidal fence: Device installed in an area with highly-changing tides that makes electricity by harnessing tidal energy.

Tidal flat: A broad, flat area of coastline alternately covered and exposed by the tides.

Tidal wave: The swell or crest of surface ocean water created by the tides. Also refers to an unusual water rise along a coastline as created by a storm or undersea earthquake.

Tide: Periodic rise and fall of sea level along coastlines caused by gravitational and rotational forces between the Sun, Moon, and Earth.

Tornado: A violently rotating column of air that is in contact with the ground.

Trade winds: Strong winds that blow from east to west in the subtropics on either side of the equator; named for their part in propelling European sailing ships to the East and West Indies to conduct trade.

Transpiration: The process where water is absorbed by a plant through its roots and passes into the air from the leaves as water vapor.

Treaty: An international agreement between two or more nations in written form and governed by international law.

Tributary: Smaller streams that flow into a larger stream or river.

Tropical storm: A low pressure storm system formed in tropical latitudes with sustained winds between 39 and 74 miles per hour (63 and 119 kilometers per hour).

Tropics: Warm, humid region lying north and south of the equator.

Trough: The lowest point in a wave; occurs between the crests.

Tsunami: Very large ocean wave created by an undersea earthquake or volcanic eruption.

Tundra: Treeless plains of the arctic and subarctic between the northern forests and the coastline of the Arctic Ocean.

Turbine: Device that converts the flow of a fluid (air, steam, water, or hot gases) into mechanical motion for generating electricity.

Twister: Common name for a tornado.

Typhoon: Tropical cyclone in the western Pacific or Indian oceans.

U

United Nations: An association of countries founded in 1945 that is devoted to the promotion of peace, security, and cooperation between nations.

United Nations Law of the Sea: International law that governs the rights and responsibilities of nations and their approach to the oceans.

Upwelling: An area where cold, often nutrient-rich water rises from the deep ocean to the surface.

U.S. Department of the Interior: Department in the U.S. government that is responsible for the conservation of natural resources and the administration of government-owned land.

U.S. Geological Survey: Division of the U.S. Department of the Interior that is responsible for the scientific analysis of natural resources, the environment, and natural disasters.

V

Vertebrate: An animal that has a bony spine that contains a nerve (spinal) chord.

W

Wall cloud: An area of clouds that extends beneath a severe thunderstorm and sometimes produces a tornado.

Wastewater: Water left over after it has been used, such as any water that empties into a drain or sewer.

Water allotment: An individual portion of water granted by a water right.

Water chemistry: The balance of nutrients, chemicals, and minerals in water.

Water footprint: The amount of water used by an individual, business, community, or nation.

Water right: Grants a right to use water but not ownership of the waterway.

Water table: The zone above which the spaces in the soil and rocks are not completely filled with water and below which the soil and rock spaces are completely filled with water.

Water treatment: A series of steps that makes water potable and removes chemicals and microoganisms that could be harmful to the natural environment.

Watershed: The land area that drains water into a river or other body of water.

Waterspout: A column of rotating air, similar to a tornado, over a body of water.

Wave base: Water depth at which water is undisturbed by a passing wave. Wave base is at a depth equal to half the horizontal distance between two neighboring wave crests (one-half wavelength).

Wave refraction: Wave fronts bending when they approach a coastline at an angle.

Wavelength: Distance of one full wave; can be measured from crest to crest or trough to trough.

Weir: A low dam built across a stream or any flowing body of water, usually with rocks, to raise its level or divert its flow.

Wet deposition: Precipitation that has become acidic as a result of air pollution.

Wetlands: Areas of land where water covers the surface for at least part of the year and controls the development of soil.

Z

Zone of infiltration: Shallow soil and rock layers with pore space that are at least partially filled with air; water table is the bottom of this zone.

Zone of saturation: Soil and rock layers with pore spaces that are completely filled with fluid; water table is the top of this zone.

Zooplankton: Small, often microscopic, animals that float in the ocean.

Research and Activity Ideas

The following research and activity ideas are intended to offer suggestions for complementing science and social studies curricula, to trigger additional ideas for enhancing learning, and to provide cross-disciplinary projects for library and classroom use.

• **Experimentation:** The following resources contain simple experiments that illustrate the physical properties of water:

Project WET (Water Education for Teachers), an international nonprofit water education program and publisher located at Montana State University. http://www.projectwet.org/index.html.

Janice VanCleave's Oceans for Every Kid: Easy Activities That Make Learning Science Fun, by Janice Van Cleave, Wiley, 1996.

Exploring the Oceans: Science Activities for Kids, by Shawn Berlute-Shea and Anthony B. Fredericks, Fulcrum, 1998.

Oceans Alive: Water, Wind, and Waves, by Doug Sylvester, Rainbow Horizons, 2001.

Why Is the Ocean Salty? by Herbert Swenson, U.S. Government Printing Office, Superintendent of Documents. Prepared by the U.S. Geological Survey to provide information about the earth sciences, natural resources, and the environment.

• **Adopt a creature:** Take a class vote to choose a freshwater or marine creature to adopt whose species is stressed or endangered. Research the life of the creature, prepare a class display, and learn about the latest efforts to conserve the species and its habitat. Suggestions for creatures to adopt include the:

Manatee: Information about adopting a manatee can be found at the Save the Manatee Club Web site, http://www.savethemanatee.org/default.html.

Humpback whale: Information about adopting a humpback whale can be found at the Whale Center of New England Web site, http://www.whalecenter.org/adopt.htm.

Sea turtle: Information about adopting a sea turtle that has been fitted with a transmitter for tracking can be found at the Seaturtle.org Web site, http://www.seaturtle.org/tracking/adopt/.

Whooping crane: Information about adopting a whooping crane can be found at the Friends of the Patuxent Wildlife Center Web site, http://www.friendspwrc.org/.

Salmon: Information about participating in the Adopt-a-salmon program can be found on the U.S. Department of Fish and Wildlife Web site, http://www.fws.gov/r5cneafp/guide.htm.

• **Newspaper search:** Locate and review newspapers for the following disasters using the dates given. Assess if reporters grasped the cause and extent of the event. Choose interesting accounts to read to the class. The events are: hurricane in Galveston, Texas, on September 8, 1900; drought in the southern plains of the United States, 1930–39 (also called the Dust Bowl); tsunami in the Gulf of Alaska on March 28, 1964; Arno River floods in Florence, Italy, on November 4–5, 1966; and *Amoco Cadiz* oil spill off the coast of Brittany, France, on March 16, 1978. Old issues of local newspapers are likely available at your public library, a nearby college or university library, or from the local newspaper office itself.

• **At the movies:** Watch one of the following popular movies, each of which contains content about Earth's water sources or its ecosystems. *20,000 Leagues Under the Sea* (1954), *Jaws* (1977), *Into the Deep* (1991), *A River Runs Through It* (1992), *Free Willy* (1993), *The Living Sea* (1995), and *Finding Nemo* (2003). Applying your knowledge of water science, how was the issue portrayed in the movie? Whether the movie was a drama, comedy, or documentary, was the science portrayed accurately? Were there misconceptions about water science issues that it relayed to the audience?

• **Debate #1:** Divide the class into two groups, one in favor of the United States ratifying the United Nations Law of the Sea and the other against. Students should defend their positions about the environmental, economic, and political benefits or hardships that adopting the law would bring the United States, and whether U.S. ratification would change the state of the world's oceans.

• **Debate #2:** Divide the class into two groups, one in favor of large dam projects on major rivers and the other against. Students should research China's Three Gorges project, the Sardar Sarovar Project in India, and the Hoover and Glen Canyon dams. Debate the issue, with students defending their positions on hydroelectric power, water supply, flood control, and recreation enabled by dams, along with the environmental impacts, displaced persons, and detriments of flooding an area for a reservoir that occur when large dams are constructed.

• **Interviews:** Make a list of persons who have visited or lived near beaches, lakes, rivers, or wetlands for a long period of time. Parents or grandparents would be good candidates. Interview them about the changes in the area that they have noticed over time, such as changes in the water quality or quantity, new or reduced populations of water creatures, habitat change, and encroaching development. Develop questions ahead of time. Tape record the interview if possible or take careful notes. Transcribe the recording or notes into a clear written retelling of the interview. This process is known as taking and recording an oral history. Share the oral history with the class.

• **Aquarium:** Plan a class trip to a local aquarium. Notice the environment required for particular species such as water salinity, depth, temperature, presence of other unique features (coral reef, rocks, caves, plants) and available food sources. Design a model aquarium of several compatible species, labeling the particular features needed by each species. If a home aquarium sounds like an interesting hobby, the following Web sites provide helpful information for getting started: "Aquariums as a Hobby" from SeaWorld's *Animals: Explore, Discover, Connect* Web site at: http://www.seaworld.org/infobooks/Aquarium/Aquarium.html and "Starting a New Aquarium" from the *World of Fish* Web site at: http://meltingpot.fortunecity.com/oltorf/729/id18.htm.

• **Conserve water:** Make a checklist of ways to conserve water in the home. Include: using low-flush toilets (or placing a closed container of water in non-low-flush toilet tanks), checking faucets for leaks, using aerators on faucets, collecting rainwater for watering gardens, watering landscapes during early morning hours, landscaping with native plants that demand less water, installing low-flow shower heads, and using other water-saving measures found while researching the topic of water conservation. Inspect your home according to the checklist to learn ways that your family can help conserve water and discuss this with family members. Make checklists to distribute to other students at your school.

• **Stay informed:** Three current challenges facing the world's oceans are often featured in the news media. Watch and listen for reports about diminishing coral reefs in the Caribbean Sea and in the Pacific Ocean, about warming ocean temperatures, and for reports about noise pollution interfering with marine mammal communication. Get the details of one of these current issues with research. Web sites of oceanographic institutes and universities are good places to begin collecting information.

• **"Water Science for Schools"** The U.S. Geological Survey maintains the Web site "Water Science for Schools," which provides teachers and students with information and activities for learning about water science and water resources. The Web site is located at: http://ga.water.usgs.gov/edu/ and includes excellent information about the water cycle, Earth's water resources, and how humans use water. The site includes pictures, data, maps, and an interactive center.

• **Map project:** Research the watershed areas of local rivers, lakes, and streams. Using colored chalk or highlighters, color-code and shade the watershed areas on a large street map. Post the map in the community to raise awareness of the watershed, along with measures people can take to protect it from contamination.

U·X·L ENCYCLOPEDIA OF
water science

Chapter 7
Science and Technology

Aqueducts

Aqueducts are man-made conduits constructed to carry water. The term aqueduct comes from words meaning "to lead water" in Latin, the language of the Romans who were the first builders of large aqueducts. Aqueducts carry water from natural sources, such as springs, into cities and towns for public use.

The first aqueducts

Wells, rivers, lakes, and streams are the oldest sources of water. In the ancient world however, rivers and lakes were also sometimes used as places to dispose of sewage and trash. Water from rivers that flowed though several villages often carried disease-causing organisms. Aqueducts provided a way for a plentiful supply of clean water to be piped into cities.

The earliest aqueducts were also used to transport water for irrigation (watering crops). Aqueducts were used in ancient India, Persia, Assyria, and Egypt as early as 700 B.C.E. The Romans, however, are regarded as the most famous ancient aqueduct builders. Between 312 B.C.E. and 230 C.E., the most complex and efficient ancient system of aqueducts was built to supply the city of Rome with water. Outside of the capital city of Rome, the Romans built aqueducts throughout their large empire. Ruins of ancient aqueducts can still be seen in Italy, Greece, North Africa, Spain, and France.

How ancient aqueducts functioned

Ancient aqueducts used tunnels and channels (passages for water to flow) to transport water. The earliest irrigation aqueducts were simple canals and ditches dug into the ground. In

◆**Cistern:** A man-made reservoir for storing water, usually underground.

◆**Irrigation:** Water channeled to lands for growing crops.

◆**Terra cotta:** Ceramic materials made from baked clay used in Ancient Rome for aqueduct pipes, dishes, and some tools.

order to keep water for use by people clean, aqueducts that supplied people with water featured covered channels or pipes. The first aqueduct made of stone-covered waterways was built by the Assyrians around 690 B.C.E. Centuries later, Roman aqueduct builders perfected the closed channel design, building thousands of miles (kilometers) of stone aqueducts throughout the Roman Empire.

Ancient aqueducts were carefully planned before they were constructed. Water flowed through the channels by the force of gravity alone. The rate of flow (how many gallons could flow through the conduit in a day) was determined by the force of the spring that fed the aqueduct. Aqueduct channels were constructed with a gradual slope (angle) so that water from the source could flow downhill to its destination. There were no pumps that could move water up a hill or slope. Thus, when crossing hilly terrain, aqueducts were built on stone bridges and in tunnels. Pipes made of stone or a type of baked clay called terra cotta carried water through carved out tunnels. Aqueduct bridges (or elevated spans) were required to withstand the heavy weight of water. Spectacular Roman aqueduct bridges featuring several stories (or tiers) of strong arches can still be seen today. Some are still in use!

After the aqueducts entered the city, water flowed into public cisterns (large pools or wells that store water) or flowed from public fountains. In Rome, some citizens had water from the aqueducts piped directly to their homes. Wastewater was carried by sewer systems that emptied into outlying streams that normally did not feed into the aqueduct.

Like modern water supply systems, ancient aqueducts required constant maintenance. Where aqueducts ran underground, shafts (tunnels) were built to provide access to the aqueduct for repairs. Chalk and other minerals built up in the conduits and required regular cleaning. Wars, earthquakes, storms, and floods sometimes damaged whole sections of aqueducts. Fixing aqueducts was an expensive undertaking and required the work of strong laborers and skilled engineers.

Innovations in aqueduct technology

After the fall of the Roman Empire in the fifth century, aqueduct building ceased in Europe. For centuries, the scientific knowledge necessary to build aqueducts, aqueduct bridges, and sewers was lost. Rome and some other cities continued to use their ancient aqueducts. However, during the Middle Ages (500–1500 C.E.), people mostly used wells and rivers as a source

Roman Aqueducts

Built by the ancient Romans, the three tiered Pont du Gard aqueduct spans the Gard River in France. © Archivo Iconografico, S.A./Corbis. Reproduced by permission.

The Romans were the greatest aqueduct builders of the ancient world. In fact, when one mentions the word aqueduct, most people think of the beautiful, ancient, arched aqueduct bridges throughout southern Europe that were built by the Romans. However, these aqueduct bridges or spans were only a small fraction of the Roman aqueduct system. For example, of the aqueducts that served the city of Rome, only 30 miles (48 kilometers) out of nearly 300 (483 kilometers) miles of aqueducts crossed valley and hills on arched bridges.

The aqueduct system that served Rome was the largest and most complex in the ancient world. Until the late 1800s, it remained unsurpassed in terms of both distance and the amount of water carried. Over a period of 500 years, (from 312 B.C.E. to 230 C.E.), 11 aqueducts were built to serve the city of Rome. The longest aqueduct brought water from a spring over 59 miles (95 kilometers) away into the heart of the city.

When water from the aqueduct reached the city, it was carried to cisterns that were built on high ground. Cisterns are large, deep pools used for storing water. From the cisterns, water was carried to public fountains or private homes by a system of lead or terra-cotta pipes. Sometimes water was carried directly from the aqueduct conduits to public baths or pools. However, taking water directly from the aqueducts was usually illegal. Only the emperor and very wealthy citizens were permitted to construct special conduits that took water directly from the aqueduct to their private residences.

The aqueducts were one of Rome's most prized possessions. The army guarded the water system and almost one hundred engineers supervised maintenance and repairs. Over two hundred towns in the Roman Empire also had their own water systems featuring aqueducts.

of water. During the Renaissance (1300s–1600s), a renewed interest in classical architecture and engineering led scholars of the day to rediscover how ancient water systems worked and how aqueducts were constructed.

In the 1600s, aqueducts were once again included in public water systems. In France, a system of pumps moved water from a river to an aqueduct system that began on the crest (high point) of a nearby hill. An aqueduct spanning 38 miles (61 kilometers) carried water into the city of London, England. The

An aqueduct and canal near Bakersfield, California. © *Yann Arthus-Bertrand/Corbis.* Reproduced by permission.

Chadwell River to London aqueduct flowed over 200 small bridges.

In the eighteenth and nineteenth centuries, innovations such the steam pump permitted water to be pressurized. Pressurized water is water that is mixed with air or steam that, with the help of a pump, can be moved forcefully through pipes and conduits. This allowed water systems to move water over any terrain. Aqueducts and water pipe systems carried water over greater distances with the aid of pressurized water. Pressurization also created a need for stronger pipes. Instead of terra-cotta, pipes were made of metals or concrete.

Between the 1830s and 1900, the growing city of New York constructed several aqueducts to bring spring and river water into the city from sources over 120 miles (193 kilometers) away. These aqueducts incorporated new and old aqueduct technology. They employed pumps and deep underground pipe systems, but the Old Croton aqueduct, in use until 1955, also featured a Roman-like aqueduct bridge. Today, the three major aqueduct systems that serve New York City deliver nearly 1.8 billion gallons (approximately 6.8 billion liters) of water per day.

Aqueducts today

Aqueducts remain an important and efficient means of delivering clean water to cities. Today's aqueducts are longer and able to carry more water than ancient aqueducts. Pumps and pressurized water flow permit aqueducts to flow up a slope. Improved pipe materials allows today's aqueducts to be completely hidden deep underground. The largest modern aqueduct system in the world has been under construction since the 1960s. When finished, the aqueduct will carry water 600 miles (966 kilometers) through the state of California, from the northern part of the state south to the Mexican border.

Adrienne Wilmoth Lerner

For More Information

Books

Hodge, A. Trevor. "Roman Aqueducts and Water Supply." London: Gerald Duckworth & Co., 2002.

Websites

"Aqueducts." *British Waterways.* http://www.britishwaterways. co.uk/responsibilities/heritage/aqueducts.html (accessed on August 24, 2004).

"Roman Aqueducts." *InfoRoma.* http://www.inforoma.it/ feature.php?lookup=aqueduct (accessed on August 24, 2004).

"The Water Science Picture Gallery—Aqueducts Move Water." *United States Geological Survey.* http://ga.water.usgs.gov/ edu/aqueduct1.html (accessed on August 24, 2004).

Dams and Reservoirs

Dams are structures that restrict the flow of water in a river or stream. Both streams and rivers are bodies of flowing surface water driven by gravity that drain water from the continents. Once a body of flowing surface water has been slowed or stopped, a reservoir or lake collects behind the dam. Dams and reservoirs exist in nature, and man-made water control structures are patterned after examples in the natural word. Many lakes are held back by rock dams created by geologic events such as volcanic eruptions, landslides or the upward force of Earth that creates mountains. Humans and beavers alike have discovered how to modify their natural environment to suit their needs by constructing dams and creating artificial lakes.

Dams are classified into four main types: gravity, embankment, buttress, and arch.

- Gravity dams: Gravity dams are massive earth, masonry (brick or stone work), rock fill, or concrete structures that hold back river water with their own weight. They are usually triangular with their point in a narrow gorge (deep ravine). The Grand Dixence dam in the Swiss Alps is the world's tallest gravity dam.

- Embankment dams: Embankment dams are wide areas of compacted earth or rock fill with a concrete or masonry core that contains a reservoir, while allowing for some saturation and shifting of the earth around the dam, and of the dam within the earth.

- Buttress dams: Buttress dams have supports that reinforce the walls of the dam and can be curved or straight. Buttresses on large modern dams, such as the Itaipu dam in Brazil, are often constructed as a series of arches and are made of concrete reinforced with steel.

- Arch dams: Arch dams are curved dams that depend on the strength of the arch design to hold back water. Like gravity dams, they are most suited to narrow, V-shaped river valleys with solid rock to anchor the structure. Arch dams, however, can be much thinner than gravity dams and use less concrete.

Dams in history

Humans have used dams to trap and store fresh water in reservoirs for more than 5,000 years. Although water is ultimately a plentiful, renewable resource on Earth (Earth is after all "the water planet"), fresh water is scarce or only seasonally available in many regions. Left unregulated, the rivers and streams that provide humans' most essential natural resource are often hazardous to human life and too unpredictable to provide a constant source of fresh water. The ancient civilizations of Egypt, Assyria, Mesopotamia, and China grew and prospered in part because construction of dams and reservoirs allowed for irrigation (watering) of arid (extremely dry) lands, control of seasonal floods, and water storage during dry weather. If Earth's streams and rivers are veins that support human survival, dams are valves that regulate the flow of water through those vessels.

Humans today depend on dams to store water for irrigation, drinking water, and flood control just as they did in the ancient Middle East. Mesopotamians and Sumerians used weirs (low dams built across streams or rivers) and channels (passage for water) to irrigate the land between the Tigris and Euphrates Rivers, called the Fertile Crescent, about 6,500 years ago. Earthen dams that hold drinking and irrigation water in reservoirs for small towns and farms around the world today resemble the earliest known remains of dams. Archeologists estimate that a rock weir and series of small dams and reservoirs near the modern-day town of Jawa in Jordan were constructed about 5,000 years ago. Systems of aqueducts (artificial channels for conveying water) and canals (man-made watercourses designed to carry goods or water) like those constructed during the Roman Empire (1500–2000 years ago) carry water from reservoirs to modern farmlands and cities.

Dams and reservoirs have a second important use beyond water storage and regulation of river flows. They can be used to generate hydropower, one of humans' oldest, simplest, and cleanest forms of renewable and reusable energy. Water that is held in a reservoir above the elevation of the river downstream has stored energy called hydrologic potential. When water is released through the dam from the reservoir, its motion can be used to turn a wheel that can then power a mill or an electrical generator. The farther the water falls, the more energy it releases. Water scientists and engineers use the height of the reservoir surface, called the hydraulic head, to estimate the amount of potential energy stored behind a dam.

The technology to harness the mechanical power of falling water is almost as old as that for water storage and flood control. Ancient Sumerians and Egyptians used waterwheels with buckets on their blades, called norias, to dip water from streams or rivers. By 2,500 years ago, waterwheels drove grain mills and pumped water from wells in the Greek and Roman Empires. During the late Middle Ages, water mills in the industrial centers of Germany and Italy ground grain, pulped wood for paper, spun silk for textiles, pounded metal, tanned hides, and crushed ore (mineral deposits) from mines. During the Industrial Revolution of the nineteenth century, British civil and mining engineers constructed 200 dams taller than 49 feet (15 meters, which is about the height of a five-story building) to store water for Britain's rapidly growing cities and to provide hydropower for mining and transport of coal, the energy source that powered industrialization.

Modern dams

Today's dams and reservoirs provide many of the same benefits to humans and rely on the same basic technology as they did in ancient times. However, the size and complexity of modern water control and structures and systems would have astounded ancient Greeks and nineteenth century engineers. In developed nations like the United States, all of the major rivers have been dammed and almost every river system has been altered by humans. Worldwide, there were over 45,000 dams taller than 49 feet (15 meters) in 150 countries at the end of the twentieth century. Today, dams hold water for irrigation, control flooding along rivers, provide water for cities, and generate about one-fifth of the world's electricity. In the countries with the most dams—China, the United States, and the nations of the former Soviet Union—engineering has given humans almost complete control over the rivers. In fact, one of the main reasons humans can no longer depend on hydropower to meet rising electricity needs is that there are very few large rivers left on Earth to be dammed.

Dams are, by nature, destined to fail. A river erodes (wears away) and deposits sediment (particles of sand, silt, and clay) along its path from where it originates to the ocean in an attempt to create a constant slope (slanting contour of the land) called a graded profile. When a dam, natural or otherwise, blocks a river, the river adjusts to a new pattern of erosion and deposition in an attempt to return to its graded profile. In essence, the river attempts to remove the obstacle; reservoirs fill with sediment, and downstream erosion cuts under dams. Dams built before the 1930s were constructed with little knowledge of how rivers work or how structures can be designed to resist failure. One in ten dams built in the United States before 1930 has collapsed. In 1889, more than 2,200 people were killed when the earthen embankment above Johnstown, Pennsylvania failed and the town was flooded. By the 1930s, use of concrete and metal in dams, arched designs, and an understanding of rivers allowed engineers to build safer, stronger dams. The new technology also led to an era of construction of ever-larger dams that has lasted until the present.

Environmental and social implications of superdams

The world's largest dams are massive structures over 492 feet or 150 meters tall (more than three times the height of the Statue of Liberty) that hold back reservoirs that cover a total land area about the size of Nebraska and Kansas combined. Construction of more than 300 super dams since the early

Three Gorges Dam: Triumph or Travesty?

Barges now travel over the remains of cites flooded after the construction of the Three Gorges Dam in China. © *James Whitlow Delano/Corbis. Reproduced by permission.*

In 1993, seventy-four years after Sun Yat Sen, the "Father of the Chinese Revolution," first proposed a dam across the Yangtze River, preparation began for construction of a massive hydropower plant in the Three Gorges region of China. The Yangtze River is known as the "mighty dragon" that has brought both prosperity and tragedy for the estimated four hundred million people living along its banks. The same unpredictable floods that replenish the fertile soil of central China have destroyed millions of homes, drowned millions of acres of crops, and killed thousands of people over the last century.

When the Three Gorges Dam is complete, it will be the world's largest and tallest dam, and it will hold back a 360-mile (579 kilometer) long reservoir. The dam will be 610 feet (186 meters) tall, 1.3 miles (2 kilometers) long, and will be visible from the Moon. Chinese government officials and other supporters of the project say that the Three Gorges structure will "tame the dragon" by protecting millions of people downstream of the dam from dangerous flooding and by improving navigation on the river. The hydroelectric plant will generate enough inexpensive electricity to power most of central China.

Opponents of the Three Gorges project argue that its costs far outweigh its potential benefits. In addition to its $29 billion price tag as of 2004, the project has already been plagued with corruption, shoddy construction, and cost overruns. Construction of the reservoir will force about 1.9 million people from their homes and drown tens of thousands of significant natural, archeological, and historical sites. A billion tons of untreated industrial waste and sewage will flow into the new lake. Other potential problems include erosion and loss of fertility in farmlands, coastal erosion, and contamination of water and food.

twentieth century has created both benefits and problems for people living nearby. The economic, social, and environmental costs of major dams like the Grand Coulee dam on the Columbia River in the United States, the High Aswan dam on the Nile in Egypt, the Itaipu dam on the Paraná River between Brazil and Paraguay, the La Grande dams in Canada, and the Three Gorges Dam across the Yangtze River in China are extremely high and could possibly, according to many geologists, exceed the long-term benefits of the projects.

Aswan High Dam

The Aswan High Dam and Lake Nasser in Egypt, as seen from the space shuttle *Discovery*. © 1996 *Corbis. Reproduced by permission.*

The modern Aswan High Dam, like the ancient Pyramids at Giza, is a marvel of Egyptian engineering and government organization. It is a massive embankment dam across the Nile River at the first set of rapids in the Egyptian city of Aswan near the Sudan-Egypt border. The dam, known as *Saad al Aali* in Arabic, was completed in 1971 after 10 years of work by more than 30,000 people. Since then, the Aswan High Dam has controlled flooding on the Nile, provided hydroelectric power to millions of Egyptians, and dramatically increased the amount of useable farmland along the banks of the Nile. The waters of Lake Nasser, the 500-mile (805-kilometer) long reservoir contained behind the dam, sustained Egypt through droughts, floods, and economic downturns that brought famine, poverty and war to the rest of northeastern Africa in the 1980s and 1990s.

Greek Historian Herodotus wrote, "Egypt is the gift of the Nile" in the fifth century B.C.E. This is as true today as it was then. (About 95% of Egyptians live within 12 miles of the Nile.) Recognizing a need for Egypt's growing population to make more efficient use of the Nile, Egyptian President Gamal Abdel Nasser commissioned a new dam at Aswan as a government project in the late 1950s. (The original Aswan dam was built by the British in 1889. It was reinforced several times before the need for a larger, stronger dam became apparent.) The high dam was extremely costly and the project's financing placed Egypt in the middle of Cold War controversy. (The Cold War was a prolonged conflict for world dominance between the democratic United States and the communist Soviet Union. The weapons of conflict were commonly words of propaganda and threats.) When the Americans and British withdrew their support after a conflict between Israel and Egypt, Nasser turned to the Soviet Union for help to complete the dam.

Like all superdams, the Aswan High Dam has also had significant environmental and social drawbacks. Tens of thousands of people, mostly Nubian nomads of the Sahara Desert in Sudan, were forced from their homes and land. Ancient artifacts and historical sites were drowned beneath the waters of Lake Nasser. Archeologists and historians located and moved many invaluable sites and objects, including the Great Temple of Abu Sibel, before the lake was flooded, but many treasures were lost. Without annual floods of the Nile, Egyptian croplands no longer receive new nutrient-rich layers of silt, and their fertility has diminished, leaving Egyptian farmers dependent on chemical fertilizers. The Nile delta and beaches of the Mediterranean Sea are shrinking without sand supplied from the mouth of the Nile. Sediment has, instead, collected in Lake Nasser and reduced its capacity. About 15% of the water in Lake Nasser evaporates into the atmosphere or seeps through the dam. The Aswan Dam has been a source of prosperity for Egypt and, in the eyes of the Egyptian government and general public, its benefits have outweighed its costs.

Problems associated with very large dams are now becoming apparent to geologists. According to the World Commission on Dams (WCD), between 30 and 60 million people, mostly poor farmers and people in India and China, have been displaced by large hydropower projects. Irreplaceable natural, archeological, and historical sites are drowned beneath huge reservoirs. Drowned vegetation contaminates reservoir water and fish. Dams like Hoover and Glen Canyon dams on the Colorado River in the United States, or the Aswan High Dam on the Nile, disrupt river systems so large that the ecology (living environment) of an entire region has to adjust. Downstream, agricultural lands may lose their fertility, water quality is poor, and natural ecosystems (interactions between living organisms and their environment) are harmed. Coastal erosion results when rivers no longer replenish deltas (land area before river enters larger body of water) with sediment.

Many environmental groups, scientists, and even some governments have begun to seek solutions to the problems presented by large dams. Decreasing the size and number of new dams, discovering new energy alternatives, managing river flows to counteract harmful environmental and social effects, and even removing some dams have all been considered. With the new goal of using dams and reservoirs to create a sustainable human and natural environment, modern and ancient water management technology combined could serve well far into the future.

Laurie Duncan, Ph.D.

For More Information

Books

Postel, Sandra, and Brian Richter. Washington, DC: Island Press, 2003.

World Commission on Dams. London: Earthscan Publications, Ltd., 2001.

Websites

"Benefits of Dams to Society—Did You Know?" http://www. ussdams.org/benefits.html (accessed on August 24, 2004).

"Rivers, Dams, and Climate Change." http://www.irn.org/ programs/greenhouse (accessed on August 24, 2004).

"U.S. Army Corps of Engineers Education Center—Water Resources Management." http://education.usace.army.mil/ water/resmgmt.html (accessed on August 24, 2004).

Desalination

Approximately 97% of Earth's water is either sea water or brackish water (a mixture of salt and fresh water). Humans and other animals cannot drink salt water and to do so can bring on dehydration (the loss of the body's existing water) that can lead to illness and in extreme cases, death.

Desalination is the process of removing salt from seawater to make it drinkable (drinkable water is also called potable water) or to make it useable for irrigation (watering fields and crops).

Natural desalination occurs everyday as a part of the world's hydrologic cycle. As salt water from the oceans evaporates (changes from liquid to gas), the salt is left behind and the water that moves into the atmosphere is fresh water. Thus, the water in clouds that eventually falls as rain is fresh water.

Salt can also be removed from water by a series of processes known as manipulated desalinization, desalting, or saline water reclamation (salt water reclamation). All of these manmade processes are expensive in terms of how much money and energy they each require to produce a gallon of water.

Salt is composed (made up) of sodium and chorine atoms (the smallest particles of each element). Seawater contains the same kind of salt (sodium chloride) used everyday on food and in cooking. In addition, seawater also contains many small particles of the chemicals such as calcium and magnesium that also form chemicals called salts. Some of these salts come from chemicals used by industry, others from natural processes. Between three and four pounds out of every 100 pounds of atoms in saltwater (the hydrogen and oxygen atoms that together form water plus the atoms of all chemicals dissolved in the water) are combined into salts. Public health officials who test water use a different scale and label the salt in water as parts (particles) per million (ppm). Using this scale, seawater contains 35,000 ppm of dissolved salts. Brackish water typically contains less than half the amount of salt that is found in seawater, about 5,000–10,000 ppm of salt. Safe drinking water for humans, and water for most types of crops, must contain only 5,000–10,000 ppm of salt.

Methods to remove salt

There are several ways to remove salt from seawater and the method used is determined by the intended use of the water. Salt can also be removed from groundwater contaminated with saltwater. For example, if the water is to be drinkable then more salt needs to be removed than if the water is to be used for crops. Cost is also an important consideration because the more salt that needs to be removed, the greater the cost.

Stories from ancient Greece tell of how sailors obtained fresh water by first removing salt from seawater by evaporating the seawater, and then condensing (changing from a gas to a liquid) the air carrying the evaporated water. This process, because it uses the heat of the Sun is now called solar distillation. Solar distillation is similar to the natural process of the heat of the Sun evaporating water from the oceans that later condense into fresh water drops in clouds. When the water evaporates, only fresh water moves into the surrounding air because the salts are too heavy and are left behind in the ocean. Only fresh water went into the surrounding air (for example, the air over a bucket of seawater). As the air came into contact with cooler sheets or sails spread over the bucket, drops of fresh water would form and could then be collected in a separate bucket.

A worker samples water from the Doha, Kuwait desalination facility. © *Ed Kashi/Corbis. Reproduced by permission.*

Other, but far less efficient ways to obtain fresh water included the use of filtering seawater. One method of filtering included the use of a wool wick (a length of rope made of wool) to absorb (siphon) the water. The salts were trapped in the wool and fresh water dripped out. Water was also poured through sand or clay to remove salts.

By the fourth century (400 A.D.) onward, people obtained fresh water by boiling salt water and using sponges to absorb the fresh water in the air above the pot. The first scientific paper on desalting was published by Arab scientists in the eighth century.

The first desalination efforts for industry started in 1869, as land-based steam distillation plants were established in Britain to prepare fresh water for ships going to sea.

Methods of distillation and filtering are still the most widely used methods of desalination used in most areas of the world.

Other modern techniques use complex machines that change the temperature at which water boils away by lowering the pressure of the atmosphere over a sealed container of water.

This methods reduces the formation of crusty white salts, which appear similar to the sticky white powder found at the bottom of a pan from which all water has boiled away. These crusty white salts can clog machinery and make it more difficult to heat water. In industry, the crusty residue is called scaling, and the method of lowering the temperature at which water boils is called multistage distillation (multiple stages of distillation). The goal of multistage distillation is to reduce the boiling point of water to a temperature where it will still boil (evaporate) into a collection flask, but that it will not form a crusty salt residue. The residue forms at about 160°F (71°C) so the goal is to reduce the boiling point of water to less than 160°F. In some desalinization plants, distilled water is also filtered of other pollutants to make it ready to drink.

A process called reverse osmosis can also be used to remove salt from water. Water molecules are forced through a plastic membrane (a barrier) with very small pores (openings) that allow the passage of water, but not of salts.

K. Lee Lerner

For More Information

Books

Farndon, John. *Water (Science Experiments)*. Salt Lake City, UT: Benchmark Books, 2000.

Postel, Sandra, and Brian Richter. *Rivers for Life: Managing Water for People and Nature*. Washington, DC: Island Press, 2003.

Websites

"Chemistry Tutorial. The Chemistry of Water." *Biology Project. University of Arizona.* http://www.biology.arizona.edu/biochemistry/tutorials/chemistry/page3.html (accessed on August 26, 2004).

"Water Basics." *Water Science for Schools, United States Geological Survey.* http://ga.water.usgs.gov/edu/mwater.html (accessed on August 26, 2004).

Hydropower

Hydropower is energy that is generated by moving water. Today, hydropower facilities make electricity by converting kinetic (moving) energy into mechanical (machine) energy as water flows in a river or over a dam. Electricity made at hydropower facilities can be carried away, via power transmission lines, and sold to homes and businesses. Hydropower is a relatively inexpensive, non-polluting form of renewable energy.

Canada and the United States are currently the world's top hydroelectric producers. Other countries that use hydropower on a large scale include Brazil, China, Russia, Norway, Japan, India, Iceland, Sweden, and France. Hydropower produces about 10% of United States' electricity, in contrast to Norway, who generates nearly 99% of its electricity from hydropower. Hydropower is used nationwide, but is primarily used in the western coastal United States where other energy resources such as coal are limited. Hydropower is important to the United States economy because it supplies electricity to a growing population and industry.

Hydropower in history

Humans have harnessed water power for thousands of years, using the mechanical energy of moving water to turn wooden wheels to power mills that sawed lumber and processed grains. Water either fell onto the wheel and caused it to turn or the wheel was placed in the river and the river's current (a steady flow of water in a prevailing direction) turned the wheel. The wheel was attached to other levers and gears inside the mill that did the work needed. During the 1700s to 1800s, mechanical hydropower was used extensively in the United States and elsewhere for milling and pumping. It began to be widely used to supply electricity in the late 1800s. In 1882 the world's first hydropower facility was built on the Fox River in Appleton, Wisconsin. The Fox River facility generated electricity for local industries.

By the 1920s, following the development of the electrical motor and the demand for electricity that followed, hydropower accounted for about 40% of the U.S. electricity supply. Since then, other energy technologies have developed that are less expensive than hydropower.

In 1933, President Franklin D. Roosevelt (1882–1945) signed the Tennessee Valley Authority (TVA) Act. The purpose of the TVA was to construct dams on the Tennessee River that would aid in river navigation, control flooding, provide water for irrigation (watering crops) and drinking, and provide hydropower to Tennessee River Valley residents. In the American West, hydropower aided in the production of the

Swimmers enjoy geothermally heated pools at Svartsvehring, Iceland. © Bob Krist/Corbis. Reproduced by permission.

dams themselves, moving and lifting construction materials and providing energy for lights to make round-the-clock work possible. Surplus energy was sold to neighboring farms and homes, which in turn paid for the operation and building costs of the dams. Hydropower facility development was at its peak during the 1930s and 1940s. The Hoover Dam on the Nevada-Arizona border and the Grand Coulee dam located on the Columbia River in Washington state were constructed during this period. The Grand Coulee dam remains the largest concrete structure in the United States.

Hydroelectric technology

Electricity is one of the most important types of energy because it allows people to perform the work needed to light homes and power appliances and computers. Hydropower generation utilizes the principles of electromagnetic induction (creating an electrical current, the flow of electricity, by moving a magnet through a wire coil), first described by English chemist and physicist Michael Faraday (1791–1867) in 1831 when he made the first generator. A generator is a machine that converts mechanical energy to electrical energy. Energy is the power to do work. Energy cannot be created or destroyed; it merely changes state, as occurs when electrical energy is harnessed from the mechanical energy of moving water.

No matter the type or size of the hydropower facility, electricity is generated in much the same way in each one. The dam or the natural elevation drop in a river creates head, or a certain height over which the water flows as it is released from the dam or as it flows downstream. As water is released from a reservoir in an impoundment or pumped storage facility, or diverted from a river through a control gate, it flows by gravity (the attraction between two masses) to a turbine. A turbine is a device that transforms the energy in moving fluid or wind to rotary mechanical energy. As the water flows past the turbine blades, the turbine blades spin and turn a rotor (the moving part of an electric generator) much like wind spins a pinwheel. Giant magnets inside the rotor move past coils of copper wire and create an alternating current. An alternating current (AC) is produced when electrons wiggle back and forth between atoms. The used water returns to the river through pipes.

The alternating current moves through a series of devices called transformers that can increase the voltage (energy required to move a charge from one point to another, similar to pressure). The increase in voltage allows the electricity to travel faster and more efficiently through power lines (important when the hydropower facility is in a remote location) from the hydropower facility to a town's electricity facility. At the local facility transformers are used again to reduce the voltage to a level that is safe for the electricity to be used in homes and businesses.

Types of hydropower facilities

There are three types of hydropower facilities: impoundment, pumped storage, and diversion. Impoundment and pumped storage facilities require dams. In the United States, hydropower is a very small percentage of the primary purpose of dams. Usually a dam is built first for other reasons, such as water storage and flood control, and a hydropower facility is incorporated later if there is a demonstrated need for electricity.

Impoundment facilities require a large dam that allows river water to be stored in a reservoir. When water is released from the reservoir, the water flows downward through a penstock (pipe) in the dam and spins turbines, thereby creating mechanical energy that is then used to power electric generators. Transmission lines carry electricity away from the impoundment facility to local distributors who sell the electricity to homes and businesses.

Pumped storage hydropower facilities also require dams to operate. In periods of low electricity demand water is pumped from a lower reservoir to a higher reservoir. When electrical demand increases, water is released from the higher reservoir back into the lower reservoir through a penstock, turning tur-

Iceland

The northern island of Iceland is known for generating geothermal power (power derived from heat found under Earth's surface) rather than hydropower. Yet when large glaciers (large, slow-moving mass of ice) melt in the spring it supplies water to large rivers and provides favorable conditions for hydropower development. Long, dark, and cold winters contribute to Iceland's high rate of energy consumption, second only to Norway.

In the early 1900s, Icelanders primarily used peat (plant debris and moss from bogs that is dried) for fuel. By 1940 imported coal and oil were used. Geothermal and hydropower accounted for only approximately 9% of Iceland's energy. About 87% of houses in Iceland are currently heated with geothermal energy. The rest are heated with electricity, 83% of which is generated using hydropower. Orkustofnun, Iceland's National Energy Authority, estimates that only about 10–15% of Iceland's potential hydropower sites have been developed.

Tennessee Valley Authority

Prior to 1933, residents of the Tennessee River Valley lived without water and power. Many people lived in poverty without jobs following the Great Depression, which began in 1929. In 1933, President Franklin D. Roosevelt signed the Tennessee Valley Authority Act as part of his New Deal plan, a series of social programs that reformed American financial practices and offered relief and jobs to struggling Americans during the Depression. This act created the Tennessee Valley Authority (TVA), a federally funded utility company incorporating approximately 80,000 square miles (207,200 square kilometers) in Tennessee and parts of Kentucky, Virginia, North Carolina, Georgia, Alabama, and Mississippi.

The TVA was initially charged with making rivers more navigable and bringing water and electricity to homes and farms throughout the seven southern states. Since its founding, the TVA has also been responsible for developing flood control through dam construction, improving and maintaining water quality, replanting forests, developing roads and providing recreation opportunities on lakes and rivers. The TVA improved the Tennessee River Valley economy by providing construction and maintenance jobs to the region and supporting farm and industry development.

Originally, tax dollars provided funding for TVA projects, but today the TVA supports its staff and maintains its facilities by making and selling electricity. Today the TVA is the largest public power company in the United States, supplying power for more than eight million people. The TVA currently operates twenty-nine hydroelectric and one pumped-storage dam, eleven coal-fired plants, three nuclear power plants, and several solar, wind, and other renewable energy sites.

bines that power electric generators. Pumped storage and impoundment hydropower facilities provide a reliable source of electricity because water flow from reservoirs can be controlled so that electricity production meets demand.

Diversion hydropower facilities (sometimes called run-of-river systems) are smaller than impoundment facilities and do not require a dam. Instead, diversion facilities use a river's natural flow to generate electricity. The amount of electricity produced depends upon the river's rate of flow (volume of water flow within a period of time) and the river's elevation change at the diversion facility site. In diversion hydropower facilities, river water is channeled through a canal (artificial waterway that controls water flow, in this case, to a turbine) or penstock. Diversion facilities are less reliable than impoundment or pumped storage facilities because flow rates in rivers can change drastically depending on the amount of rainfall or spring meltwater that supplies the river.

Hoover Dam

The Hoover Dam hydropower plant is driven by waters of the Colorado River. © Royalty-Free/CORBIS. Reproduced by permission.

Hoover Dam was built on Black Canyon, about 30 miles (48 kilometers) southeast of Las Vegas on the Colorado River. The dam took less than five years (1931–36) to complete and employed an average of 3,500 people each year. At 726.4 feet (221.4 meters) tall, Hoover Dam was the largest dam of the time. Today, Hoover Dam is a National Historic Landmark and heralded as one of America's Seven Modern Civil Engineering Wonders. The dam and Hoover Power plant (the hydropower facili-

ty) are currently operated and maintained by the Bureau of Reclamation. The reservoir (Lake Mead) is maintained jointly by the Bureau of Reclamation and the National Park Service.

Hoover Dam was built to control waters of the Colorado River Basin, including the Green, San Juan, Virgin, and Gila Rivers, which are all tributaries (smaller streams that feed into a larger stream or river) of the Colorado River. Rivers of the Colorado River Basin drain a 242,000-square-mile (626,777-square-kilometer) area of the western United States between Colorado and the Gulf of California. Arizona, California, Colorado, Nevada, New Mexico, Utah, and Wyoming are allocated water from the Colorado River Basin.

The Hoover power plant is a U-shaped facility located at the base of the dam. The power plant was installed in 1961 and upgraded between 1986 and 1993. Water from the river is taken through 30-foot (9-meter) wide penstocks to sixteen 13-foot (4 meter) wide penstocks to the turbines. Electricity generated in the Hoover power plant supplies the operations of the dam and plant and provides low-cost power to Arizona, Nevada, and Southern California. Revenues from the sale of power have allowed for its $165 million dollar dam construction cost to be repaid to the Federal Treasury. Revenue monies now pay for operation and maintenance of the dam.

Sizes of hydropower facilities

The size of a hydropower facility depends upon the amount of energy that can be generated at the facility. Some hydropower plants may produce electricity for only one to a few homes. These facilities are called micro-hydropower plants. In micro-hydropower facilities the total change in elevation of the flowing water is only about 100 feet (30 meters). Energy output can be increased, however, with higher water flow. Larger hydroelectric power facilities such as the Hoover power plant in Nevada, however, can provide electricity to more than one million consumers.

Benefits and drawbacks of hydropower

Hydropower is an efficient, clean, and reliable source of energy. Once hydropower plants are constructed and the technology is in place, the cost of hydropower is the lowest of all energy sources. No fuel is used during hydropower production; water returns to the river. No pollutants are released into the air during electrical generation, so the air around hydropower plants remains clean. Hydropower facilities can respond to high demands for electricity through reservoir storage, even in times of water shortage.

The negative effects of hydropower generally come from large-scale facilities. Impoundment or pumped storage facilities often alter wildlife habitats along rivers because large dams must be built to provide a reservoir. Dams can flood areas close to a river or lake, obstruct fish migration (periodic movement from one region to another), and affect water quality and flow downstream. Humans are sometimes displaced from their homes when dams are built. In diversion facilities, seasonal and annual fluctuations (variations) in water supply can negatively affect electrical production if river flow rates become too low. Regulations and licensing permits for dams and hydropower facilities as well as electrical transportation from remote hydropower are often costly.

The future of hydropower

Recent energy shortages in the United States has spurred the government to study hydropower's future potential. The Department of Energy has identified 5,677 sites in the United States that have potential for large-scale hydropower development, but many of these sites are not possible because of economic drawback, such as their remote location, environmental issues, and other circumstances. Because a change to hydropower as a primary energy source could help lessen air pollution and reduce demands for fossil fuels (oil and gas), hydropower will likely be further explored.

Laurie Duncan, Ph.D., and Marcy Davis, M.S.

For More Information

Books

Mann, Elizabeth, and Alan Witschonke. *Hoover Dam: The Story of Hard Times, Tough People, and the Taming of a Rough River.* New York: Mikaya Press, 2001.

Websites

"Energy in Iceland." *Ministries of Industry and Commerce.* http://brunnur.stjr.is/interpro/ivr/ivreng.nsf/0/344886a871936f30002568d30038828d?OpenDocument (accessed on August 26, 2004).

"Hydro Facts." *National Hydropower Association.* http://www.hydro.org/hydrofacts/index.asp (accessed on August 26, 2004).

"Hydropower." *Energy Efficiency and Renewable Energy, U.S. Department of Energy.* http://www.eere.energy.gov/RE/hydropower.html (accessed on August 26, 2004).

"The Story of Hoover Dam." *United States Bureau of Reclamation.* http://www.usbr.gov/lc/hooverdam/History/index.htm (accessed on August 26, 2004).

"TVA: Electricity for All." *Tennessee Valley Authority.* http://newdeal.feri.org/tva (accessed on August 26, 2004).

Ports and Harbors

Peoples of ancient civilizations often built their cities on the shores of natural harbors. A harbor is place on the coastline that is protected from the full effects of tide and currents (a steady flow of ocean waters in a prevailing direction). Harbors are often shaped like horseshoes. They are surrounded by land with a narrow opening through which ships can pass. Man-made harbors use structures such as walls or barriers built into the water to protect anchored ships from tide or storm damage.

Building cities near harbors permitted the construction of ports for trade. A port is a place on a shoreline for the loading and unloading of cargo from shipping vessels. Ports can be located on the ocean coast or on the shores of lakes and rivers. Cities with working ports are also called seaports or port cities.

Many of the great cities of the ancient world were seaports. Seaports allowed cities to grow and flourish. Trade made them wealthy. Ports also sheltered ships of war, sometimes a necessi-

◦Barrier Island: Long, narrow coastal island built up parallel to the mainland.

◦Export: Raw materials or goods that are shipped, traded, or sold to other nations.

◦Import: Raw materials or goods that are produced in a foreign country and brought into another.

◦Jetty: Structure built out into the sea, a lake, or a river to protect the harbor or shore against waves or tides.

◦Navigation channel: Passage in a waterway that is naturally deep or dredged to permit the passage of ships, or a defined, well-marked passage that leads from the docks to open waters; also called ship channel.

ty to guard desirable seaports from invasion. The ancient seaport of Alexandria (Egypt), located along a man-made harbor along the Mediterranean Sea and the end of the Nile River, thrived for centuries. Alexandria was invaded several times and ruled by the Egyptians, Greeks, and Romans. The modern city of Alexandria, Egypt, is located a few miles (kilometers) from the underwater ruins of the ancient seaport.

Modern ports and harbors

Improvements in technology has allowed ships to travel faster, carry more cargo, and load with greater ease. Ports have grown in size to accommodate today's bigger, faster ships. However, many parts of modern ports closely resemble their ancient counterparts.

In modern day, there are over 185 seaports in the United States. Trade with other nations, called overseas trade, is important to a nation's economy. Two types of overseas trade occur, imports and exports. Imports are goods and materials that are shipped into United States from other countries. Exports are goods and materials from the United States that are shipped to other nations. Ships move most U.S. overseas trade, and shipping on waterways remains one of the least expensive means of transporting goods.

Modern ports have several special structures that help with the movement of cargo between land and ships. Navigation channels or ship channels that ships travel into port are marked "roadways." Docks and piers permit vessels to moor (secure to the dock) and for cargo to be loaded and unloaded from ships. Cranes and ramps aid the movement of cargo. On land, ports have large warehouses to store cargo. The waterside port area is connected to inland transportation systems such as roads, railways, pipelines, and airports. This allows cargo from ships to be loaded onto trucks, trains, or airplanes for transport to inland destinations. Cargo is often stored in containers that can be loaded from trucks to trains to ships. For example, metal boxes on railroad cars can be detached and loaded directly onto barges or ships. Liquid cargo, such as oil or gasoline, can be piped from large reservoirs onboard ships into tanker trucks or tanker train cars.

Building and maintaining successful ports

Modern ports must be built to accommodate several types of ships, from oil tankers and tugboats, to barges and passenger ships. Ports not only aid trade; they are also important centers

The Port of Hong Kong

A junk, a form of boat popular in the waters, sails into the port of Honk Kong, China. © *Nik Wheeler/Corbis. Reproduced by permission.*

Hong Kong, China, is one of the major ports of the world. A large natural harbor with deep waters and several barrier islands (narrow coastal island parallel to the mainland) protect the city of Hong Kong from the tides. The port serves commercial, military, and passenger vessels. During the year 2001, nearly 40,000 seagoing vessels used Hong Kong's port.

(In the nineteenth century, Great Britain took control of Hong Kong. In 1898, a treaty with China gave Great Britain control of Hong Kong for 99 years. On July 1, 1997, the treaty expired and Hong Kong reverted to Chinese control.)

Over the past century, Hong Kong grew into one of the wealthiest most productive ports in the world. When the port was established, it had a sparse population and no industry. In modern day Hong Kong is a major industrial center and one of the most densely populated cities in the world. Hong Kong must import raw materials for construction and manufacturing. However, the city prospers because of its factories that produce clothing, shoes, toys, electronics, plastics, and jewelry for export to other countries.

of travel for people. Passenger ferries and cruise ships carry people from one port to another. Ports usually have separate docks, piers, and places to moor for passenger vessels.

Even if a port is located in a natural harbor, river, or lake, the waterways must be maintained. Ship channels must be kept sufficiently deep to permit the passage of ships, barges, and tugboats. Dredging makes waterways deeper by removing the silt (tiny particles of rock, soil, and plant material) and mud that clogs channels. Docks, piers, and jetties (protective rock barriers) need continual maintenance. The U.S. government and local port authorities oversee daily operations at United States ports.

Problems, concerns, and the future of ports

Ports are vital to the economies of the cities in which they are located. However, the warehouses, docks, cranes, and shipyards of a working port are generally not considered attractive. Ports occupy large amounts of land near waterways. Commercial ships, vessels used for trade, are large and difficult to navigate. They can pose a danger to small recreational boats. Laws often prohibit or limit recreational boats in ship channels and other key port waters. Thus, ports can sometimes restrict individuals' use of shorelines, coastal areas, and waterways. City planners work to carefully balance the needs of the port with the interests of citizens and businesses.

Ports also pose special challenges for marine (ocean) and coastal environments. The constant presence of large vessel traffic can disturb plants, animals, and microorganisms that live in port and harbor waters. The construction of jetties and breakwaters changes the effect of tides and currents within a harbor or port area. This alters the water chemistry of water within the jetties. Water chemistry is the balance of temperature, minerals, salts, and even pollutants in water. Even a slight change in the temperature, muddiness, or salinity (saltiness) of water can harm marine life.

As ships require fuel to operate, port areas have to store and transport large amounts of gas and oil. Leaks, spills, and shipwrecks damage underwater and coastal habitats. Ports also increase the amount of other types of pollutants, such as litter. However, ships produce less air pollution than airplanes, trucks, or trains loaded with the same tonnage of cargo.

Transportation systems are always changing and improving. Ships, trains, and airplanes are becoming bigger, faster, and more efficient. Trucks and airplanes, only invented a century ago, are already essential means of moving goods and materials. Yet a port, an idea centuries old, remains an efficient link for land and ocean transport.

Adrienne Wilmoth Lerner

For More Information

Books

Bone, Kevin, et al. *The New York Waterfront: Evolution and Building Culture of the Port and Harbor.* New York: Monacelli Press, 2003.

Websites

NOAA National Ocean Service. "Marine Navigation" *National Oceanic and Atmospheric Administration.* http://oceanservice. noaa.gov/topics/navops/marinenav/welcome.html (accessed on August 24, 2004).

Tide Energy

Tides are twice-daily rises and falls of water level relative to land. Ocean tides can produce strong currents (a steady flow of ocean waters in a prevailing direction) along some coastlines. Humans have sought to harness the kinetic (motion-induced) energy of the tides for hundreds of years. Residents of coastal England and France have used tidal energy to turn water wheels and generate mechanical energy for grain mills since the eleventh century. In modern day, tidal currents are used to generate electricity. Tidal energy is a non-polluting, renewable energy source. Modern day technologies for exploiting tidal energy are, however, relatively expensive and are limited to a few coastlines with extremely high and low tides. Tidal energy may, in the future, become more widely used and economically practical.

The power in tides

Tides result from the gravitational pulls of the Moon and Sun on the surface of the spinning Earth. Gravity is the force of attraction between all masses. The shape of the shore and adjacent seafloor affects the tidal range (difference between high and low tides) along specific coastlines. Some places, like the English Channel between France and England, and the Bay of Fundy in Nova Scotia, Canada, experience very high and low tides. The tides protected Medieval monasteries in the English Channel since the eighth century. Mont-St.-Michel in western France and Lindisfarne (Holy Island) in northern England are churches built on small islands surrounded by miles of tidal flats (a broad, flat area of coastline alternately covered and exposed by the tides). Today, they are connected to the mainland by roadways but in Medieval times, only devout pilgrims rushed to make the hurried trip across miles (kilometers) of shifting sand between roaring tidal pulses.

For tidal energy to be a practical source for electricity generation, the tidal range in a coastal area must be at least 16.5 feet (5 meters). The greater an area's tidal range, the more electricity will be produced. Although tidal energy is reliable and plentiful, only a handful of suitable tidal power station locations have been proposed worldwide. Two large tidal power plants are in operation today at La Rance in Brittany, France, and in the Canadian town of Annapolis Royal, Nova Scotia. In the United States, tidal energy as a power source is realistic only in Alaska and Maine.

WORDS TO KNOW

Barrage: Artificial obstruction such as a dam constructed in a water channel to increase water depth or divert flow.

Tidal fence: Devices installed in an area with highly-changing tides that make electricity by harnessing tidal energy.

Tidal flat: A broad, flat area of coastline alternately covered and exposed by the tides.

Tide: Periodic rise and fall of sea level along coastlines caused by gravitational and rotational forces between the Sun, Moon, and Earth.

Turbine: A spinning wheel or other device that converts the kinetic (motion-induced) of a fluid such as water to mechanical motion, which in turn generates electrical energy.

Exploiting tidal energy

Devices used to exploit tidal energy may be shore-based or ocean-based systems. Both systems use a fluctuating column of water to propel turbine blades and generate electricity. This means that the water on one side of the dam is higher than on the other side. As the water falls from the high side of the dam to the other, turbines turn and produce electricity.

A barrage is a shore-based, dam-like structure that is built across a narrow-mouthed estuary (the part of a river where it nears the sea and fresh and salt water mix). As the tide ebbs and flows (moves in and out) through tunnels in the barrage, the water turns large fan-like turbines and generates electricity. Barrages are expensive to build and can harm estuarine life by restricting water flow over the tidal flats. Electricity produced by tidal energy has no harmful wastes or emissions such as greenhouse gases. Once built, the barrage is easy to maintain and inexpensive to run.

Ocean-based systems include tidal fences and offshore turbines. Tidal fences are like giant subway turnstiles built across the sea floor between the mainland and an island or between two islands. When a tidal fence is built across an open body of water, water is forced to pass through the vertical turbine gates and electricity is generated. Tidal fences may restrict tidal flow and the ability of wildlife to pass through. Offshore turbines are like giant propellers placed on large posts that are set in a line across the sea floor. Ocean currents flow past the turbines and cause the blades to spin and generate electricity. Offshore turbines are like giant propellers placed on large posts that are set in a line across the sea floor. Ocean currents flow past the turbines and cause the blades to spin and generate electricity.

Tidal fence turbines have a much lower initial cost when compared to barrages and are much less harmful to the environment because they do not restrict tidal ebb and flow. Tidal turbines also allow wildlife and small boats to pass through the area. Offshore turbine blades are smaller and less protected than those housed in barrages or tidal fences and so they are more prone to damage from strong tidal currents. Ocean-based systems are much less expensive to install than barrages, but are more expensive to maintain due to their remote location.

Laurie Duncan, Ph.D., and Marcy Davis, M.S.

For More Information

Books

Sylvester, Doug. *Oceans Alive: Water, Waves, and Tides.* San Diego: Rainbow Horizons Publishing, 2001.

Websites

Baird, Stuard. "Energy Fact Sheet: Tidal Energy." *International Council for Local Environmental Initiatives.* http://www.iclei.org/EFACTS/TIDAL.HTM (accessed on August 24, 2004).

"Ocean Energy." *California Energy Commission.* http://www.energy.ca.gov/development/oceanenergy/ (accessed on August 24, 2004).

Wastewater Management

Wastewater is any water that requires cleaning after it is used. This includes water that has been used for laundry, bathing, dishwashing, toilets, garbage disposals, and industrial purposes. Wastewater also includes rainwater that has accumulated pollutants as it runs into oceans, lakes, and rivers. Pollutants are unwanted chemicals or materials that contaminate air, soil, and water.

The goal of wastewater management is to clean and protect water. This means that water must be clean enough so that it can be used by people for drinking and washing, and by industry for commercial purposes. It also must be clean enough to release into oceans, lakes, and rivers after it has been used.

Wastewater is usually divided into two major groups: point source wastewater and non-point source wastewater. Point source wastewater includes wastewaters that enter natural waters (such as lakes, rivers, and oceans) from defined locations. The most common point sources are sanitary sewers and storm drains. Non-point source wastewater is wastewater that is not connected to a specific source. This includes runoff (water that drains away) from agriculture and urban (city) areas, and acidic waters from mines. In many ways, point source wastewater is much easier to manage because its source and the pollutants it contains are known. Non-point source wastewater, on the other hand, is both hard to identify and treat.

◆**Erosion:** The wearing away of land by air, wind, or water.

◆**Estuary:** Wide part of a river where it nears the sea; where fresh and salt water mix.

◆**Non-point source waste-water:** Wastewater that is not connected to a specific source.

◆**Pathogen:** Organisms (such as bacteria, protozoa, and viruses) that can cause disease.

◆**Point source wastewater:** Wastewater that enters natural waters from defined locations.

◆**Sedimentation:** The process when sediments settle to the bottom of a liquid.

◆**Sludge:** A semi-solid residue, containing microorganisms and their products, from any water treatment process.

Sewage treatment

One of the largest sources of wastewater is that which comes from homes and industries. These wastewaters all flow into sanitary sewers, which direct them into sewage treatment plants. Wastewaters from homes contain human waste, food, soaps, and detergents. They also contain pathogens, which are organisms that can cause diseases. Industrial wastewaters contain toxic (poisonous) pollutants, which can endanger human health and harm other organisms. These include pesticides, polychlorinated biphenyls (PCBs,) and heavy metals like lead, mercury, and nickel. These metals are generally toxic to plant and animal life. The goal of sewage treatment is to remove all of these pollutants from the wastewater so that it can be returned to natural waters.

Sewage treatment involves three stages: primary treatment, secondary treatment, and tertiary treatment. Primary treatment physically separates solids and liquids. The wastewater passes through a grating that strains out large particles. The remaining water is left to stand in a tank, where smaller sediments (particles of sand, clay, and other materials) settle to the bottom. These sediments are called sludge. At this point, the liquid part of the wastewater still contains many pollutants and is not safe for exposure to humans or the environment.

In the second step, called secondary treatment, the liquid part of the wastewater passes through a trickling filter or an aeration tank. A trickling filter is a set of pipes with small holes in it that dribbles water over a bed of stones or corrugated plastic. Bacteria in the stones or plastic absorb pollutants from the water and break them down into substances that are not harmful. An aeration tank is a tank that contains bacteria that break down pollutants. The liquid part of the wastewater from primary treatment is pumped into the tank and mixed with the bacteria. Air is bubbled through the tank to help the bacteria grow. As bacteria accumulate, they settle to the bottom of the tank and form sludge. The sludge is removed from the bottom of the tank and buried in landfills.

After secondary treatment, the water is generally free from the majority of pathogens and heavy metals. It still contains high concentrations of nitrate and phosphate, minerals that can overstimulate the growth of algae and plants in natural waters, which can ultimately cause them and the surrounding organisms to die.

Circular pools or treatment ponds of a sewage treatment plant.
© *Lester Lefkowitz/Corbis. Reproduced by permission.*

Tertiary treatment removes these nutrients from the wastewater. One method of tertiary treatment involves using biological, chemical, and physical processes to remove these nutrients. Another method is to pass the water through a wetland or lagoon (shallow body of water cut off from a larger body).

Storm sewers

In most cities in the United States, the sewers that carry storm waters are routed through sewage treatment plants. Much of the runoff from storms contains fertilizers, oils, and other chemicals that should be removed from the water before it enters lakes, rivers, and oceans. When there are very heavy rainfalls, however, the sewage treatment plants can become overwhelmed by the volume of water entering the facility. At these times, sewage and wastewater from storms may be dumped directly into natural water bodies. Many cities have programs underway to separate the storm sewers from sanitary sewers, but these projects are very costly and time consuming.

Agricultural runoff

Agricultural runoff occurs when rain falls to the ground and then runs through agricultural fields or livestock-raising farms. The rainwater can accumulate fertilizer, oils, and animal wastes before it runs into rivers, lakes, and oceans. These materials pollute natural waters and can cause fish to die, contaminate drinking water, and speed up the rate of sedimentation (particles settling to the bottom of a waterway) in lakes and streams. In the summer of 1995, runoff from hog farms in North Carolina caused the rapid growth of the algae *Pfisteria*. This algae released toxins that affected the nervous system of fish as well as humans in the area.

In an attempt to manage agricultural runoff, the Office of Wastewater Management (OWM) of the U.S. Environmental Protection Agency has designated farms as Animal Feeding Operations (AFOS). As of 1998, nearly half a million AFOS had been identified. By designating AFOS, the OWM can regulate the disposal of animal waste products. This moves a large portion of agricultural runoff from the non-point source category to the point source category, and allows for better management of agricultural pollutants.

Acid mine drainage

In places where coal is mined, the mineral pyrite is a waste material. A series of complex reactions between pyrite, oxygen, and water result in acid mine drainage. Acid mine drainage is wastewater that is extremely acidic and contains high concentrations of heavy metals. Acid mine drainage is one of the major sources of stream pollution in the Appalachian mountain region. Acid mine drainage has severely damaged more than half the streams in Pennsylvania and West Virginia. There are at least 200,000 abandoned mines throughout the United States that produce acid mine drainage.

Acid mine drainage can be treated using chemical treatments that decrease the acidity of the water, and allow the heavy metals to precipitate (separate from the water). This type of treatment is often very expensive. Another way to treat acid mine drainage is by passing it through a lagoon or wetlands, which removes heavy metals and decreases the acidity of the water. Acid mine drainage is also treated by passing it through a channel of limestone (a rock that is very alkaline), which also neutralizes the acidity of the water.

Urban runoff

When rain falls on natural lands such as forests and meadows, some of it soaks into the soil and then slowly makes its way to rivers, lakes, and oceans. In cities, much of the land is paved with cement and asphalt, and water is unable to sink into the ground. Instead, it quickly moves to storm drains and then into natural waterways. This great volume of water causes much erosion (wearing away of the land) and sedimentation. In addition, as the rainwater runs over paved surfaces, it gathers oil and grease from cars, fertilizers and pesticides from gardening, pathogens form animal wastes, road salts, and heavy metals. These are dumped directly into natural waters with urban wastewater. Runoff from urban areas is the largest source of pollution in estuaries (the wide part of a river where it nears the sea) and the third largest source of pollution in lakes.

Controlling urban runoff is extremely difficult because its sources are hard to identify. The Environmental Protection Agency works to influence developers to take into account urban runoff when planning new buildings. Some ideas to minimize runoff include adding vegetation and drainage areas to new construction sites. Some cities have instituted sewer-stenciling programs that remind people that rainwater flows directly into natural waters. Gas stations have also been targeted as businesses that can help control car oils and grease. Schools have also developed programs to teach students about urban runoff and non-point source wastewater.

Juli Berwald, Ph.D.

For More Information

Books

Cunningham, William P. and Barbara Woodworth Saigo. *Environmental Science: A Global Concern.* Boston, WCB/McGraw-Hill, 1999.

Raven, Peter H, Linda R. Berg and George B. Johnson. *Environment,* Second Edition. Orlando, FL: Saunders College Publishing, 1998.

Websites

"Agricultural Runoff Management." *Wisconsin Department of Natural Resources.* http://www.dnr.state.wi.us/org/water/wm/nps/animal.htm (accessed on August 24, 2004).

"Managing Urban Runoff." *United States Environmental Protection Agency.* http://www.epa.gov/OWOW/NPS/facts/point7.htm (accessed on August 24, 2004).

"The Science of Acid Mine Drainage and Passive Treatment." *Pennsylvania Department of Environmental Protection.* http://www.dep.state.pa.us/dep/deputate/minres/bamr/amd/science_of_amd.htm (accessed on August 24, 2004).

"Wastewater Primer." *United States Environmental Protection Agency.* http://www.epa.gov/owm/primer.pdf (accessed on August 24, 2004).

Wave Energy

The oceans store large amounts of kinetic (moving) energy from the wind. The wind generates waves as it blows across the sea's) surface. The larger the wave, the more energy the wave contains. Wave energy provides a continuous source of renewable, non-polluting energy that can be converted to electricity at wave power plant sites around the world.

Where the waves are

Windy coastlines around large oceans are the best places to build power plants that harness wave energy. Strong winds that blow continuously over long stretches of open water create the largest waves, which contain the most energy. Strong, steady winds that blow in Earth's major wind belts (zones of wind in a prevailing direction) generate massive waves. In the subtropical zone on either side of the equator (imaginary circle around Earth halfway between the North and South Poles), suitable wind power sites are along east-facing coastlines in the path of the westerly trade winds, such as the east coast of Florida. (Winds are named for the direction from which they blow; the trade winds are strong winds that blow from east to west in the subtropics on either side of the equator.) In mid-latitudes (imaginary lines on Earth that tell how far north or south a place is from the equator), storms along the course of Easterly jet streams, a current of fast-moving air in the upper atmosphere, produce waves that pound west-facing coastlines such as the Pacific Coast of the United States. At higher latitudes, sub-polar easterly winds produce some of the largest waves in the world, up to 100 feet (30.5 meters) high in the North Atlantic Ocean.

Harnessing wave energy

There are two types of energy technologies used to capture wave energy and generate electricity: fixed devices and floating devices. Fixed devices are attached to the shore or sea floor. Tapered channels (TAPCHANS) are fixed devices that direct large waves into raised pools on the shore. Water draining from the pools turns turbines that generate electricity. (Turbines are spinning wheels or other devices that convert the energy in falling water to mechanical and electrical energy.) A power plant on the North Coast of Norway uses a TAPCHAN to harness wave energy. TAPCHANS are relatively easy and inexpensive to maintain. Water can be stored in the reservoir (body of water) so that power can be generated when needed. An appropriate TAPCHAN site however, is difficult to find because it must have consistent waves, small tidal variations, deep water close to the shoreline, and a place to build a reservoir.

Oscillating water channels (OWCs) are fixed devices that consist of a small opening, where waves can enter and retreat, attached to a vertical closed pipe. As a wave flows into the OWC, the water forces air up the pipe, turning turbine blades as it passes. When the wave ebbs (pulls back) the air is sucked back down the pipe and turns the turbine blades again. Adequate locations for oscillating water channels are also difficult to find, in part, because the relatively new technology requires that OWCs be embedded in the shoreline, limiting OWC usage to rocky coasts.

Floating devices have several advantages over fixed devices: they have less visual impact on the shoreline, are less likely to change wave patterns and disrupt wildlife, and are quieter than TAPCHANS. Floating devices use the cyclic motion of waves to generate electricity. A Salter Duck (developed by University of Edinburgh professor Steven Salter in the 1970s) looks like a row of floating ducks that are anchored to the sea floor. As a wave passes, the duck rotates about a central turning point. This rotational motion causes fluid within the duck to move thereby generating electricity.

Japan, Denmark, Norway, England, Spain, and Portugal are all developing new technologies to use wave energy to generate power. As technologies for generating electricity from wave energy are developed, costs for these systems will decrease, and commercial wave power plants will most likely become more common.

Laurie Duncan, Ph.D. and Marcy Davis, M.S.

For More Information

Books

Penney, Terry R., and Desikan Bharathan. "Power from the Sea." *Scientific American* (January 1987).

Websites

"Ocean Energy." *California Energy Commission.* http://www.energy.ca.gov/development/oceanenergy (accessed on August 26, 2004).

"Wave Energy." *U.S. Department of Energy: Energy Efficiency and Renewable Energy.* http://www.eere.energy.gov/RE/ocean_wave.html (accessed on August 26, 2004).

"Wave Power." *The Chartered Institution of Water and Environmental Management.* http://www.ciwem.com/policy/factsheets/fs7.asp (accessed on August 26, 2004).

Chapter 8
Science and Research

Aquariums

An aquarium is any water-filled tank, pool, or pond in which fish, underwater plants, or animals are kept. An aquarium can be as small as a glass bowl for a goldfish and as large as a pool for a whale or a marine museum.

History of fish keeping

The ancient Sumarians (2500 B.C.E.) were the earliest fish keepers. Fish keeping developed as a way to provide and store food. Fish were caught in rivers and then kept in small ponds until they were used. The ancient Egyptians also kept fish in ponds, but not all of their ponds served a practical purpose. Egyptian hieroglyphs (a system of writing that used symbols and pictures) and art depict fish and fishponds as decorative objects.

In ancient Iran, China, and Japan, fish keepers bred special types of fish for use in decorative ponds. Fish keepers created koi, a popular decorative fish, by selectively breeding carp (a fish used for food) in pleasing colors and sizes. The present-day common goldfish, a close relative of the koi, is also a result of these ancient breeding practices.

The popularity of fish keeping spread to Europe and the United States in the eighteenth century, when ornamental fish were imported from the East. Fish keepers maintained ponds of ornamental fish, but the fish could only be viewed from above the water's surface. Growing interest in the scientific study of plants and animals sparked curiosity about viewing marine life from below the surface of the water. In the nineteenth century,

◆**Aeration:** Adding oxygen, nitrogen, and other gasses necessary for respiration into water.

◆**Aquarist** Person who keeps an aquarium.

◆**Filtration:** The process by which pollutants are removed from water.

◆**Ichthyology:** The scientific study of fish.

◆**Water chemistry:** The balance of nutrients, chemicals, and minerals in water.

zoos, circuses, and natural history museums began to add fish and other marine creatures and plants to their exhibits.

Development of modern aquariums

The first public aquarium opened in London, England, in 1853. The aquarium was an instant success and several other public aquariums opened in England over the next 10 years. Although popular, these aquariums faced several difficulties. Tanks were limited in size because there were not strong enough materials to construct very large tanks. The tanks also lacked adequate support systems to keep the fish healthy. Without support systems to clean and heat the water, most fish did not survive. Aquariums had to frequently replace the fish in their exhibits.

In the 1870s, the first successful long-term aquariums opened. Improvements in glassmaking and metalwork permitted the construction of larger tanks to house marine exhibits. Scientists began to study aquatic habitats, the water environments in which plants and animals live, to gather information about water chemistry. When caring for fish, water chemistry concerns the temperature of water and its balance of minerals, salt, oxygen, and other particles. Aquarists (people who keep an aquarium) and scientists experimented with the water chemistry of aquarium tanks. New technologies allowed scientists to copy the water chemistry of marine and river environments. Filtration systems cleaned pollutants such as fish waste from the water. Aeration systems added air to the water to aid respiration (breathing) and keep the water moving. Moving water stayed cleaner. Heaters kept water in the tanks at appropriate temperatures. These support systems helped fish and other marine creatures in aquariums remain healthy.

By 1900, support systems permitted aquariums to house exotic tropical fish. Public aquariums competed for the most spectacular creatures and exhibits. Most of the creatures on display came from the ocean. Exotic marine creatures from far-away places were a favorite of aquarium visitors and few exhibits featured local or non-ocean species. The fish and other creatures were the focus of the exhibits. Tanks contained few plants.

Several technological advances in the second half of the twentieth century heightened scientific and public interest in the sea. Personal breathing systems for marine divers, nicknamed scuba (self-contained underwater breathing apparatus), permitted more lengthy underwater exploration. Small submersibles, sub-

Aquariums in the Home

Aquariums in the home are a popular hobby. © *Michael Pole/Corbis. Reproduced by permission.*

Many people keep fish and other marine creatures in aquariums as pets. With proper planning and care, home aquariums can be successful and healthy environments for fish.

Before starting an aquarium at home, home aquarists should research which size of tank and species of fish will that live in the aquarium. All the chosen species must be able to live in the same underwater environment and the same water chemistry. Often this will mean deciding between a freshwater and saltwater aquarium. For example, common freshwater goldfish cannot live in the same tank as tropical saltwater fish. Also, some popular fish, such as colorful betas, need to live alone because they will attack or eat other fish.

Like public aquariums, home aquarists are encouraged to copy their pet's natural habitat and place plants, rocks, and corals in the aquarium. Before adding fish, an aquarium should be filled with water and plants. Aeration, filtration, and heating systems should run for at least one day before adding fish. It might be helpful to take a sample of the home aquarium water to the store where fish will be purchased. The water could then be tested to make sure it provides a proper environment for the fish.

Like all pets, taking care of an aquarium requires responsibility. Most fish need to be fed daily, but cannot be overfed. Sick or injured fish must be removed from the main tank and placed in a separate tank. Maintaining proper water chemistry, including aeration and temperature, is essential to the health and survival of fish. Water must be tested regularly and adjusted carefully. Home aquarists should also clean filters, aerators, and tanks when needed. Routine care for a home aquarium leads to better health for the fish and more enjoyment for their keepers.

marine-like vessels usually driven by one to four persons, permitted some of the first glimpses of deep waters inaccessible to scuba divers. Cameras that could film underwater captured underwater images for both scientific study and public broadcast. A television series created by marine biologist Jacques-Yves Cousteau (1910–1997) featured underwater habitats, fish, and animals. The series made aquariums even more popular.

Greater scientific and public awareness of underwater life changed aquarium exhibits. Tanks began to copy whole marine habitats. Instead of featuring one type of fish, single tanks would recreate a part of the ocean. Coral reefs (underwater

A girl pets a dolphin at Sea World in San Diego, California. © *Carl & Ann Purcell/Corbis. Reproduced by permission.*

ridges of compacted coral), underwater rocks and coves, and plants were part of ocean landscapes featured in exhibits. Aquarists displayed many species of fish and other marine creatures together in tanks in groupings that appeared in nature. By recreating marine habitats, aquariums sought to show visitors a whole picture of life underwater.

Unlike the ornamental fishponds of ancient times, exhibits in aquariums are now designed and managed by scientists, such as marine biologists and ichthyologists (scientists who study fish). Today's aquariums also feature a variety of underwater habitats including oceans, lakes, rivers, bays, and swamps. Some aquariums provide visitors with a look at underwater environments from two angles, above the water and below its surface. Many include exhibits where visitors can touch and handle underwater creatures such as sea stars, clams, and mussels.

Today's aquariums still encourage visitors to have fun, but they also educate visitors about the preservation and protection of underwater habitats and species. Aquariums can show visitors healthy habitats in tanks next to pictures of natural habitats destroyed by pollution. Aquarium exhibits and programs educate the public about threats to natural underwater habitats and species from litter, chemicals, oil, and over fishing. Captive breeding programs in aquariums help preserve animals endangered by habitat loss or over fishing. Rescue programs provide medical care and shelter for animals and fish injured by litter, pollution, and oil spills.

Adrienne Wilmoth Lerner

For More Information

Books

Kisling, Vernon N., Jr. *Zoo and Aquarium History: Ancient Animal Collections and Zoological Gardens.* Boca Raton, FL: CRC Press, 2000.

Taylor, Leighton. *Aquariums: Windows to Nature.* New York: Prentice Hall, 1993.

Websites

Aquarium of the Pacific. http://www.aquariumofpacific.org/index.html (accessed on August 24, 2004).

"Aquariums as a Hobby." *SeaWorld/Busch Gardens.* http://www.seaworld.org/infobooks/Aquarium/Aquarium.html (accessed on August 24, 2004).

"Audubon Aquarium of the Americas." *Audubon Nature Institute.* http://www.auduboninstitute.org/aoa (accessed on August 24, 2004).

National Aquarium in Washington, D.C. http://www.national-aquarium.com (accessed on August 24, 2004).

Ecology

Ecology is the study of the relationships between organisms and the relationships between organisms and their environment. Ecology was first recognized as an academic subject in 1869 when German naturalist Ernst Haeckel (1834–1919) first coined the term ecology. The word is derived from the Greek words *eco*, meaning "house" and *logy*, meaning "to study," indicating that ecology is the study of organisms in their home.

Ecologists often distinguish between two parts of environment as a whole: the living or biotic part and the nonliving or abiotic part. The biotic part of the environment includes all organisms such as animals, plants, bacteria, and fungi. The abiotic part includes all physical features like temperature, humidity, availability of light, as well as chemical components, such as the concentrations of salts, nutrients, and gases. Ecology, then, is the study of the relationships between and among the biotic and abiotic environments.

Ecology as part of the biological sciences

The components of the biological world are often organized along a spectrum. Assuming the spectrum is laid out from left

WORDS TO KNOW

⬥**Abiotic:** Nonliving part of the environment.

⬥ **Autecology:** Ecological study of individual organisms or individual species.

⬥**Autotroph:** Organism that uses inorganic substances to produce energy.

⬥**Biosphere:** All the communities that exist in the world.

⬥**Biotic:** Living part of the environment.

⬥**Community:** All of the organisms that live in a certain locations.

⬥**Ecology:** Study of the relationships among organisms and between organisms and their environment.

⬥**Ecosystem:** Relationships between the living and nonliving parts of an environment.

⬥**Heterotroph:** Organism that consumes another organism to obtain energy.

⬥**Homeostasis:** Tendency for a system to resist change.

⬥**Population:** Group of organisms all belonging to the same species that live in a specific location.

⬥**Saprotroph:** Organism that decomposes another organism into inorganic substances and in the process obtains energy for itself.

⬥ **Synecology:** Ecological study of groups of organisms and how they work together.

to right with the left being the smallest, atoms are at the far left. When atoms combine together they organize into molecules, which are just to the right of atoms on the spectrum. Moving right along the spectrum, next comes cells, which are the smallest unit of life. Next come tissues, such as muscle tissue and nervous tissue, which are collections of cells that work together to perform a function. These tissues are then organized into organs, such as the heart and the brain, and these are found to the right of tissues on the spectrum. Organs work together as organ systems, such as the cardiac system, which includes the heart as well as the blood vessels that transport blood throughout the body. Farther to the right along the biological spectrum are organ systems, which come together to form an individual organism, such as a human, fish, or kelp.

Towards the center of the biological spectrum, individual organisms are grouped together into populations. These populations are all the members of a species that live together. Even farther to the right of the biological spectrum, populations are grouped into communities, which are all the organisms that are found in a specific location. Communities include members of different species. Communities depend upon the nonliving world in order to survive, so an ecosystem, also called an ecological system, represents all the relationships between a community and the abiotic world.

All the communities of the world together make up the biosphere, which is found near the right side of the biological spectrum. The biosphere interacts with all of the abiotic parts of Earth, including the atmosphere, which are the gasses surrounding the planet; the hydrosphere, which is the water on Earth; and the lithosphere, which is the soil and rock on Earth. The biosphere and its relationships with the atmosphere, hydrosphere and lithosphere make up the ecosphere. The ecosphere is on the extreme right hand side of the biological spectrum.

Ecologists generally focus their research on the part of the biological spectrum that is to the right of the individual. For example, a population ecologist may study the ways that populations of sardines off the coast of California differ in their mating habits from populations of sardines off the coast of Chile. On the next level, community ecologist will study the diet of the various populations of sardines. An ecosystem ecologist may study how the populations of sardines are affected by the changes in temperature associated with the warming or cooling of the oceans.

Subdivisions and important concepts of ecology

The field of ecology is often subdivided because it incorporates so many different disciplines. Two large groupings within ecology are autecology and synecology. Autecology is the study of the individual organism or an individual species. This part of ecology might focus on the life history of an animal or plant. For example, one could study how the caddis fly grows from an egg into a larva (early stage of insect's life) that builds a house of sand at the bottom of a river and then metamorphoses (changes form) into a fly. Autecology might also investigate how the caddis fly adapts to its environment. For example, a study of how well the caddis fly larvae houses are hidden from predators (animals that hunt others for food) would be an autecological study. Synecology focuses on groups of organisms and how they work together. If a study estimated the amount of energy fish obtained by eating caddis fly larvae, it would be synecological. Synecology tends to ask questions that study the ecosystem on a large scale.

Another way to subdivide the subject of ecology is by the kind of environment. Commonly, environments are grouped into freshwater (lakes, rivers, and streams), marine (oceans), or terrestrial (land-based). Although the fundamental principles of ecology hold in all of these environments, the specific animals and plants vary and it is often convenient to study each type separately.

Finally, ecology can be divided into different types of organisms. This is called a taxonomical grouping. For example, one might study plant ecology, bacterial ecology, or insect ecology. This allows the study to be focused on a specific group and to use similar methods to study the different organisms in the group. For example, in order to study the environmental factors that influence the growth of marine algae, one could develop several growth environments with different light and different concentrations of the nutrients phosphate and nitrate. These same growth environments could be used to grow several species of algae. The results might be useful in predicting where and when the rapid growth of algae might occur in the ocean.

The ecosystem. Every living thing has requirements in order to exist: food, water, gases, stable temperatures and a place to live. Living organisms depend the nonliving environment for many of these requirements. The relationships between the biotic and the abiotic are called an ecological system, or an ecosystem.

Inorganic (non-living) substances such as carbon, nitrogen, phosphorous, carbon dioxide, and oxygen are required for all organisms to produce the molecules in their bodies.

Autotrophs are organisms that use inorganic substances to make energy. (The root word *auto* means "self" and the root word *troph* means "to eat.") Most often plants are autotrophs, using sunlight, water, and carbon dioxide in a process called photosynthesis to produce energy in the form of carbohydrates that their cells need. Heterotrophs are organisms that consume autotrophs in order to get their energy and grow. (The root word *hetero* means "other.") Heterotrophs include animals that eat plants as well as animals that eat other animals. Finally there are the decomposers or saprotrophs, such as bacteria and fungi. (The root word *sapro* means "to decompose.") These organisms break down dead organisms into inorganic substances, which may then be used by autotrophs. Understanding the ways that substances and energy flow through ecosystems is one of the fundamental principles in ecology.

Homeostasis. Homeostasis is used to describe the tendency for a biological system to resist change. (The root word *homeo* means "the same" and the root word *stasis* means "standing.") A principle of ecology is that ecosystems generally remain homeostatic. In other words, if there are no outside influences, the number of organisms that live in any given location will tend to remain the same, and they will have the same food supply and access to shelter over time. Even minor changes in the environment, such as temperature changes or changes in rainfall, will not greatly affect an ecosystem.

One of the ways that an ecosystem maintains homeostasis is through negative feedback mechanisms. For example, kelp forests grow off the coasts of California. Sea urchins eat the kelp, keeping its density relatively constant. In turn, sea otters eat sea urchins. If the population of sea otters were to suddenly decrease, the population of sea urchins would grow because they would not have any predators. However, the sea urchins would eat a large amount of kelp removing their food supply. Many urchins would starve, decreasing the population of urchins and allowing the kelp to grow back to its former density. Eventually the ecosystem would return to its former state. Of course, large disruptions to ecosystems can be very destructive. For example, hunting sea otters to extinction (as almost occurred during the early part of the twentieth century) would completely disrupt the homeostasis of the California kelp forest.

Energy in the ecosystem. One of the fundamental principles of physics is that energy cannot be created or destroyed. It can, however, be transformed from one form to another. Light is a form of energy. It can be transformed into heat or chemical energy that is stored in food. In fact, this is the basis for photosynthesis. Some of the energy in light is stored in the chemical bonds of the molecules in plants. Another fundamental principle of physics states that when energy is transformed from one form to another, some of the energy is lost. In photosynthesis, some of the energy in light is lost as heat. This means that the transformations of energy within ecosystems are never 100% efficient. Energy is always lost as it flows from one organism to the next.

In any ecosystem, energy is transferred between organisms as they eat and are eaten by other organisms. Usually the autotrophs or primary producers (such as seaweed and algae) capture light energy from the Sun through photosynthesis. They store this energy in the chemical bonds of the molecules that make up their cells. Herbivores (plant eaters such as urchins and snails) eat the autotrophs. These grazers convert the energy in the chemical bonds of the primary producers into energy that is stored in the chemical bonds of their own cells. Usually about 80–90% of the energy in the chemical bonds of the primary producer is lost during this process. Next, carnivores (meat eaters such as frogs and fish) eat the herbivores. They convert the energy stored in the chemical bonds of the herbivores into energy stored in the chemical bonds of their own cells. Again, about 80–90% of the energy is lost in this transformation.

The result of the energy loss each time an organism is eaten results in what is called an ecological pyramid. At the base of the pyramid are the primary producers; in the middle are the herbivores and at the top the carnivores. If one measures the weight of each of these groups after the water has been removed (called the dry weight), one gets an idea of how much energy is stored in chemical bonds at each level of the pyramid. For example, in a lake in Wisconsin, the dry weight of the primary producers is 96 grams per square meter. The dry weight of the herbivores is only 11 grams per square meter. The dry weight of the carnivores is just 4 grams per square meter. The ecological pyramid demonstrates how about 80–90% of the energy stored in chemical bonds is lost every time an organism is eaten. It also shows that there can never be as many predators as there are prey; there is just not enough energy for that to occur.

Juli M. Berwald, Ph.D.

For More Information

Books

Bush, Mark B. *Ecology of a Changing Planet.* Upper Saddle River, NJ: Prentice Hall. 1997.

Raven, Peter H., Linda R. Berg, and George B. Johnson. *Environment.* 2nd ed. Fort Worth, TX: Saunders College Publishing. 1998.

Websites

"About Ecology." *Ecology.com.* http://www.ecology.com (accessed on August 24, 2004).

"Ecology." *Wikipedia.* http://en.wikipedia.org/wiki/Ecology #History_of_ecology (accessed on August 24, 2004).

"Ecology and Environment Page." *The Need to Know Library.* http://www.peak.org/~mageet/tkm/ecolenv.htm (accessed on August 24, 2004).

Hydrology and Hydrogeology

Hydrologists and hydrogeologists are water scientists who study the properties of freshwater and its distribution on the continents. (Oceanographers study the physical and chemical properties of salt water in the oceans.) Together, hydrology and hydrogeology provide information on how to manage and protect freshwater, humans most essential natural resource. Hydrology and hydrogeology are distinct fields of study that employ different methods and techniques, but they overlap to provide a complete picture of Earth's freshwater resources.

Hydrology is a branch of engineering that deals with the physical properties of surface freshwater, such as lakes and rivers, and with its chemical interactions with other substances. Hydrogeology is a subfield of geology (study of Earth) that, by definition, specifically addresses groundwater—water moving through tiny openings in rock and soil layers beneath the land surface. In practice, ground and surface water interact as a single system. Surface water seeps into the ground and groundwater emerges to the surface. Hydrogeologists work to explain the geological effects of surface water in rivers, streams and lakes, and hydrologists lend their technical expertise to the mechanics and chemistry of moving groundwater.

Hydrology

Hydrologists use mathematics and experimental techniques to determine water's general properties, to make specific observations of freshwater environments, and to design water management systems that contain and direct water. Britain's Centre for Hydrology, a government environmental research agency, describes its mission as an effort to answer two questions about the Earth's freshwater: Why is the natural environment as it is? and What is it likely to be in the future?

Today, humans, not natural processes, manage the flow, distribution, and allocation of almost all of Earth's surface waters. Dams, levees, and reservoirs (natural or man-made lakes) direct and contain the water of the world's largest and most heavily used river systems: the Nile, Yangtze, Amazon, Ganges, and Mississippi. U.S. Army Corps of Engineers hydrologists, along with their counterparts at the Bureau of Reclamation (which has jurisdiction over rivers west of the Rockies), control the flow and distribution of all the surface waters of the United States.

Hydrological studies generally seek to understand how water moves between and through bodies of freshwater, such as lakes, streams, aquifers (water-bearing soil and rock layers), and reservoirs, and even the atmosphere (mass of air surrounding Earth) over time. Hydrologists usually begin with data from a particular region. They collect numerous measurements of water system conditions such as rainfall totals, lake and reservoir levels, river discharges (the volume of water that flows through a river in a given time), and current speeds, air and water temperatures, and humidity (amount of water vapor in the atmosphere) at specific sites. Then they merge the data into a computerized model that shows how water has moved through the region's various freshwater reservoirs in the past.

Once a hydrologist has constructed a model of a watershed (land area that contributes water to a stream, lake, or aquifer) or reservoir (body of water), the hydrologist tests it by comparing its calculated predictions with actual results in the natural environment. The model is adjusted to better match the real world. The more times the scientist repeats the process of adding new data to the model and retesting it, the more accurate it becomes. Computer models help hydrologists predict the ways that natural and man-made changes like droughts (uncommonly dry weather), heavy snows and rains, and new dams across rivers affect water supplies and flows in the future. Many models also include information about the way water physically and chemically interacts with rocks and minerals on

WORDS TO KNOW

◆ **Aquiclude:** Permeable (leaky) layers of rock or soil that confine and pressurize groundwater within aquifers.

◆**Aquifer:** Rock or soil layer that yields freshwater for human use.

◆**Computer model:** Description of a system, theory, or phenomenon entered into a computer that includes its known properties and conditions and can be used to predict future conditions and events within the system.

◆**Contaminant:** Polluting substance that has harmful effects on biological life and other natural systems.

◆**Hydrogeologist:** Scientist who studies the properties and distribution of freshwater, especially as it relates to the soil and rock structure of the Earth.

◆**Hydrologist:** Scientist who studies the properties and distribution of Earth's freshwater.

◆**Reservoir:** Natural or man-made lake or body of water, often constructed to control a body of water.

An erupting geyser displays the power of geothermal forces. © Royalty-Free/Corbis. Reproduced by permission.

its path through the system. These models can be used to track contaminants and predict water quality changes over time.

One example of how hydrologists' work can affect a regions water supply is in the city of Denver, Colorado when the city had very low reserves of freshwater in its reservoirs. There had been lower than average snowfall in the nearby Rocky Mountains and the city's water supplies ran low without their usual influx of spring melt water. Hydrologists at the U.S. Geological Survey in Denver used data and computer models to help the city distribute limited water during the drought period, and to plan for future dry periods. Models of Denver's surface water flows and seasonal patterns also help water managers protect and regulate the city's water supply from contamination by such human waste products as agricultural fertilizers and chemicals, industrial wastes, and sewage.

Hydrogeology

Hydrogeologists are concerned mostly with groundwater and how geologic features affect groundwater storage, flow, and replenishment. Like other geologists, they use observations of rock types and geologic structures on the land surface together with subsurface samples to map folded, faulted (broken), and fractured (cracked) rock layers and bodies beneath the land surface. Hydrogeologic maps show the locations and shapes of aquifers, and the distribution of less permeable (leaky) layers called aquicludes that confine and pressurize groundwater within aquifers. They identify systems of caves, cavities, and fractures where groundwater may flow more quickly along specific routes. They also show the areas where surface water enters aquifers (recharge zones), and places where groundwater reemerges at springs and seeps (discharge zones).

Once a hydrogeologist has mapped out the dimensions, physical characteristics, and "plumbing" of a groundwater reservoir, he or she sets out to understand how water moves through the system. Measurements of flows at recharge and discharge points show the rates at which water is entering and leaving the aquifer as well as the time an average water molecule (smallest part of water that has its properties) takes to travel through the system (residence time.) Water levels and pressures in wells indicate flow patterns and rates inside the aquifer.

Groundwater can become polluted. Hydrogeologists also use their understanding of groundwater flow patterns to predict how contaminants might enter an aquifer, move through the system, and reemerge in a distant spring or well. Sometimes an aquifer or soil layer acts as a filter that improves water quality as contaminants move through an aquifer. Others transport polluted water quickly to a discharge site. Some rock layers even contribute hazardous dissolved chemicals to the groundwater. Hydrogeologists collect water samples and monitor water quality within aquifers. They also conduct laboratory and computer experiments to better understand groundwater's chemical interactions.

Cities and regions that depend on groundwater require detailed hydrogeologic maps, and a good understanding of how water moves through their aquifer, to effectively manage groundwater resources. In many states and countries, groundwater is common, public property. Most rules and regulations regarding groundwater consumption and contamination were written in an era when groundwater systems were poorly understood and were considered unending sources of clean freshwater. Today, many regions with large human populations and fragile natural ecosystems (communities of plants and animals) depend on limited, shared groundwater resources. As such, the actions of some of a groundwater reservoir's users can negatively affect the water supply and quality for other people, as well as for the aquifer's plants and animals.

Laurie Duncan, Ph.D., and Todd Minehardt, Ph.D.

For More Information

Books

Postel, Sandra, and Brian Richter. *Rivers for Life: Managing Water for People and Nature.* Washington, DC: Island Press, 2003.

Websites

"Hydrologic Engineering Center." *U.S. Army Corps of Engineers.* http://www.hec.usace.army.mil (accessed on August 24, 2004).

"Water Resources of Colorado." *United States Geological Survey.* http://webserver.cr.usgs.gov (accessed on August 24, 2004).

Limnology

Limnology is the study of the chemistry, biology, geology, and physics of waters that are found within continents. In contrast, oceanography is the study of open ocean waters. Waters found within continents may be lakes, reservoirs, rivers, or wetlands (land where water covers the surface for at least part of the year) Although most limnologists specialize in freshwaters, the study of saline lakes, like the Great Salt Lake, also falls under the discipline of limnology.

One of the more important goals of limnology is providing guidelines for water management and water pollution control. Limnologists also study ways to protect the wildlife that lives in lakes and rivers as well as the lakes and rivers themselves. Some limnologists are working on construction of artificial wetlands, which could serve as habitats for a variety of animal and plant species and aid in decreasing water pollution.

History of limnology

Limnology is a relatively new academic subject. François-Alphonse Forel (1841–1912), considered the father of limnology, was a Swiss physician who dedicated much of his life to the study of the biology, chemistry, and physics of Lake Geneva. Around 1868, he coined the term limnology to mean the study of lakes. (The root word *limn* means "lake" and *ology* means "the study of.") In 1887, American naturalist Stephen Alfred Forbes (1844–1930), a pioneer in the study of lake ecology (the study of the relationships between organisms and their environment), published the paper "Lake as a Microcosm," which is still cited as an important study of lake ecosystems. An ecosystem refers to all of the relationships between the living and nonliving parts of an environment.

George Evelyn Hutchinson (1903–1991) was a British American biologist and a physicist. He made great advancements in limnology beginning in the 1950s and summarized much of the field of limnology in a three-volume text. Hutchinson was extremely influential in bringing modern ecological theories to limnology. Today, limnologists focus much of their attention on integrating ideas from geology, physics, chemistry, and biology into understanding lakes and rivers. They also focus much attention on understanding how humans impact these important ecosystems.

Geological limnology

Geological limnology is focused on the formation of lakes and rivers. Many lakes, especially in North America, were formed by the retreat of the glaciers (slow-moving mass of ice) at the end of the Ice Age. As the glaciers melted, they gouged holes in soft parts of the solid rock. When these depressions filled with water, they became lakes. Other lakes form when tectonic plates (mobile pieces of Earth's crust) pull away from each other, leaving rifts called grabens. When these rifts fill with water, very deep lakes can be formed. The deepest lake in the world, Lake Baikal in Siberia, was formed in a graben.

Rivers usually begin as springs in areas of high altitude such as mountains. As they flow downward, rivers gather water from melting snow and other streams, called tributaries, as they flow toward sea level. Geological limnologists are interested in the size and the shape, also called the topography, of the watersheds of lakes and rivers. A watershed is all of the land and water areas that drain into the lake or the river.

Physical limnology

Physical limnology deals with the physical properties of the water in lakes and rivers. This includes changes in light levels, water temperatures, and water currents. Water absorbs energy

A Russian remote submersible vehicle prepares to explore Lake Baikal, the world's deepest freshwater lake. © *Ralph White/Corbis. Reproduced by permission.*

from sunlight, which warms the surface waters. Because the intensity of the sun changes throughout the year, the amount of heat absorbed in the summer is much greater than that absorbed in the winter. During the summer, lakes become stratified or layered, with the warmer, lighter water floating on top of the cooler, deeper water. In the winters, the surface of the lake loses its heat and mixes with the cooler waters below. Understanding the cycle of mixing and stratification is extremely important to understanding the biology of the plants, animals, and microorganisms that live in lakes and the movement of chemicals throughout lakes.

Chemical limnology

Chemical limnology focuses on the cycling of various chemical substances in lakes and rivers. Several factors affect the chemistry of lakes and rivers including the chemical composition of the soil in the watershed, the atmosphere (mass of air surrounding Earth) and the composition of the riverbed or lake bottom. In modern day, human activities have had a very important influence on the chemistry of lakes and rivers, and chemical limnologists play an important role in understanding these effects. For instance, building construction near lakes and rivers changes the erosion (wearing away of soil) patterns and influences they type of chemicals that reach the water. In some areas, rainwater running into lakes and rivers contains large amounts of fertilizers, oils, and heavy metals.

The concentration of the hydrogen ion (H^+) in water is one of the most important chemicals to study. An ion has a positive

Lake Baikal

Lake Baikal, which is located in Siberia in the middle of Asia, is both the oldest (25 million years) and deepest (1 mile or 1,600 meters) lake in the world. It contains one-fifth of all the unfrozen freshwater in the world. Because of its age and its distance from other water bodies, at least 1,200 different animal species and 1,000 different plant species have evolved in it. It is estimated that at least 80% of these species are only found in Lake Baikal.

One of the most interesting animals in the lake is a seal called the nerpa. It is the only mammal that inhabits the lake. Scientists believe that they migrated to the lake about 22 million years ago from the Arctic Ocean. It is estimated that the nerpa population in the lake is about 100,000. They feed on fish that they catch in the lake. During the winter the nerpa swim under the frozen lake, making breathing holes in the ice with their sharp claws. The nerpa can stay underwater for up to 70 minutes at a time.

Crustaceans (aquatic animals with no backbone, jointed limbs, and a hard shell) have flourished in Lake Baikal. The most numerous animal in Lake Baikal is the Baikal epischura crustacean. It is extremely small, about the size of a grain of rice. It feeds on microscopic algae and bacteria by filtering water through appendages around its mouth that look like combs. The total flow of water through the mouths of these tiny animals is equivalent to ten times the flow of all the rivers that enter Lake Baikal each year. The work of these small animals is credited with keeping the lake so clear.

One of the most interesting fish in Lake Baikal is the golomyanka or oil fish. They are relatively small, about 10 inches (24 centimeters) in length, have no scales, and are transparent. About 35% of their body weight is made up of an oil that is a very pure form of vitamin A. Residents who have lived near the lake for many years say that the fish was used to treat many diseases, such as arthritis, and to soothe wounds that would not heal.

or negative charge and the hydrogen ion indicates the acidity (charge) of the water, which strongly affects which kinds of organisms can live in the water. Other important substances are the sulfate and nitrate ions, which become concentrated in freshwaters as a result of acid rain. Also, the heavy metal mercury (Hg) is a dangerous pollutant that can circulate in the water and affect the health of animals, along with the humans who eat those animals and use the lake or river.

Biological limnology

Biological limnology is directed at understanding the animals, plants, and microorganisms that live in lakes and rivers. The patterns of distribution of these various organisms depend on the geology, physics, and chemistry of the lake or river. For example, plants require light in order to grow. Because water is very effective at absorbing light, plants must either grow near the shore, where the water is shallow or they must float near the surface of the water. Because the intensity of sunlight changes with season, plants usually have a growth season in the spring when the light levels increase and they die off in the fall when light levels decrease. In the same way, animals require oxygen dissolved in water in order to breath. Warm water holds less dissolved oxygen than cold waters. As a result, trout, which require a lot of dissolved oxygen, are more often found in cold lakes and rivers. Bass, on the other hand, require less dissolved oxygen and can be found in warmer lakes and the surface waters of lakes.

One of the critical challenges facing biological limnologists is the introduction of exotic species into lakes and rivers. Often, humans introduce new species into lakes and rivers. In some cases these species grow faster than the local species and can take over much of the habitat. For example, in 1985 the zebra mussel was released into the Great Lakes of the United States, in the ballast water of a ship coming from the Caspian Sea in Asia. These mussels are able to reproduce extremely fast in the Great Lakes and have become a widespread problem, clogging sewage pipes and overgrowing docks and piers.

Juli M. Berwald, Ph.D.

For More Information

Books

Josephs, David. *Lakes, Ponds, and Temporary Pools.* New York: Franklin Watts, 2000.

Raven, Peter H., Linda R. Berg, and George B. Johnson. *Environment.* 2nd. ed. Fort Worth, TX: Saunders College Publishing, 1998.

Rowland-Entwistle, Theodore. *Rivers and Lakes.* Morristown, NJ: Silver Burdett Press, 1987.

Sayre, April Pulley. *Lake and Pond.* New York: Twenty-First Century Books, 1996.

Sayre, April Pulley. *River and Stream.* New York: Twenty-First Century Books, 1996.

Websites

"Dedicated to the Memory of G. Evelyn Hutchinson." *Soil & Water Conservation Society of Metro Halifax.* http://lakes. chebucto.org/PEOPLE/hutchins.html#Hutchinson (accessed on August 24, 2004).

"Lake Baikal Home Page." *WWW Irkutsk*. http://www.irkutsk.org/baikal/index.html (accessed on August 24, 2004).

"Understanding: Lake Ecology Primer." *Water on the Web*. http://wow.nrri.umn.edu/wow/under/primer (accessed on August 24, 2004).

Marine Archaeology

Many of the most famous archaeological sites are those of the ancient Egyptians, Greeks, Romans, and Vikings. While most all of these archaeological sites, from Egypt's pyramids to Rome's Coliseum, are on land, these cultures had strong ties to the sea, engaging in frequent trade and exploration. They also used ships in wars. These civilizations left behind shipwrecks and the ruins of port cities that have been claimed by the sea due to erosion (wearing away of land). Technological advances in the late twentieth century permitted archaeologists to begin exploration and excavation of underwater archaeological sites. This branch of archaeology is called marine or underwater archaeology.

Archaeology explores how people lived in the past through excavation and survey. An excavation is a planned, careful exploration of ancient sites. It is sometime called a dig because digging (excavation) is the most well known method for discovering clues about the past at an archeological site. Wherever people live or work, they leave traces of their life. Pieces of pottery, metal, glass, wood, bricks, and cut stone can remain behind for hundreds or thousands of years after a dwelling (house), city, or civilization has vanished. Remnants that were made or used by humans are called artifacts. Artifacts and their surroundings, called context, give scientists clues to what past peoples valued, what they ate, where they lived, and how they worked.

Exploring underwater archaeological sites

When studying a site, marine archaeologists pay close attention to the context of each artifact, carefully noting and mapping exactly where each artifact or ruin was discovered. The location on site where an artifact is found is known as its provenience. Noting the provenience of each artifact helps marine archaeologists construct maps and computer models of the site. Artifacts and features are like pieces of a puzzle and such models permit scientists to see how the various pieces fit together.

Exploration of underwater archaeological sties is more difficult than studying land-based sites. Underwater archaeology

WORDS TO KNOW

Archaeological context: The natural surroundings, physical location, and cultural origin of archaeological artifacts or sites.

Artifact: Any object made or modified by humans.

Curation: Cleaning, preserving, and storing artifacts recovered from archaeological sites for further study.

Magnetometer: Used in marine archaeology to locate shipwrecks by finding metal objects used in the ship's construction such as nails, brackets, decorative ironwork, or artillery.

Remote sensing: The use of devices to collect and interpret data; in marine archaeology, remote sensing is used to locate, map, and study underwater sites.

Sidescan sonar: Type of sonar that operates in a sideways manner and can cover wide swaths of the ocean floor.

Sonar: The acronym for SOund NAvigation and Ranging; bounces sound waves and interprets their echoes to locate objects and gather data underwater.

Alexandria Submerged

The waters of the Mediterranean now cover the spot where the ancient Pharos lighthouse stood near Alexandria, Egypt. © *Roger Wood/Corbis. Reproduced by permission.*

Alexandria was an ancient port city in the western Mediterranean Sea on the Egyptian coastline. The city was first established by the Egyptians about 332 B.C.E., and later ruled by the Greeks, and then Romans. Because of its favorable location for trade, Alexandria was one of the wealthiest and most important cities in the ancient world. It was a center for trade, ship making, and scientific exploration. Alexandria's most famous buildings were its museum and library. Before being burned down in the third century, the library held the great-est collection of work of philosophy, literature, and science in the ancient world.

Because of its importance in the ancient world archaeologists have long been fascinated with exploring and studying the remains of the ancient city. Over the past two hundred years, most of this research took place on land. However, excavation of land-based sites is difficult because the modern city of Alexandria, Egypt, stands in the same location as the ancient city.

Some of the ancient city now lies underwater. Rising water levels and the changing flows of silt and water in the Nile River delta (the sedimentary deposits where the river meets the sea) deposits altered the coastline around Alexandria. In the 1960s, archaeologists began to explore the submerged areas of ancient Alexandria. Underwater excavation located the ruins of several temples, columns, and buildings. Marine archaeologists have unearthed pieces of pottery, stone statues, and metal artifacts. They have also studied the structures built by the ancient Alexandrians to improve their port. They have found ancient Alexandrians formed a large, protected harbor by connecting several manmade walls and barriers between small islands.

requires special equipment. People who participate in underwater digs must be skilled in both scuba diving and archaeological field methods. Though often more challenging, underwater archaeologists follow the same scientific standards used on land to conduct careful studies of their sites.

Often the first step in studying an underwater archaeological site is a surface survey, a study of the visible parts of the site. A surface survey can be as simple as an archaeologist diving to the site and looking over the structure, shipwreck, or smaller artifacts. A survey can be as complex as a carefully planned removal of visible, small artifacts from specific locations. Marine archaeologists often look for clues about the origin and age of the site from this initial survey.

Exploration of an underwater site usually requires excavation. Excavation requires both divers and a crew on board the research vessel. If a site is excavated, marine archaeologists first lay out a grid, a geometric plan for the site consisting of rows and columns of small squares. The small squares, or units, are then excavated by removing one layer of silt (tiny rock, soil, and other mineral particles) and artifacts at a time. Vacuum hoses are often used to remove silt layers and carry them back to the research vessel. The silt is then pushed through a screen or mesh and is examined for small artifacts. Larger artifacts are brought up by divers conducting the dig or by the research vessel's lifting mechanism.

As excavation progresses, marine archaeologists formulate detailed maps of the site. These maps can be drawn from precise notations of each artifact's location. Maps are usually drawn of each level of each unit both before and after a layer is silt is removed. They include drawings and notes about each significant artifact within that level. Features such as changes in the color or texture of sea floor sediments (particles of sand, silt, or clay) are also noted on such drawn maps.

Special maps of a site can also be made by using remote sensing. Remote sensing involves the use of equipment to discover and map buried or underwater sites from a distance. Sonar (which is short for Sound Navigation and Ranging) sends out sound pulses and interprets their echoes to penetrate the depths of the oceans and locate objects. Different remote sensing techniques vary in what they detect and the type of data they produce. Remote sensing techniques are typically used if a site is so deep that humans cannot dive to it, if a large layer of silt covers most of the site, or if archaeologists are trying to locate the precise location or boundaries of a site. Sidescan sonar can look over an 18-mile-wide (29-kilometer) swath of the ocean floor to locate natural features and archaeological sites. Underwater cameras with night vision features penetrate dark waters. A magnetometer, another remote sensing device, finds shipwrecks by detecting metal objects used in the ship's construction such as nails, brackets, decorative ironwork, or artillery (cannons and guns). The data from remote sensing apparatuses are processed by computers, which produce maps and charts that marine archaeologists can then interpret.

Some archaeologists have employed their basic senses while investigating underwater archaeological sites. In one project requiring the exploration of a two-thousand-year-old Roman shipwreck in the Mediterranean Sea, marine archaeologists even sampled the shipwreck's cargo. They tried a sip of the ancient wine and olive oil discovered in the ship's amphorae (large pottery jars)!

Marine archaeology and conservation

Excavation is sometimes not the preferred method to explore an underwater archaeological site. Mapping, remote sensing, and surface survey are often used without digging or removing artifacts from a site. Excavation is primarily used only when a site is in danger of destruction from modern vessels, severe storms, dredging (removing sediment from the bottom of a waterway, usually to make it wider or deeper), or rapid, natural decay. Leaving a site intact permits future archaeologists to study the same site.

Artifacts can be both helped and damaged by the water that surrounds them. Some artifacts, such as the wooden hull of ancient ships, are better preserved in the salt waters in which they sank. On the other hand, the iron and metal hulls of relatively modern vessels, such as the *Titanic* that sank in 1912, are destroyed by saltwater. The temperature of water, its salinity (salt content), and depth of a site also affect preservation. Cold water with low salinity does not destroy artifacts as rapidly as salty, warm water destroys artifacts. The hulls of shipwrecks in extremely deep ocean waters can be crushed by intense pressures equal to thousand of pounds per square inch.

Artifacts removed from underwater sites require special handling, preservation, and storage, also known as curation. The goal of proper conservation and curation is to clean and protect artifacts from further damage so that they may be studied by scientists or placed on display in museums. Various pieces of broken pottery jars are grouped together. Sometimes, the pieces are reassembled to restore the object, and sometimes they are left as individual fragments. Some artifacts recovered from the sea are kept moist in special wet or humid cases, other artifacts are carefully dried out once removed. Even a small artifact, such a sailor's wooden pipe, may take months or years of conservation work before ready for a museum display.

Adrienne Wilmoth Lerner

For More Information

Books

Hackwel, John W. *Diving to the Past.* New York: Scribners, 1988.

Marx, Robert F. *The Underwater Dig: An Introduction to Marine Archaeology.* 2nd ed. Oakland, CA: Pisces Books, 1990.

Sunk! Exploring Underwater Archaeology. Minneapolis: Runestone Press, 1994.

Websites

Clement, Colin. "Mapping the Treasures: NOVA Online." *PBS.* http://www.pbs.org/wgbh/nova/sunken/mapping.html (accessed on August 26, 2004).

Marine Biology

Marine (ocean) biology is the study of the function, biodiversity, and ecology of the animals and plants that live in the ocean. An organism's function is how it lives and grows in its environment. Biodiversity refers to the wide range of species of plants, animals, and microorganisms such as bacteria that live in the ocean. Ecology is the study of the relationships between organisms as well as the relationships between organisms and their environment. In order to do their work, marine biologists incorporate information and techniques from a broad range of disciplines, including chemistry, physics, geology (the study of rocks), paleontology (the study of fossils), and geography (the study of locations on Earth).

Many factors make the marine environment a unique place for animals and plants to live. The marine environment is fluid, which affects the way organisms move and breathe. A variety of chemicals are dissolved in the water that bathes marine organisms and many have special ways to use these chemicals or to prevent them from entering their bodies. Ocean water is salty, which affects the organism's ability to obtain and hold water in its body. The ocean has relatively constant temperatures, especially compared to land. This means that animals do not need to exert a lot of energy to stay warm. Sunlight generally reaches only the surface layers of the oceans so plants must live in surface waters in order to perform photosynthesis (process where they convert energy from the Sun into food).

◆**Benthic:** Animals, plants and microorganisms that live on the floor of the ocean.

◆**Biodiversity:** Wide range of species of plants, animals, and microorganisms that live in an environment.

◆**Ecology:** Study of the relationships between organisms as well as the relationships between organisms and their environment.

◆**Mariculture:** Farming of marine animals and aquatic plants in a controlled marine environment.

◆**Necton:** Visible animals that live in the ocean.

◆**Plankton:** Small, often microscopic, organisms that float in the ocean.

◆**Phytoplankton:** Microscopic plants that float in the ocean.

◆**Virus:** Genetic material, like RNA or DNA, usually found inside a protein coat that has the ability to reproduce in the correct host.

◆**Zooplankton:** Small, often microscopic, animals that float in the the ocean.

History of marine biology

Greek philosopher and natural historian Aristotle (384–322 B.C.E.), is generally regarded as the first marine biologist. Aristotle believed that observation, along with induction and reasoning, would lead to an accurate understanding of the natural world. These pioneering ideas set the stage for the modern scientific method. Aristotle identified, described, and named 24 species of marine worms and crustaceans (animals that have a hard external covering and jointed limbs like crabs, shrimp, lobsters), 40 species of molluscs (clams, scallops, oysters) and echinoderms (a group of invertebrate animals that includes sea stars, sea urchins, and sea cucumbers) and 116 species of fish. He also correctly identified whales and dolphins as mammals (warm-blooded animals that have hair and feed young with milk).

Between Aristotle's time and the Renaissance (about 1500 C.E.), very little work was done in marine biology because most people assumed that Aristotle had already accomplished everything. In the sixteenth century, explorers made many important observations about marine life. Alexander von Humboldt (1769–1859) was a German naturalist who journeyed through Central and South America identifying marine animals and plants. British sea captain James Cook (1728–1779) was a renowned explorer who traveled throughout the Pacific describing and identifying marine organisms.

In the nineteenth century, work in marine biology became more active. British naturalist Charles Darwin (1809–1882) studied many marine organisms during his travels aboard the H.M.S. *Beagle* (1831–1836). Darwin's work led to the theory of evolution, a theory that the organisms best suited to their environment live and reproduce to eventually form new species while those not suited to the environment will die. His work also led to a theory of how coral reefs form atolls (a type of island) and to a classification of barnacles (a type of crab that attaches itself to hard surfaces) that is still in use today. Edward Forbes was a British naturalist and one of the first scientists to focus his attention on organisms in the ocean. His azoic theory put forward the idea that there was no life at depths below about 1,800 feet (554 meters). Although this theory was accepted as true for nearly a century, it was later proved to be false. The first large expedition to study life in the ocean was undertaken by the British ship H.M.S. *Challenger* between 1872 and 1876. The biologists aboard found and described a large number of new marine species.

During the twentieth century, great advances in marine biology occurred. Submersible submarines, the Self Contained Breathing Apparatus (SCUBA), and underwater photography allowed scientists to observe life throughout the oceans. Technological advances have led to electronic instrumentation that measure the characteristics of the ocean such as temperature, salinity (saltiness), intensity of light, and concentrations of dissolved gasses that provides important information on the distribution of organisms throughout the oceans. Tracking devices that use satellites (instruments sent into orbit in order to observe Earth) to report the locations of large animals, such as whales, sharks, and tuna, are used to understand migration (travel) patterns. Techniques from the fields of biotechnology (the use of modern equipment and tests to understand biological processes), molecular biology (the study of molecules within cells), neurobiology (the study of nerves), and biochemistry (the study of chemicals that are found in organisms) are used routinely to provide a greater understanding of marine organisms.

Types of organisms studied

Marine biology involves the study of all types of organisms that live in the ocean, from the very small to the very large. The patterns and distributions of microscopic organisms called plankton involve one area of research. Plankton include viruses (small molecules like DNA or RNA that have the ability to reproduce when they are in a host), bacteria, phytoplankton (small plants that float in the ocean water) and zooplankton (small animals that float in the ocean). Another focus of marine biology includes the larger animals called neckton that swim through the water. These animals include marine invertebrates (animals without a backbone) such as squid, most species of fish and marine mammals, such as dolphins and whales. Another group of marine organisms are those that live on the ocean floor. These organisms are called benthic and can include animals and plants as well as microorganisms. Some examples of benthic plants include the giant kelp, sea grasses, and algae (plant-like organisms that photosynthesize, but have simpler bodies without veins) that grow on a thin layer on rocks. Many invertebrates are benthic, like corals, sea anemones, sea cucumbers, sea stars, clams, snails, and crabs. A few fish that live close the bottom of the ocean are also considered benthic, such as halibut and some gobies. Many microorganisms, like bacteria and protozoans, are found in among the sand and clay at the bottom of the ocean.

Important research areas in marine biology

Marine biology contributes a large amount of information to the fields of environmental biology, economics, fisheries research, and biotechnology. Because the field is relatively young, there is still much to be learned from and about the animals and plants that live in the ocean.

Marine organisms influence local environmental conditions and economies. A simple, but powerful example of this is the red tide, which is usually caused by a particular type of phytoplankton called a dinoflagellate. Under certain environmental conditions, these dinoflagellates grow extremely quickly, blooming in bays and near shore regions of the ocean. In some instances they can cause fish kills and infect shellfish with poisonous substances, which could make the people that eat them sick. Much work is underway by marine biologists in order to understand the conditions that cause these harmful blooms so that they can predict their effects and when they will occur.

Many marine biologists study ways to improve mariculture, which is the farming of marine fish, shellfish, and seaweeds. Work includes developing types of animals and plants that are easy and economical to farm. For example, the triploid oyster is an oyster that has a longer harvest period than those found in nature. In addition, work is underway to improve the health of fish raised in pens and to decrease the pollution caused by marine farms.

Much research in marine biology contributes to the fields of biotechnology and molecular biology. Many marine animals and plants have been found to contain chemicals with industrial uses. For example, some phytoplankton produce sunscreens that can be incorporated into lotions. Other marine invertebrates produce chemicals that are mixed with paint to discourage the growth of barnacles on ships and moorings. Molecular probes (special molecules that can identify other molecules) are used in marine ecology to detect the presence of harmful viruses and bacteria on beaches and near-shore waters. Other techniques from molecular biology are used to determine if fish and marine invertebrates have been exposed to poisonous pollutants. Molecular biological techniques are also being used to analyze the DNA (genetic substance) in various marine organisms to try to understand the past relationships among species.

Juli Berwald, Ph.D.

For More Information

Books

Byatt, Andrew, et al. *Blue Planet.* London: DK Publishing, 2002.

Cousteau, Jacques. *Jacques Cousteau: The Ocean World.* New York: Harry N. Abrams, 1985.

Doris, Helen. *Marine Biology (Real Kids, Real Science).* New York: Thames & Hudson, 1999.

Levinton, Jeffrey S. *Marine Biology: Function, Biodiversity, Ecology.* 2nd ed. New York: Oxford University Press. 2001.

Websites

Levinton, Jeffrey. "MBRef: A Reference Source for Marine Biology Student Research." *Marine Biology Web.* http://life. bio.sunysb.edu/marinebio/mbref.html (accessed on August 26, 2004, 2004).

"Marine Biology." *SeaGrant: MarineCareers.net.* http://marine-careers.net/marbio.htm (accessed on August 26, 2004).

"Marine Organisms." *The Marine Biological Laboratory.* http://www.mbl.edu/marine_org/index.html (accessed on August 26, 2004).

"Scripps Research." *Scripps Institute for Oceanography.* http://sio. ucsd.edu/research (accessed on August 26, 2004).

Shaner, Stephen W. "A Brief History of Marine Biology and Oceanography." *University of California Extension Center for Media and Independent Learning.* http://www.meer.org/ mbhist.htm (accessed on August 26, 2004).

Marine Geology and Geophysics

Marine geology and geophysics are scientific fields that are concerned with solving the mysteries of the seafloor and Earth's interior. Marine geologists, like all geologists, seek to understand the processes and history of the solid Earth, but their techniques differ from geologists who work on land because they study geologic (Earth's) features that are underwater. The oceans cover more than 70% of Earth, and water obscures a wealth of information about the rocks and sediments (particles of rock, sand, and other material) in the ocean basins. Marine geologists rely mainly on physical techniques to uncover the features and processes of the seafloor.

◆**Autonomous underwater vehicle (AUV):** Remote controlled motorized crafts that are designed to study and withstand the pressure of the deep ocean.

◆**Bathymetry:** The three-dimensional shape of the seafloor.

◆**Dredge:** Device for scooping or digging rock and sediment from the seafloor.

◆**Plate tectonics:** The theory that Earth's lithospheric plates move over time.

◆**Remotely operated vehicle (ROV):** Motorized crafts designed to withstand the increased pressure of the deep ocean.

◆**Seismic waves:** Vibrations emitted by earthquakes and large explosions that travel as waves through the Earth.

◆**Subduction:** Process by which oceanic seafloor is recycled into Earth's interior at deep ocean trenches.

◆**Submersible:** A craft designed to carry a pilot and scientists for underwater study of the deep ocean.

Geophysicists are scientists who study the physical properties of the solid Earth, and often work closely with marine geologists. Geophysicists use experiments and observations to determine how Earth materials such as rock, magma (molten rock), sediments, air, and water affect physical phenomena such as sound, heat, light, magnetic fields (a field of magnetic force), and earthquake tremors (seismic waves). Marine geologists and geophysicists make images and maps of the seafloor, along with maps of sediment and rock layers below the seafloor. They also use instruments to measure changes in Earth's gravity (the attraction between two masses), magnetic field, and the pattern of heat flow arising from deep in the Earth that help to explain geologic features of the ocean basins.

Marine geology and geophysics involve many different fields of science. Many marine geoscientists (a group including both marine geologists and marine geophysicists) have backgrounds in such diverse academic fields as physics, chemistry, oceanography, engineering, and paleontology (study of biological life in the fossil record). Most marine geologists are familiar with the theories and techniques of geophysics, and most geophysicists understand the geological significance of the processes and features they are working to clarify. Marine geology is also closely linked to the sciences of oceanography and marine biology. Oceanographers study the physical and chemical properties of the water in oceans and marine biologists study the living organisms in oceans. In order to completely understand the cycles, structures and processes of the oceans, scientists from many fields must collaborate.

Why study the seafloor?

The ocean basins hold keys to understanding the two most important theories of geological science: plate tectonics and the sedimentary record of geologic history. Marine geologists and geophysicists were the first to discover the globe-encircling chain of volcanic mountains, called the mid-ocean ridge system, where new ocean floor is created.

Using their observations of the seafloor, these scientists developed the theory of plate tectonics, the idea that Earth's outer shell (lithosphere) is made of rigid pieces (plates) that move relative to one another over time. Plate tectonic theory explains the worldwide distribution of mountain ranges, ocean trenches (deep, arc-shaped valleys along the edges of the ocean basins), volcanoes, rock types, and earthquakes. By studying plate tectonics, scientists can better understand and predict geologic actions of today, such as volcanic activity and earthquakes.

Scientists also know from studying plate tectonics that the moving seafloor is recycled into Earth's interior at trenches, a process called subduction. Like the theories of evolution (change over time) in biology and relativity in physics, plate tectonics is a unifying theory that has general significance to all of science. Marine geologists and geophysicists also study layered sedimentary rocks (strata) on the seafloor that hold clues to the chemical, biological, and geographic history of the oceans.

The ocean basins hold a vast wealth of economically important minerals, such as manganese and nickel, and hydrocarbons (oil and natural gas). Petroleum (oil and gas) and mining companies hire marine geologists and geophysicists to find offshore sources of petroleum. They rely heavily on marine scientific techniques to locate petroleum reservoirs and mineral deposits.

Studying the seafloor

Marine geology and geophysics use a number of technologies uniquely adapted for ocean exploration. Many of the methods used are geophysical because they allow a "hands off" approach to seafloor observation. In other words, geophysical technologies allow marine geoscientists to "see" through water, rock, and sediment. (Techniques that involve observing or measuring the properties of land, sea, and seafloor surface from a distance are generally termed remote sensing.)

Like all geologists, marine geologists collect rock and sediment samples. They use dredges, which are metal buckets or claws that are lowered from a ship and dragged along the sea floor, and coring (drilling) devices to bring materials up from the bottom of the sea. Scientists then examine the materials' physical, chemical, and biological properties. Seafloor samples are, however, difficult and very expensive to obtain, especially in very deep water. Marine geologists usually collect them from a few critical locations within a study area and then use geophysical images to generate a big picture of the study area. Sediments and deep rock samples are collected using shipboard drills that bring back cores (metal tubes) that are filled with several meters of sample. By using samples together with seafloor maps and profiles (cross-sections) through the rock and sediment layers below the seafloor, marine geologists construct three-dimensional representations of their study areas.

Although most features that interest marine geologists, such as submarine (underwater) volcanoes, massive sand dunes, and deep trenches are too large to observe from the seafloor, direct observations by divers, submersibles, and remotely-operated

Deep Ocean Drilling

Deep ocean drilling allows scientists to recover cores of ocean sediments and underlying oceanic crust for mapping the ocean floor. The core is brought back to the surface where scientists analyze the sediments' history and composition. Deep ocean drilling can be expensive and in 1964, several U.S. institutions interested in studying the sea floor pooled their resources and formed an organization called Joint Oceanographic Institution for Deep Earth Sampling (JOIDES). JOIDES directed the first Deep Sea Drilling Project (DSDP) that used a ship named the *Glomar Challenger*. The *Glomar Challenger* was a customized ship that had powerful thrusters that kept the ship centered over the top of the ocean floor target. The *Challenger* could lower the drill through up to 20,013 feet (6100 meters) of ocean water and drill up to 2,500 feet (760 meters) of sediment once it hit the sea floor.

Over 15 years the DSDP drilled more than 600 core holes during 96 legs (voyages) worldwide. Seismic and magnetic surveys of the ocean floor were made while the ship was in motion. When the cores were brought up they were analyzed in ship-board laboratories. Data from the DSDP project proved that Earth's ocean basins are relatively young when compared to the continents and contributed to an understanding of sea floor spreading and plate tectonics.

In 1984 a group of 21 nations formed the Ocean Drilling Program (ODP). ODP used the drillship JOIDES' *Resolution* for drilling in poorly sampled areas, especially along the margins of continents and ocean trenches. The ODP also drilled holes in which instruments were lowered to the seafloor, providing a global network to study earthquake movements (seismic waves) on the ocean floor. The JOIDES *Resolution* drilled 650 holes over 110 legs.

In October 1993, ODP became the Integrated Ocean Drilling Project (IODP). IODP has two ships, the *Chikyu*, built by Japan, and an upgraded *Resolution*. *Chikyu* will drill in areas where plates converge, slide beneath one another, and produce earthquakes. *Resolution* will concentrate on recovering sediment cores worldwide to help scientists study climate.

vehicles (ROVs) can be useful in some cases. Geologists use waterproof cameras and other instruments carried by divers, lowered on cables from ships, or attached to remotely operated watercraft to capture details of the seafloor environments. Submersibles are small submarines that are capable of carrying passengers to the deep seafloor. ROVs and autonomous underwater vehicles (AUVs) are unmanned robotic submarines equipped with cameras and instruments that operators control from a ship, much like a remote controlled car.

Marine geologists rely on sonar (short for "sound navigation and ranging"), which is the use of underwater sound waves. Sound travels at a constant velocity (speed) in water, so the time it takes for the sound wave to travel through the water and echo back to the ship illustrates variations in the seafloor. Sonar is

Submersibles, ROVs, and AUVs

Submersibles, remotely operated vehicles (ROVs), and autonomous underwater vehicles (AUVs) are motorized crafts that are designed to withstand the pressure of the deep ocean. Submersibles carry passengers, usually a pilot and two scientific observers, while ROVs and AUVs are remotely operated. These crafts were originally built of steel, but now are built of light materials such as titanium. Although these type of deep-diving craft are expensive to build and can be dangerous to people riding in the submersibles, they offer scientists a unique look at the deep oceans. Several of the important capabilities of these crafts include cameras that record underwater conditions in real-time; instruments that record temperature, pressure, and chemistry; and robotic arms that can retrieve specimens.

The first submersible, named *Alvin,* was built in 1964 and is still operated by Woods Whole Oceanographic Institute (WHOI). *Alvin* was the first deep-sea submersible that could carry passengers. Lowered from a ship platform, *Alvin* can dive to a depth of 14,764 feet (4,500 meters) and remain under water for 10 hours. In case of emergency, *Alvin's* life support system can sustain three people for 72 hours. Alvin is 23 feet (7 meters) long and can travel 6 miles (9.6 kilometers) from the ship platform with maximum speed of 2 knots. Alvin is responsible for important observations of hydrothermal vents (geysers on the ocean floor) near the Galapagos Islands, and helping to find the wreckage of the *Titanic,* a passenger ship that sank in 1912 and resulted in the deaths of over 1,500 people.

ROVs are small crafts that carry video cameras deep and record or transmit live footage back to a screen on a ship. ROVs like *Jason,* also operated by WHOI, do not carry passengers, but are driven like a remote control car. As images are transmitted from the ROV back to the ship, the ROV operator can steer the ROV in the direction he or she wants.

AUVs are used for longer-term projects. While submersibles and ROVs are good for intensive short-term studies, AUVs can remain in one location for up to a year. An AUV operator can program a computer inside the AUV to sit on the sea floor for a predetermined time and can "wake up" to perform surveys then return to sleep mode until the next scheduled survey. AUVs can record changes that occur in one location over time and are often used in between ROV or submersible visits in one location.

used to measure bathymetry, the topography or layout of the sea floor. A "chirp" is transmitted from a ship hull and travels until it reaches the sea floor and bounces back to a receiver on the ship where the travel time is recorded. To determine the distance from sea level to the ocean bottom, scientists multiply the time it takes for the sound wave to travel to the ocean floor and back by the rate (speed) at which the sound wave travels in water.

Scientists can also map ocean floor bathymetry using satellite (vehicles in orbit around Earth) instruments. The ocean surface is not completely flat, but mimics the sea floor by bulging upward and downward. Satellite observations reveal detailed patterns of mid-ocean ridges and trenches and underwater volcanoes, thus confirming plate tectonics. Magnetometers, towed behind a ship, measure small changes in Earth's magnetic field. Sensitive shipboard gravimeters record subtle changes in Earth's field of gravity (the attraction between the Earth and another body).

Marine geoscientists also use seismology (earthquake waves) to make an image of the seafloor. A ship tows several air guns that make an underwater explosion using compressed air. The shock waves from the explosion are the same type as waves made in an earthquake. These waves penetrate layers of rock underlying the surface of the ocean and bounce back to hydrophones (receivers). The waves travel at different speeds depending on the type of rock.

Laurie Duncan, Ph.D., and Marcy Davis, M.S.

For More Information

Books

Fowler, C. M. R. *The Solid Earth, An Introduction to Global Geophysics.* Cambridge, UK: Cambridge University Press, 1990.

Kennett, James. *Marine Geology.* Washington, DC: Prentice-Hall, 1981.

Websites

"Exploring with Satellite Altimeter Data." *Satellite Geodesy.* http://topex.ucsd.edu/marine_grav/explore_grav.html (accessed on August 26, 2004).

"Integrated Ocean Drilling Program." *IODP Website.* http://www.oceandrilling.org (accessed on August 26, 2004).

"Ocean Explorer, Technology." *National Oceanographic and Atmospheric Administration.* http://oceanexplorer.noaa.gov/technology/subs/subs.html (accessed on August 26, 2004).

Oceanography

Oceanography, also called marine science, is the study of the ocean. Its goal is to discover unifying principles that can explain data measured in ocean waters, in the organisms that live in the ocean, and on the land surrounding the ocean. Oceanography is a broad subject, drawing on techniques and theories from biology, chemistry, physics, mathematics, geology, and engineering. Oceanography is usually divided into four different areas of research. Marine biology or biological oceanography focuses on life (animals, plants, and bacteria) in the ocean. Chemical oceanography studies the substances that are dissolved in the ocean. Physical oceanography attempts to understand the movement of water and the relationships between oceans and the atmosphere (mass of air surrounding Earth). Marine geology is directed at understanding geological features of the ocean floor, such as the composition of the seafloor and the movement of tectonic plates (moving plates of Earth's crust).

History of oceanography

Oceanography as an academic subject is relatively young, probably dating from the 1950s. But interest and study of the ocean has existed for thousands of years. Fifth century Greek historian Herodotus recorded the first documented ocean exploration. He wrote that the Phoenicians sailed from the Mediterranean Sea through the Red Sea and along the coast of Africa before 600 B.C.E. As early as 2000 B.C.E. the Phoenicians may have sailed as far as England. The Polynesians were also great ocean explorers, crossing the Pacific as early as 1500 B.C.E. in order to colonize many Pacific islands. Much of this early exploration was associated with trade, however in the process of sailing the oceans, sailors accumulated knowledge of navigation, currents (the movement of water), tides, and geography.

European ocean exploration blossomed in the 1400s when Christian armies invading Spain discovered Greek and Arab writings and maps of the oceans in Islamic libraries. This stimulated a period of oceanographic exploration by the Portuguese, Dutch, English, and Spanish. Many of the oceanographic advancements made during this time were aimed at solving practical problems, such as sailing faster, navigating more accurately, and avoiding nearshore obstacles. With the skills they developed, the Europeans dominated ocean exploration for nearly 400 years.

The first expedition focused entirely on collecting scientific data of the ocean took place from 1872 to 1876 and was funded by The Royal Society of London. The H.M.S. *Challenger* was a war ship that was remodeled to accommodate scientific research. The *Challenger* expeditions explored the biology and physics of every ocean except the Arctic during a journey of 68,000 miles (109,000 kilometers). The data from the expedition took 23 years to analyze and fills 50 volumes.

In the 1800s, the United States began establishing government agencies to improve the safety of sailing vessels, protect fisheries, and defend its coasts. The Naval Depot of Charts and Instruments was established in 1830, followed by the Fish Commission in 1871. Two important oceanographic institutions were founded on Cape Cod: the Marine Biological Laboratory in 1888 and the Woods Hole Oceanographic Institute in 1930. Both of these institutions are still active places of research today.

In the 1950s, government support of oceanographic research and education increased. Universities became involved in competing for government and international grants to study various aspects of oceanography. This cooperative effort between educational institutions and governments is what drives oceanographic research in modern day.

Biological oceanography

Biological oceanographers (or marine biologists) focus on the patterns and distribution of marine organisms. These scientists work to understand why certain animals, plants, and microorganisms are found in different places and how these organisms grow. A variety of factors influence the success of a certain species in any location, including the chemistry and physical properties of the water. In turn, the biological organisms in the ocean affect the oceans on a global and local level.

Biological oceanographers study all types of organisms that live in the ocean, from the very small to the very large. They investigate patterns and distributions of the microscopic organisms including viruses (which are not really organisms, but genetic material such as DNA that do have the ability to reproduce), bacteria, and plankton (free-floating animals and plants). They also study the larger animals and plants, like kelp, seaweed, marine invertebrates (animals without a backbone), fish, and marine mammals. They incorporate information and techniques from a broad range of disciplines including chemistry, physics, remote sensing (the use of specialized instruments, such as satellites, to relay information about one location to another location for analysis), paleontology (study of fossils), and geography (study of Earth's surface) for their research.

Chemical oceanography

Chemical oceanographers study the chemicals that are dissolved in the ocean waters. Different parts of the ocean contain varying concentrations of gasses, salts, and other chemical com-

ponents. These variations are due to the impact of the atmosphere, surrounding lands, seafloor, and biological organisms in the ocean water. Chemical oceanographers work to develop theories that explain the various patterns throughout the oceans.

One of the more important problems facing chemical oceanographers today is understanding the concentration of and changes in carbon dioxide in the ocean. Carbon dioxide is a major greenhouse gas, meaning it holds a lot of heat when it is found as a gas in the atmosphere. Burning fossil fuels for industry and in cars releases carbon dioxide into the atmosphere, where it contributes to global warming. The ocean, however, can remove a lot of carbon dioxide from the atmosphere. Carbon dioxide readily combines with seawater. It then goes through a series of complex chemical reactions before it becomes a solid material called calcium carbonate. Calcium carbonate can be buried in the sediments (particles of gravel, sand, and clay) at the bottom of the ocean. This means that the ocean has the potential to act as a "sink" for a lot of the carbon dioxide in the atmosphere. Chemical oceanographers are working to determine just how large the sink is and how quickly it can act.

Physical oceanography

Physical oceanographers study the physical properties of the ocean. These include temperature, salinity, density, and ability to transmit light and sound. In turn, these fundamental physical characteristics affect the way that ocean currents move, the forces associated with waves, and the amount of energy absorbed by the ocean.

Float Research: Athletic Shoe and Rubber Duck Spills

A major area of research for physical oceanographers is understanding how currents flow throughout oceans. There are two major ways that they study currents. The flow method involves putting a piece of equipment in the water that measures the speed and direction of the current. By using this equipment to record the flow of water in many different places in the ocean, maps of the currents can be constructed.

A second method of studying currents is called the float method. This method depends on dropping an object that floats into the water and tracking its movement. Usually special instruments called drogues are released into the water, where they float along with currents. These drogues have transmitters that send radio or satellite signals back to scientists identifying their location.

Not all float studies are as technical as drogue studies, however. In May 1990, a terrible storm hit a freighter traveling from Korea to Seattle, Washington. The ship lost 21 cargo containers during the storm, some of which contained more than 30,000 pairs of Nike gym shoes. About six months later, the shoes began washing up on beaches along the northwest coast of the United States and the west coast of Canada. Physical oceanographers asked people who found the shoes to notify them and they used the data to adjust their models of currents in the North Pacific Ocean. In January 1992, another storm hit a cargo ship, which lost a container carrying nearly 30,000 bath toys including rubber ducks and turtles. A number of these toys were studied and recovered along a 500-mile (800-kilometer) stretch of the Alaskan coast.

The temperature and salinity of the water affect the density of the water. Cooler and saltier water sinks while warmer and fresher water floats. This seemingly simple property of the ocean drives much of the water circulation throughout the globe. Density also affects the way that sound travels through water and the buoyancy (ability to float) of marine organisms.

Some of the projects that physical oceanographers are studying include understanding trends in climate. Satellites measure ocean temperatures over the whole globe to try to discriminate between local changes in ocean temperature, like the El Niño-La Niña, a cycle that brings warm water and storms to the Eastern Pacific every 5 to 7 years, from more large scale changes, like global warming.

Marine geology

Marine geologists study the geological features of the ocean. These scientists try to determine the composition of the inner Earth by looking at special places on the seafloor where the tectonic plates are moving away from each other. In these places, called spreading centers, material from the inner Earth rises to the seafloor. Marine geologists analyze the chemical and physical makeup of this material to gain an understanding on how the Earth was formed. The shifting of tectonic plates also can cause earthquakes. Marine geologists also study the movements of the tectonic plates in the ocean to try to predict where and when earthquakes will occur.

Another focus for marine geologists is the sediments found on the seafloor. These sediments are made up of particles from the land, dead marine plants and animals, precipitates (solid material) from chemical reactions, and even material from space. Studying the chemical and physical composition of sediments provides information on how the Earth's climate has changed over time and where valuable resources, like oil and minerals, can be found.

Juli Berwald, Ph.D.

For More Information

Books

Littlefield, Cindy A. *Awesome Ocean Science: Investigating the Secrets of the Underwater World.* Charlotte, VT: Williamson Publishing, 2002.

Thurman, Harold, and Alan P. Trujillo. *Essentials of Oceanography,* 7th ed. Upper Saddle, NJ: Prentice Hall, 2001.

Websites

"History of Oceanography." *About.com.* http://inventors. about.com/library/inventors/bloceanography.htm (accessed on April 7, 2004).

"Oceanography." *SeaGrant: MarineCareers.net.* http://marine-careers.net/ocean.htm (accessed on August 26, 2004).

"Polynesian History and Origin." *PBS: Wayfinders: A Pacific Odyssey.* http://www.pbs.org/wayfinders/polynesian2.html (accessed on August 26, 2004).

Shaner, Stephen W. "A Brief History of Marine Biology and Oceanography." *University of California Extension Center for Media and Independent Learning.* http://www.meer.org/mbhist.htm (accessed on August 26, 2004).

◆**Decibel:** Unit that measures the loudness or intensity of sound.

◆**Electromagnetic spectrum:** The range of light wavelengths that includes radiation that is invisible to the eye, as well as colors that we can see.

◆**Sensor:** Device that can detect the waves that have bounced back from the object they contacted..

◆**Sonar:** Also known as remote sensing, technique that determine the presence and location of objects underwater; term stands for sound navigation and ranging.

◆**Wavelength:** Distance of one full wave; can be measured from crest to crest or trough to trough.

Remote Sensing

Remote sensing is a technique that gives information about the surface of the Earth and the underwater world without touching the surface. The technique bounces energy off of non-living or living objects and analyzes the returning signal to collect information.

Remote sensing has many uses in water. Common uses of remote sensing include charting the depth of a lake or ocean bottom. It is vital to the fishing industry and in locating objects at the bottom of the water. Treasure hunters and researchers would find it much harder to detect lost shipwrecks if not for remote sensing. People interested in finding out where water pollution is occurring can take remote sensing images of water from planes or satellites (orbiting spacecraft) to detect microorganisms such as algae that thrive in polluted water. People who are trying to find deposits of oil and natural gas under the ocean floor also use remote sensing.

Energy of remote sensing

The first step in remote sensing is to have a source of energy that will be beamed toward the target. The energy comes in the form of light waves of different sizes. Like the waves in an ocean, energy waves can range from waves whose top point (crest) to lowest point (trough) are very tiny to those that are hundreds of feet (meters) long. The distance of one full wave, from crest to crest or trough to trough, is known as the wavelength. The range of waves is known as the electromagnetic spectrum.

At one end of the electromagnetic spectrum lie the tiny waves such as gamma rays and X rays. These waves tend to carry large amounts of energy and can penetrate into solid or liquid material more so than other waves. That is why X rays can pass right through skin to reveal images of the bones and teeth underneath. At the other end of the spectrum lie waves such as the microwaves that can penetrate a short distance to heat up foods, and radio waves that beam music through a radio speaker. Radio waves are not efficient for remote sensing operations. Microwaves are the longest waves with enough energy to be used for remote sensing.

The regions of the electromagnetic spectrum that is useful for remote sensing contain the waves known as ultraviolet rays (the same rays that give a suntan or sunburn). The term ultraviolet means that the waves are just beyond the portion of the

The Nile River and Nile River Delta as seen from the space shuttle *Columbia* in 1991. *Corbis/NASA. Reproduced by permission.*

spectrum that contains the waves that are visible, in particular the region of the spectrum that contain violet-colored waves. Indeed, for the visible portion of the electromagnetic spectrum, our eyes are the remote sensors!

Shorter, higher energy wavelengths are preferred for remote sensing because the waves have to move through air or water on their way to the target. Passing through air and water causes some of the waves to be absorbed or deflected (bounced) off the target. (The deflection of different wavelengths of light as they pass through Earth's atmosphere, the mass of air surrounding Earth, is the reason why the sky appears blue. Colors with relatively long wavelengths pass straight through the atmosphere. Blue light has a shorter wavelength and the atmosphere scatters it.) A higher energy wave will be better able to blast through any interference to the target, and to bounce back from the target.

The absorption of waves can be useful when trying to figure out the nature of the target. For example, microwaves tend to be absorbed by the gas form of water known as water vapor. The pattern of absorption detected by scientists on their instruments can provide important clues about the amount of water contained in the air above the ground or water.

How remote sensing works

In order to illustrate how remote sensing works, imagine a bathtub full of water. If a bar of soap is dropped into the water, waves will move outward over the surface of the water. As the waves contact the sides of the tub, some the energy will rebound back into the tub. So it is with the energy that is beamed from a satellite, ship or plane. The returning energy is captured by a detector (also known as a sensor). Instruments and computers that are connected to the sensor can analyze the pattern of the returning waves to help scientists understand the distance and shape of the object on the ground or the ocean floor that deflected the waves.

History of remote sensing

It has been known since the early nineteenth century that sound can move through water. In 1822, scientists measured how fast sound moved underwater in Lake Geneva in Switzerland by suspending a bell from one boat and having someone in another boat listen through a tube lowered down into the water. Their calculations turned out to be very close to those obtained using modern day sensitive electronic technology.

The use of underwater sound became known as sonar, which is a short form for "sound navigation and ranging". Like many technologies, sonar became used in warfare. In World War I (1914–18), British, French, and American forces used sonar to locate submarines and to detect icebergs (massive chunks of ice) that could rip open the hulls of their ships. By World War II (1939–45), sonar had become much more accurate and sophisticated.

During the first half of the twentieth century, scientists realized that sound waves do not move through all ocean water in the same manner. The depth of the water, the amount of salt in the water, and the ocean temperature can all affect wave movement. For example, a technique called acoustic tomography measures the movement of ocean currents (the circulation of ocean waters that produces a steady flow of water in a prevailing direction) by examining the differing properties of the current from the surrounding water.

Sending energy underwater

To chart the depth of a lake or ocean bottom, a transmitter on a boat will beam energy for a short time (a pulse transmission) straight down into the water. A sensor on the boat detects the returning signal. Using a mathematical formula to account for the presence of water, scientists can then determine the one-way distance of the signal. Other uses of vertical (up and down) sonar include detecting other ships and as an aid in navigating.

The energy pulse can also be sent out horizontally through the water, rather than straight down. This is called sidescan sonar, and is useful in determining what lies around a ship. Some systems are so sensitive that they can detect an object in the water that is less than 0.4 inches (1 centimeter) in size. Sidescan sonar is also useful in investigating underwater archaeological sites.

Brian Hoyle, Ph.D.

For More Information

Books

Earle, Sylvia. *Atlas of the Ocean: The Deep Frontier (National Geographic)*. Washington, DC: National Geographic, 2001.

Johnson, Andrew K. *Earth From Space*. Richmond Hill, Ontario, Canada: Firefly, 2004.

Locker, Thomas. *Water Dance*. New York: Voyager, 2002.

Websites

"Acoustics and Sonar Primer." *Institute for Marine Acoustics*. http://www.marine-group.com/SonarPrimer/SideScanSonar.htm (accessed on June 21, 2004).

"Fundamentals of Remote Sensing." *Natural Resources Canada* http://www.ccrs.nrcan.gc.ca/ccrs/learn/tutorials/fundam/fundam_e.html (accessed on June 21, 2004).

Impact of Sound on Marine Animals

The U.S. Navy uses powerful sound waves that can travel great distances through the water to detect submarines. The damaging effects of these energy waves on marine life is under study by marine scientists. Some researchers claim that damage from sound waves in large marine mammals such as whales is a short-term event, such as when sound waves may temporarily interfere with the whales' ability to communicate within their group. Other scientists claim that fish and entire populations of whales could suffer long-lasting consequences from the use of sound waves.

The newest Navy active-sonar devices result in a sound of 235 decibels (a unit of measure for sound), about as loud as a space shuttle launch. When several groups of whales beached themselves after exposure to this sonar in 2001–3, scientists found that some of the whales died from decompression sickness or "the bends," the same condition that can affect scuba divers who rise to the surface from deep water too quickly.

There is no clear answer yet as to what level of underwater sound is too much for marine mammals but overall, underwater noise in the oceans is increasing. Although the Navy has reached agreements with environmental groups to limit the use of the powerful active-sonar devices, several other countries are developing similar systems, and control of excess sound in the oceans is a world-wide concern.

Chapter 9
Economic Uses of Water

Agricultural Water Use

The images of seemingly endless crop fields of the American Midwest and the lush San Joaquin Valley of central California are powerful symbols of the agricultural might of the United States. In the past century, the United States has become the greatest producer of food in the world.

Water has always been a vital part of agriculture. Just like humans, crops need water to survive and grow. The process where dry land or crops are supplied with water is called irrigation. A century ago, the relatively small fields of a local farmer in many areas of the United States could receive enough moisture from rainwater, along with water that could be diverted from local streams, rivers, and lakes. The growth of huge corporate farms that are thousands of acres in size has taken the need for water to another scale. For these operations, water needs to be trucked in, pumped up from underground, and obtained from surface water (freshwater located on the surface) sources in large quantities.

In modern times, in countries such as the United States and Canada, agriculture is not the largest user of water but is the largest consumer of water. Other activities such as the oil industry use more water than does agriculture. But, in these other industries, much of the water is put back into the ground or surface water after being used. Agriculture consumes water; the water does not go back to the surface or to the groundwater.

Uses of water in agriculture

There are four main areas of water use in agriculture: growing of crops, supplying drinking water to livestock, cleaning farm

WORDS TO KNOW

Evaporation: The change of liquid water to water vapor.

Groundwater: Fresh water that resides in rock and soil layers beneath Earth's land surface.

Irrigation: In agriculture, a process where dry land or crops are supplied with water.

Surface water: Freshwater that is located on the surface in the form of streams, rivers, lakes and other waterways, or in reservoirs, swimming pools and other containers that have been built.

Transpiration: The change from liquid water to water vapor that occurs at the surface of leaves.

Agriculture in the San Joaquin Valley

The San Joaquin Valley is located in the central region of California. It is bound by the coastal mountains on the west, the region containing Yosemite, Kings Canyon, and Sequoia National Parks on the east, and the state capital city of Sacramento to the north. The fertile soil carried down from the rivers and streams that emerge from the mountains have made the valley soil fertile for growing crops, and the region is sometimes known as the "salad bowl" of America.

Crops grown in the San Joaquin Valley include grapes for the state's famous wine industry, lettuce, peppers, cherries, almonds, peaches, tomatoes, and asparagus. These and other crops and livestock make for a $4 billion a year industry. Many valuable farmlands are also valuable to developers, who build new neighborhoods as the population in the San Francisco Bay area and other urban centers grow. California officials predict that by 2020, the population in the San Joaquin Valley will increase by over 50%, adding additional strain to the remaining farmland and water supply. While many California citizens welcome the new growth, local governments are working to meet the needs of growth while preserving farmlands.

buildings and animals, and supplying drinking water for those who work on the farm. The amount of each category varies according to the type of farm. For example, farms in the eastern part of North America usually receive enough rainfall and water from melting snow to meet most of the water needs. But drier areas, such as the U.S. and Canadian prairies, regions of Mexico, and some mountainous regions of the West do not receive sufficient natural moisture. On these farms, water must be supplied through irrigation.

Irrigation

Nearly 60% of the world's freshwater that is used by humans is used for irrigation. Of this water that is applied to crop fields, only about half returns to surface water or groundwater sources. The rest is lost by natural processes such as evaporation (when liquid water changes to water vapor) and transpiration (when water from plant leaves is transformed into water vapor), and accidental occurrences such as leakage from pipes or spillage.

There are various methods to irrigate crops. The oldest, "low-tech" way is to flood the field. This flood type of irrigation has been used for centuries and remains popular for crops like rice. Field flooding is very wasteful, since only about half of the water used actually gets to the plant. The efficiency of flood irrigation can be improved by making the land contoured, such as eliminating small hills and putting steps (terraces) on larger hills to prevent water from flowing over certain portions of the field and gathering in another part of the field. The flooding of a field can also be controlled by releasing water from dams (barriers) alongside the field, adding water to the field only when needed. Water that flows off of a field can be captured in a pond and re-used.

A newer and much more efficient technique of water use is called drip irrigation. In drip irrigation, water runs through pipes that have tiny holes in them. When buried underground, water can ooze out of the pipe into the soil near the roots of the

plants. The loss of water is reduced and less water is required to grow the crops.

A popular means of irrigation is spraying. Water flows through a tube and is shot out through a system of spray nozzles positioned along the length of the tube. The tube can be fixed in one position or can be moved manually or automatically from place to place. A visual example of a spray irrigation system is a green circle seen from an airplane passing over farmland. The green circles are crops that are being irrigated by a circular sprayer. Spray irrigation is sometimes wasteful, as water that is sprayed can evaporate or be blown away before hitting the crop. Some farmers now use an irrigation method where water is gently sprayed from pipes that are suspended over the crop. This method allows about 90% of the water to reach the crop.

With the knowledge that surface and groundwaters are resources that can be overused, agricultural scientists and modern farmers are paying attention to methods of conserving and re-using water while maintaining the growth of their crops.

Brian Hoyle, Ph.D.

Sprinkler irrigation can be an essential addition to natural rainfall. © *Royalty-Free/Corbis. Reproduced by permission.*

For More Information

Books

Wild, Alan. *Soils, Land and Food: Managing the Land During the Twenty-First Century.* New York: Cambridge University Press, 2003.

Websites

"Agriculture's Effects on Water." *Agriculture and Agri-Food Canada.* http://res2.agr.gc.ca/publications/hw/01b_e.htm (accessed on August 24, 2004).

United States Geological Survey. "Irrigation Techniques." *Water Science for Schools.* http://ga.water.usgs.gov/edu/irmethods.html (accessed on August 24, 2004).

Aquaculture

Aquaculture is the farming of animals or plants under controlled conditions in aquatic environments. Aquaculture usually refers to growing animals and plants in fresh or brackish water (water that has a salt content between that of freshwater and that of ocean water). Mariculture indicates the farming of animals and plants in ocean waters. (Marine means seawater.) Just as on land, aquaculture and mariculture farmers try to control the environmental factors surrounding their crops in order to make them grow quickly and in good health. Some of the factors that aquaculture and mariculture farmers manipulate are the diet of their animals, the nutrients provided to their plants, the reproductive cycles of both animals and plants, and the chemistry and physical properties of the water where the farms are located. They also try to develop methods to minimize diseases in their crops, to keep their crops safe from predators (animals that hunt them for food), and to reduce the pollution produced by their crops.

The aquaculture and mariculture industry

The combined industry of aquaculture and mariculture represents one of the fastest growing economic areas in the world. According to the United Nations Food and Agricultural Organization (FAO), aquaculture and mariculture have increased by nearly 10% per year since 1970. China has become a world leader in both aquaculture and mariculture. Between 1970 and 2000, China had an annual growth rate of 11.5% in aquaculture and 14% in mariculture. In China, farms produce

three times more fish and shellfish for human consumption than fishermen catch.

FAO estimates that aquaculture and mariculture revenues were $56.5 billion in 2000, half of which was generated by China. The crops that generated the largest amounts of revenue were the finfish (catfish, salmon, and talapia), which accounted for about half the world's aquaculture and mariculture production. The other two large crops are mollusks (mostly oysters; mollusks are soft bodied aquatic animals generally having a shell) and plants (mostly kelp). Excluding China, FAO estimates that about one-fifth of the world's fish and shellfish supply comes from aquaculture and mariculture.

Major aquaculture and mariculture crops

A large variety of animals and plants are grown by aquaculture and mariculture. Animals are grown for human consumption, for consumption by other animals, for use in aquaria, for stocking of natural waters and as research animals. Catfish are the most important aquaculture crop in the United States with an estimated 750 million fish grown per year. More than half of

Japanese farmers tend commercial oyster beds.
© *Michael S. Yamashita/Corbis. Reproduced by permission.*

WORDS TO KNOW

◆**Anadromous:** Fish that are born in fresh water and then move to marine water as adults.

◆**Brackish:** Water with a salinity between that of freshwater and ocean water.

◆**Invertebrate:** Animals without a backbone.

◆**Mariculture:** Farming animals and plants under controlled conditions in marine waters.

Catfish Farming

The North American channel catfish is no fragile beauty. Catfish are the hardy, whiskered garbage collectors of sluggish rivers and muddy lakes in the southeastern United States. They can survive in almost any type of fresh or brackish water, and they are scavengers that feed on everything from dead animals to human garbage. In the past, catfish was sometimes considered an unfortunate person's meal. Though plentiful and easily caught, the channel catfish's putrid diet gave its meat the taste of, well, garbage.

In modern day, thanks to aquaculturists in Mississippi, Alabama, Louisiana, and other southern states, mild-tasting catfish is an appealing, inexpensive item on menus at restaurants and grocery store shelves in the United States. When catfish eat feed instead of garbage, their meat tastes good. They are easy to raise in ponds or tanks, and farms have relatively few negative effects on their environment. Unlike other species like salmon or shrimp, they tolerate all kinds of conditions, don't mind living in densely packed ponds, and will eat anything, including inexpensive plant-based feed. Catfish farms do require a lot of water, and they are less welcome in areas where a large-human population is sharing a limited water supply.

these are produced in Mississippi. The next most important fish grown as a crop are the salmon, which are usually raised in pens in bays in the ocean. In 1999, the world mariculture industry grew by more than 1 million tons of salmon. Norway leads the world in salmon farming, followed by Chile. Tilapia is a finfish with mild, tender meat that is becoming an increasingly important mariculture crop.

Shellfish are also grown on farms. The most important crops are oysters, which are grown both for human consumption and for the pearls that they generate. Shrimp, clams, mussels, and abalone are also farmed in marine waters. In freshwaters, the largest shellfish crop is crawfish, followed by shrimp.

Many species of aquatic plants are raised on farms. The major saltwater food crop is kelp, also called wakame in Japan, which is a type of brown algae. This brown algae is also harvested to make agar, a thickening agent used in salad dressings, paint and ink. A red algae, called purple laver or nori, is used in many types of sushi. The most commonly grown freshwater plants for human consumption are watercress and Chinese water chestnuts. Other algae are raised as animal feeds and as mulches and fertilizers (products used by gardeners). Water hyacinth, which efficiently removes excess pollutants from water, is grown for use in wastewater treatment plants.

Drawbacks to aquaculture

Although aquaculture and mariculture have the potential to make great contributions to the world's food supply, there are some drawbacks to the growth of these industries. In some developing countries, natural habitats are destroyed in order to build pens for crops. For example, shrimp farmers often cut down large areas of trees called mangroves. These trees have the ability to live in salt water. The roots of these trees serve important purposes in the tropical marine ecosystem (community of organisms and their environment). They provide habitats for a

Salmon Farming

A fish farm worker nets salmon in British Columbia, Canada. © Natalie Fobes/Corbis. Reproduced by permission.

Salmon is a delicacy. Like bears, humans find its firm, pink meat tasty and nutritious. The very qualities that make salmon desirable—they have firm muscles from swimming long distances and high protein content from feeding on other fish—make them relatively rare in the wild and expensive to grow on farms. Wild salmon meat has always been an expensive luxury that, like a diamond ring or a fur coat, comes with an environmental cost.

Raising salmon in tanks and pens is a way to provide salmon to restaurants and grocery stores while preserving wild fish. Most species of Atlantic and Pacific salmon are born in cool freshwater streams and lakes, travel down rivers to oceans where they spend their adult years in salt water, and then return to their home streams to lay eggs and die. (Fish that live in both fresh and salt water are called anadromous. Coho, Chinook, Chum, Pink, and Sockeye are all anadromous Pacific salmon.) Human alterations to river systems including dams, water pollution, changes to the amount of silt and mud in the water, and over-fishing have threatened most species of wild salmon.

In modern day, most of the salmon humans eat is raised on farms in cool northern and far southern countries like Norway, Canada, Scotland, Russia, Chile, and Argentina. In the United States, aquaculturists (fish farmers) raise salmon in Washington State and Maine. Aquaculture has made salmon more widely available, but it is still expensive because the fish are difficult to raise in captivity. Salmon farmers accommodate salmon's anadromous life style by spawning and raising young fish in freshwater tanks, and then moving the adult fish to outdoor saltwater pens along coastlines. Salmon are carnivorous (meat-eaters) and it takes about 5 pounds (2.3 kilograms) of fish to produce one pound of salmon meat.

Salmon farming, like most other types of economically-profitable food production, has several drawbacks that concern environmentalists and biologists. Salmon's carnivorous diet threatens other wild species because their feed is made from wild fish. (Raising the feed fish makes farm-raised salmon more expensive than wild salmon.) Environmentalists also worry that salmon pens pollute coastal waters and affect the pristine beauty of northern coastlines. Finally, adults that escape the pens may compete with the wild salmon for resources, spread disease, or mate with wild fish to have babies that cannot survive the rigorous life of wild salmon. (Farm-raised salmon don't have the skills they need to travel thousands of miles [kilometers] in the ocean and then back to their home stream to lay eggs.) Aquaculturists, scientists, and environmentalists are working to find solutions that both protect the wild fish and provide salmon for human consumption.

Algae and fish are grown in cages by the sea in this Israeli aquaculture center. © *Jeffrey L. Rotman/Corbis. Reproduced by permission.*

variety of juvenile fish and invertebrates (animals without a backbone) that hide from predators in their crevasses. They also prevent erosion (wearing away of soil) during floods and storms, by holding soil in place. Finally they use some pollutants, like nitrogen and phosphorus, that are generated by aquatic organisms as they grow.

Pollution is a second problem that aquacultural and maricultural farmers have to confront. Having a large number of animals concentrated in a small area produces much waste. These wastes can stimulate the growth of microorganisms such as phytoplankton and bacteria, which harm animals that live nearby. Some newer technologies involve growing animals in enclosed tanks where water is cleaned and recycled rather than simply released into the environment. Although not yet financially practical, these techniques may represent a cleaner way to farm fish and shellfish in the future.

Finally, the economics of mariculture and aquaculture play a large role in the expansion of these industries. Building and running a facility that grows freshwater or marine organisms is not always profitable. Just as in farming on land, animals and plants that are grown on farms in the water must have traits that allow for domestication. For example, animals that exhibit territoriality or aggressive behaviors are not good candidates for aquaculture or mariculture. Disease can ruin crops, and expensive antibiotics may need to be used to keep animals healthy. Controlling the reproductive rate of farmed animals is extremely important. If animals reproduce too fast, some can become stunted and unable to be sold. If animals reproduce to slowly, costs can overcome profits.

Juli Berwald, Ph.D.

For More Information

Books

Davenport, John, et al. *Aquaculture: The Ecological Issues.* Malden, MA: Blackwell Publishers, 2003.

Southgate, Paul, and Lucas, John S., eds. *Aquaculture: Farming Aquatic Animals.* Ames: Iowa State University Press, 2003.

Websites

Harrell, Reginal M. "Finfish Aquaculture Workbook Series." *Maryland Sea Grant Extension.* http://www.mdsg.umd.edu/ Extension/finfish (accessed on August 24, 2004).

"State of the World Fisheries and Aquaculture: 2002." *Food and Agricultural Organization of the United Nations.* http://www.fao.org/docrep/005/y7300e/y7300e00.htm (accessed on August 24, 2004).

Commercial and Industrial Uses of Water

Besides being vital for human survival, water is also necessary in commerce and in industry. Commercial operations are those that generally do not manufacture a product, but provide a service, such as hospitals, restaurants, and schools. Industry usually involves manufacturing a product. In industry, water helps keep machinery needed for the making of products running smoothly and efficiently. Water can also be a vital part of the product, such as in sports drinks or soft drinks. In the United States, the total amount of fresh and salt water used every day by industry is nearly 410 billion gallons. To illustrate such a huge number, think of that amount of water in terms of weight. A gallon of water weighs a little over 8 pounds (3.6 kilograms). The daily water usage in the United States totals almost 3.5 trillion pounds (1.6 trillion kilograms), about the same as 200 million 200-pound (90.7 kilogram) people!

WORDS TO KNOW

Groundwater: Freshwater that resides in rock and soil layers beneath Earth's land surface.

Surface water: Freshwater that is located on the surface, naturally in the form of streams, rivers, lakes and other waterways, or in reservoirs, swimming pools, and other containers that have been built.

Commercial water use

In modern day, water is essential to people's daily lives. Without water, restaurants could not supply meals or even clean up after the meals, cars would go unwashed, and fires could be disastrous, with no means of dousing the blaze. Green parks, recreational fields, and golf courses rely on water to keep the grass and soil moist and healthy. Roadways would become dirty and grimy in the absence of any water-based cleaning program. Offices would grind to a halt with no water available for drinking and bathrooms, and office buildings, stores, and public and private centers would also be dark places without the water necessary to generate electricity for lighting.

The water for these and other commercial uses comes from the surface and from underground (groundwater) sources. The extent to which a community uses a surface or a groundwater source depends on which source is more abundant in the particular area. For example, the drier central portions of the United States and Canada do not have as much surface water as the eastern and western coasts. In the prairies, wells that reach down to tap underground water sources are more common than in coastal regions such as California.

Some of the water that is used for commercial purposes can be reused. The water used in a car wash is one example. Another example is the water that is applied to golf courses. Surface water that is obtained from a lagoon (shallow body of water cut off from a larger body) can be suitable for keeping a

Commercial Fishing

Pollack fish spill onto the deck of a commercial fishing trawler in the Bering Sea off Alaska. © *Natalie Fobes/Corbis. Reproduced by permission.*

Both fresh and salt waters have long supported commercial fisheries in North America. Rivers on the eastern and western portions of the United States and Canada once were the basis of a productive commercial salmon fishery. However, in the past few decades, the number of salmon that return from the ocean to their river homes has been steadily declining. One reason is over-fishing; the catching of more fish than is produced. But other factors may be playing a role. The decline in water quality is one suspected factor.

A century ago, the Grand Banks off the coast of Newfoundland, Canada was the world's premier cod fishing ground. Nets would strain under the weight of untold numbers of cod, often the source of fish used in preparing fish sticks and the traditional 'fish and chips'. However, over-fishing by local fishers and by large factory trawlers have greatly reduced the cod stocks. In the 1990s, the government of Canada ended fishing for cod off the east coast of Canada so that the numbers of cod could again increase in their natural habitat. A decade later, the numbers of cod fish had not recovered, and the cod fishery industry in the area was, at least temporarily, lost.

golf course lush and green. Other commercial water uses, such as drinking water, demand water that is free of chemicals and harmful microorganisms.

Fresh and salt water is home to many living creatures that are harvested by humans. Whether for sport or as a business, fisheries are completely dependent on water.

Industrial water use

Industries require large supplies of water. Machinery relies on water to cool it to a temperature that allows the manufacturing process to keep going. The mining industry needs water to wash off the material that has been brought up from underground in order to sort out the genuine product from other particles. Water is also used to clean machinery, buildings, and even, in the case of the meat processing industry, the carcasses of the cattle, pigs, and other animals that will be trimmed into the items found in the meat section of the local supermarket.

In oil producing regions, vast amounts of water are used. As oil wells get older and the underlying oil reserve is tapped, it becomes more difficult to pump out oil that is hiding in cracks in the rock deep underground. One way of getting this oil is to pump water down into the oil formation. The water can make its way into cracks and crevasses and push the oil out in front of it. The oil is then pumped up using another well. Without this industrial use of water, oil and gasoline would be more scarce and more expensive.

The generation of electrical power also makes use of water, to cool equipment and to push the turbines that are the heart of the process that produces electricity. Turbines are turning wheels with buckets, paddles or blades that turn as water moves by converting the energy of moving water to mechanical power. According to the U.S. Geological Survey, in the year 2000 about 20 billion gallons (76 billion liters) of water were used each day to make electricity. This represents about 53% of all water use in the country. The vast amount of this water comes from surface water sources. Much of this water is eventually returned to the environment for reuse. In contrast, water that is used to irrigate (water) crops usually cannot be recovered after being applied to the crops.

Another big user of water is the pulp and paper industry; millions of gallons of water is used in the various processes that turn a log into a piece of paper. Clean water is also required for papermaking. If the water contains too many solid particles, the paper will not be smooth and the paper-making machinery could be damaged.

For other industries, water may not be a key part of the actual making of the product, but it is nevertheless, required. In the steel making industry, water is needed for cooling equipment. Like in the oil industry, this use of water does not require water of the same quality as drinking water. Care must be taken in disposing of the water, however. For example, water cannot be disposed of immediately after it is used to cool equipment, as the high temperature of the water would damage fish and other life in the natural environment. This water is usually cooled in a holding pond or container before being released.

Brian Hoyle, Ph.D.

For More Information

Books

U.S. Environmental Protection Agency. *The Water Sourcebooks: K-12*. Washington, DC: USEPA, 2000.

Vickers, Amy. *Handbook of Water Use and Conservation: Homes, Landscapes, Industries, Businesses, Farms*. Amherst, MA: Waterplow Press, 2001.

Websites

United States Geological Survey. "Industrial Water Use." *Water Science for Schools*. http://wwwga.usgs.gov/edu/wuin.html (accessed on August 24, 2004).

Economic Uses of Groundwater

Groundwater is one of humans' most valuable natural resources. Groundwater is the water contained in the rock and soil layers beneath Earth's surface, and it makes up most of Earth's supply of fresh, liquid water. (The oceans and ice in the North and South Poles contain 99% of Earth's total water supply. Groundwater accounts for almost all of the remaining 1%.) Throughout history, humans have settled in areas with plentiful and pure groundwater, and have fought to own and protect wells and springs. Today, human water needs in many arid (dry) or heavily populated regions far exceed surface water supplies. Earth's rapidly-growing human population is becoming increasingly reliant on groundwater.

Groundwater fills wells and city water supplies. Groundwater irrigates (waters) crops, feeds livestock, and produces farm-raised fish. Groundwater is used to cool nuclear reactors that generate electricity, mix concrete, and manufacture millions of consumer products. In short, groundwater plays a vital role in almost every facet of people's lives, from drinking water, foods, and products people buy to roads and the buildings in which people live and work.

Groundwater reservoirs: aquifers

Water enters underground reservoirs by soaking in through soils, stream beds, and ponds in areas termed recharge zones. Water flows, often very slowly, through interconnected pore (tiny opening) spaces and then remerges onto the land surface at natural discharge points called springs and seeps. When discharge from natural springs and/or human wells exceeds the

Aquifer: Underground rock or sediment layer that yields water of adequate quantity and purity for human use.

Artesian flow: Water that rises to the land surface from confined aquifers without pumping.

Discharge zone: Land area where groundwater flows out of aquifers on to land surface.

Dowsing: Practice of using spiritual powers and a divining rod to locate underground water.

Recharge zone: Area where water enters groundwater reservoirs by infiltrating through soils, stream beds, and ponds.

Water table: Level below which all pore space is filled with water.

rate of recharge, the groundwater level falls, shallow wells and springs dry, and eventually, the reservoir empties. Many groundwater reservoirs, particularly those beneath arid deserts and semi-arid grasslands, filled with water many centuries ago when regional climate was wetter.

Groundwater reservoirs that yield water for human use are called aquifers. In part, human economics determine which water-bearing units are exploited as aquifers. In regions where clean surface water is plentiful and inexpensive, groundwater may go unused. In arid regions with scarce or polluted surface water, and in places where human water needs exceed the water supply in streams and lakes, groundwater extraction and purification become economically worthwhile. When conditions change, as during periods of drought (prolonged dry weather) or increased population growth, new groundwater supplies are tapped, thereby elevating them to aquifer status.

Wells

In addition to collecting groundwater from springs, humans extract water from aquifers by digging or drilling wells that extend from the ground surface to the water table, the level below which all the empty space in the rocks and soil are completely full of water (saturated). When a well reaches the water table, groundwater fills the hole like water filling a hole dug in beach sand. In wet regions, the water table may lie only a few feet (meters) below the surface. In arid regions, groundwater wells are often hundreds of feet (meters) deep. Most wells require a bucket system or pump to raise the water to the land surface. Some aquifers, however, contain pressurized groundwater that flows to the land surface on its own. Such free-flowing groundwater discharges are called artesian wells and springs.

There are a number of ways to construct wells. Some common types of wells are hand-dug, driven, and drilled wells.

*   Hand-dug wells: Historically, wells were dug into soil and even rock by hand. Well diggers with shovels or picks would dig a hole below the water table by bailing water faster than it flowed into the well. Once a well was complete, its builders reinforced its walls and fitted it with a bucket system or pump to bring water to the surface. Hand-dug wells are still regularly constructed in many parts of the world, but they are uncommon in developed nations like the United States.

Dowsing

Groundwater can be hard to find. Today, hydrogeologists use scientific methods to locate aquifers and productive water wells. Aquifers can be extremely complex and groundwater flow patterns difficult to predict, and it is not uncommon for hydrogeologists to drill dry wells. In the past, water-seekers consulted with spiritually-guided water prospectors called dowsers or water witches.

Dowsers profess special powers that allow them to sense or divine water beneath the ground. While a hydrogeologist searches for groundwater by taking measurements, making observations, and drawing maps, a dowser strolled across the client's land holding a metal or wooden Y- or L-shaped divining rod or a pendulum. When water was present, the rod or pendulum was said to be attracted to the water beneath. Some dowsers even claimed that their divining rods would locate groundwater on maps of the land surface.

The practice of dowsing has its roots in ancient Egypt and China, and its first published reference appeared in 1430. Early dowsers and water witches probably relied on a combination of spiritual guidance and astute scientific observations of groundwater discharge features such as springs, seeps, and vegetation patterns to locate underground water. Like witch doctors in ancient cultures, dowsers used all their available tools, including scientific knowledge, to help their clients solve problems. As such, modern hydrogeologists are perhaps their closest professional descendants.

Modern-day dowsers claim to find water entirely with their spiritually enhanced extrasensory powers. They assert that groundwater has a magnetic field that pulls on their dowsing rods, a theory that has never been scientifically proven. Dowsers do successfully locate groundwater, but without clues to the local groundwater system, their results are statistically no better than random well drilling.

- Driven wells: Driven wells are constructed by forcing or hammering a narrow pipe into soft ground. These wells are inexpensive and can reach very deep aquifers, but can only be used in areas that have loose soil or sediment (particles of sand, gravel, and silt).

- Drilled wells: Today, most water wells are drilled using rotary (turning) or percussion (hammering) machines that are mounted on large trucks. Drilled wells that penetrate loose material are lined with plastic or metal pipe called casing, which keeps the sides of the hole from collapsing. An electric pump is placed at the bottom of the well to bring the water to the surface.

Historical groundwater use

Humans in arid regions such as northern Africa, the Middle East, and central Asia have relied on groundwater to provide drinking water and irrigate crops for thousands of years.

Archeologists have discovered the remains of hand-dug wells, oasis (areas in the desert with a source of water) settlements, and groundwater distribution systems throughout the ancient world. Humans have drunk from groundwater springs at the Oasis of Bahariya in the Sahara desert of western Egypt since the early stone age (Paleolithic Age) more than one million years ago.

Knowledge of groundwater supplies and extraction technologies was critical information for ancient desert empires such as Mesopotamia, Sumeria, and Egypt. Nomads (wandering tribes) in the Saharan and Arabian deserts relied upon fiercely guarded knowledge of groundwater springs and seeps to survive. Egyptians, Mesopotamians, and Chinese who first practiced agriculture dug wells to provide irrigation for water-intensive crops such as rice and cotton, and drinking water for permanent settlements. Groundwater availability affected patterns of conquest and settlement in Greek and Roman Empires. European explorers sought groundwater and white settlers excavated wells that supported settlement and farming throughout North and South America.

Modern groundwater use

Today, people use groundwater for agricultural irrigation, industrial processes, municipal (city) and residential (home) water supplies. In the United States, groundwater accounted for about one quarter (26%) of total water use in the year 2000. (Surface freshwater made up the other 74%.) Groundwater use, however, varies by location, and many U.S. residents and industries depend almost completely upon water drawn from regional aquifers. More than one-third of U.S.' 100 largest cities, including Miami Beach, San Antonio, Memphis, Honolulu, and Tucson get all their water from aquifers. Almost all rural households (98%) draw their water from private wells.

Farmers and ranchers in Midwestern and Western states make heavy use of groundwater for irrigation of crops. In the eastern and southern U.S., most drinking and agricultural water comes from lakes and streams, but industries use vast quantities of groundwater for such activities as refining petroleum, aluminum, and other ores; manufacturing steel and chemicals; producing plastics; and mining. Aquaculture (fish farming) is big business and a significant groundwater consumer in Southeastern states like Mississippi, Alabama, and Louisiana.

In the United States, groundwater is particularly important in arid and semi-arid agricultural states in the western half of the nation. Heavily agricultural states such as California, Oregon, and Texas use large quantities of groundwater for irrigation of food crops. The livestock industry also draws heavily upon groundwater supplies in states such as Texas, Nebraska, Kansas, and Colorado. Water drawn from wells not only fills watering troughs, but also irrigates vast tracts of midwestern cropland that produce material for cattle, poultry, pig, and fish feed. Meat processing plants also require water. (It takes about 13 gallons [49 liters] of water to produce 1 pound (0.45 kilogram) of beef, and about 4 gallons [15 liters] of water go into producing 1 gallon [3.8 liters] of milk!)

Laurie Duncan, Ph.D., and
Todd Minehardt, Ph.D.

For More Information

Books

Pipkin, Bernard W., and Trent, D. D. "Fresh-water Resources." In *Geology and the Environment.* Pacific Grove, CA: Brooks/Cole, 2001.

Press, Frank, and Siever, Raymond. "Hydrologic Cycle and Groundwater." *Understanding Earth.* New York: W. H. Freeman and Company, 2003.

Periodicals

Hansen, George P. "Dowsing: A Review of Experimental Research." *Journal of the Society for Psychical Research* (October 1982): pp. 343–67. Available online at http://www.tricksterbook.com/ArticlesOnline/Dowsing.htm (accessed August 24, 2004).

Websites

"Ground Water and Drinking Water." *U.S. Environmental Protection Agency.* http://www.epa.gov/OGWDW/index.html (accessed August 24, 2004).

U.S. Geological Survey. "Earth's Water." *Water Science for Schools.* http://ga.water.usgs.gov/edu/mearth.html (August 24, 2004).

"Water Resources." *U.S. Department of Agriculture, National Resources Conservation Service.* http://www.nrcs.usda.gov/technical/water.html (accessed August 24, 2004).

WORDS TO KNOW

Black smoker: Underwater seep of magma that deposits minerals.

Element: A substance that cannot be divided by ordinary chemical means.

Hydrothermal deposit: Mineral-containing geologic unit that was formed by hot waters percolating through source rocks.

Metal: Substance that is a conductor of electricity and heat.

Open-pit mine: Large craters dug into the earth to extract ore that is near the surface.

Ore: Naturally occurring source of minerals.

Placer deposit: Water-deposited mineral source, such as gold nuggets in streams.

Stope (adit) mine: Mines with large, vertical shafts for miners to enter the mine and horizontal shafts (adits) for miners to reach the ore.

Strip mine: Large, underground swaths dug through ore-rich zones with shafts for miners to enter and for deposits to exit.

Minerals and Mining

Minerals are defined as naturally occurring solids found in the earth that are composed of matter other than plants or animals. Ore is a naturally occurring source of minerals, such as a rock. A mineral can be composed from one element, such as diamond, which contains only carbon, or several elements, such as quartz, which contains silicon and oxygen. An element is a substance that cannot be divided by ordinary chemical means. Even ice is considered a mineral. Minerals are found everywhere on Earth, from the bottom of the ocean to the highest mountains. Mineral deposits are frequently located underground, and thus they must be mined. South Africa and Russia hold the largest amount of minerals in the world. Minerals are vital to people's lives, and many of these minerals are critical to countries' industries and economies.

The United States is relatively poor in critical minerals, including platinum, cobalt, and gold, but there are sand deposits of titanium ore in Florida and the Pacific Northwest. In the central United States, minerals that contain lead and gallium (used in computer chips) are abundant, and iron ore is found in the states near the Great Lakes. Most of the diamonds are mined in Africa, as is gold, although gold is found in many other locations as well.

Importance of minerals

Minerals are essential in every aspect of life for humans. Humans need to ingest minerals in order for our bodies to function normally. Most of these required minerals come from the foods people eat. Gold and silver have been valued by civilization since ancient times. Metals became useful for purposes other than money during the Bronze Age, when weapons and tools could be made from metal as people became more educated with how to process the minerals and extract (remove) metals. As metals were not evenly dispersed around the globe, the more powerful nations became that way through military might from weapons made from metal.

Industry also depends upon minerals. Without aluminum (mined mostly in Jamaica), people could not manufacture airplanes, much less soda-pop cans. Titanium is used in the aerospace industry for constructing spacecraft and in medicine for the construction of artificial limbs and joints. Copper is required to make wire that carries electricity to homes and factories.

Right: Swimmers enjoy geothermally heated pools in Svartsvehring, Iceland. See "Hydropower" entry. © *Bob Krist/ Corbis. Reproduced by permission.*

Below: Sailboats moor off the Tahitian islands, a popular tourist destination in the South Pacific. See "Tourism on the Oceans" entry. © *Neil Rabinowitz/ Corbis. Reproduced by permission.*

Left: Built by the ancient Romans, the three tiered Pont du Gard aqueduct spans the Gard River in France. See "Aqueducts" entry. © *Archivo Iconografico, S.A./Corbis. Reproduced by permission.*

Below: A junk, a form of boat popular in the waters of east Asia, sails into the port of Hong Kong, China. See "Ports and Harbors" entry. © *Nik Wheeler/Corbis. Reproduced by permission.*

Right: Supplying water to densely packed New York City requires a complex municipal water supply system. See "Municipal Water Use" entry. © 1996 Corbis. Reproduced by permission.

Below: Oil storage tanks line the channel from the Gulf of Mexico to the Port of Houston, Texas. The ship in the foreground is painted orange to indicate it carries flammable or hazardous cargo. See "Petroleum Exploration and Recovery" entry. © Ray Soto/ Corbis. Reproduced by permission.

Right: A scuba diver encounters a stingray in the waters off the Cayman Islands. See "Recreation in and on the Oceans" entry. © *Stephen Frink/Corbis. Reproduced by permission.*

Below: In the modern world, water is used as a form of art. The Trocadero fountains in Paris compliment the form of the Eiffel Tower. See "Commercial and Industrial Uses of Water" entry. © *Royalty-Free/Corbis. Reproduced by permission.*

Right: The Hoover Dam hydropower plant is driven by water from the Colorado River. See "Arid Climates" entry. © *Royalty-Free/Corbis. Reproduced by permission.*

Below: An erupting geyser displays the power of geothermal forces. See "Hydrology and Hydrogeology" entry. © *Royalty-Free/ Corbis. Reproduced by permission.*

Left: An aqueduct and canal near Bakersfield, California. See "Aqueducts" entry. © *Yann Arthus-Bertrand/Corbis. Reproduced by permission.*

Below: A group of whales swimming off Tomiura, Japan. See "Whaling" entry. *AP/Wide World Photos. Reproduced by permission.*

Right: A girl pets a dolphin at Sea World in San Diego, California. See "Aquariums" entry. *© Carl & Ann Purcell/Corbis. Reproduced by permission.*

Below: Maintaining an aquarium at home is a popular hobby. See "Aquariums" entry. *© Michael Pole/Corbis. Reproduced by permission.*

Above: Large container ships
carry freight across the world's
oceans. See "Shipping on the
Oceans" entry. © *Lester Lefkowitz/*
Corbis. Reproduced by permission.

Mineral reserves are of great importance in the marketplace and it is not uncommon to stockpile (save) certain metals extracted from mineral ores. Because large mineral deposits are located in regions of the world that are, at times, politically and economically unstable, the supply of critical minerals is not guaranteed. The United States stockpiles metals such as platinum, palladium, cobalt, chromium, manganese, and vanadium. These metals are used in the high-technology industries and the military. Chromium, for instance, is used to produce stainless steel. Vanadium is used, along with aluminum, to make forms of titanium that are resistant to fracture (breaking), enabling the manufacture of jet planes that can withstand extreme conditions. Platinum is used in removing the impurities from oil. Palladium is used in the exhaust systems of automobiles to reduce the amount of pollutants. It is advantageous for a highly-industrialized country such as the United States to have these resources at hand, and to purchase reserves when prices are low.

Water-laid ores and minerals

The formation of mineral deposits always involves water. Water is part of the chemical processes of mineral formation and also changes the mineral content of rocks by dissolving certain elements in the ore and transporting them elsewhere. Heat is another ingredient in the formation of many mineral deposits.

Hydrothermal deposits. Many metal-bearing ores are found in veins (cracks in rock filled with minerals) that cut through surrounding rock. In these cases, very hot water reacted with elements and other minerals in the rock, and burst through the layers of rock where there was a weakness. These mineral deposits are called hydrothermal deposits. Hydrothermal deposits form gold, silver, and the platinum-group metals, which are commonly found in veins. The metals themselves are hosted in a vein that

Manganese Nodules

Manganese nodules (solid, raised bumps) are tennis-ball sized mineral nodules that litter the ocean floor, mostly in the Pacific Ocean. They form much like pearls, with a small center that can be a grain of sand or even a tooth from a fish, and over millions of years, manganese, along with iron and other minerals build-up as shells. There are numerous manganese nodules yet they are hard to extract, largely due to the depths from which they must be brought to the surface. This is an expensive proposition, and until other sources of the minerals contained in manganese nodules are exhausted, will not likely be a source of minerals for human use.

Because the nodules are in international waters, there has been debate over who can claim ownership. Many nations formed the United Nations Convention on the Law of the Sea, which in turn led to the formation of the International Seabed Authority in 1994, which controls international ocean mining rights. The reason for making these laws and forming a governing body was to ensure that all nations could share in the wealth stored in the nodules. The International Seabed Authority has granted several areas for exploration and recovery to many public and private concerns, but the United States does not abide by these directives because, as of 2004, it does not observe the Law of the Sea.

is often quartz. Miners follow the vein, extract the ore, and remove the host rock to extract the metals contained within. Mining minerals from veins is an expensive process that is seldom used today.

When hot water flows through porous rock (rock with many small holes), the rock can become a host to a kind of deposit known as porphyry. The host rock containing a porphyry deposit is filled with small veins of (usually) quartz that contain the minerals. Although the mineral content is low, porphyry deposits are large, and most of the copper that is mined comes from these unique deposits. Fool's gold (iron sulfide) is often found in porphyry deposits as well.

Volcanogenic deposits. Volcanogenic deposits form when magma (molten or melted rock beneath the Earth's surface) from miles (kilometers) down in the earth is transported to the surface in volcanoes. There are two kinds of volcanic eruptions that most concern scientists. One of these brings iron-rich magma to the surface (such as in Hawaii) and one brings explosive plumes of ash and magma to the surface (such as in Mt. Saint Helens). Elements in the water that is in contact with the magma, along with the rock through which the water travels on its way to the surface, determine the kinds of minerals found in volcanogenic deposits. For the most part, lead and iron ore are found in volcanogenic deposits, along with smaller amounts of cadmium, antimony, and copper.

On the floor of the ocean, the same kinds of deposits can form where magma seeps through a crack in the seabed. These features are called black smokers, because the iron-rich magma makes the plume appear like black smoke. The mineral deposits collect near the smoker until the hole becomes plugged or the magma is diverted elsewhere.

Mining for minerals

The process of mining for minerals begins after a mineral deposit has been identified. The common types of mines used to excavate minerals are open-pit mines, strip mines, and stope and adit mines.

- Open-pit mines: These mines are large craters dug into the earth to extract ore that is near the surface. Open pit mines are usually associated with porphyry deposits, and minerals such as galena (which contains lead), chalcopyrite (which contains copper), and sphalerite (which contains zinc) are commonly mined at open pits. The open pit is excavated using very powerful and large earth-moving equipment, and processing of the ore (crushing, grinding, partial refinement) is often done near the open pit. Open pits are less environmentally friendly than conventional mines because any native vegetation in the area is lost, and abandoned open pit mines eventually pool waters that are frequently contaminated. Open-pit mines are used for copper in Arizona.

- Strip mines: These mines are large swaths dug through ore-rich zones (common for coal). Most mines are located below the surface of the Earth, and require drilling shafts to enable workers to reach the ore below and transport it to the surface. Strip mines are used for coal in many states and other areas where the ore is buried deeply, as in Montana, where platinum and palladium ore is extracted (removed).

- Stope and adit mines: These mines are bored into the ground. Shafts are bored vertically, and horizontal offshoots (adits) from the shafts that lead into ore-containing portions of the subsurface are dug. Large mining vehicles that crush the rock move along veins of ore, and this byproduct is transported to the surface by rail or cable lifts. Temperatures in conventional mines are high, and the conditions are dangerous—cave-ins occur often—so safety measures are very strict. The shafts and other structures are reinforced with concrete or metal supports.

Panning for gold near Sutter's Mill, California. © *Robert Holmes/Corbis. Reproduced by permission.*

Other ore and mineral deposits

Placer deposits are concentrated metals that have been transported to streambeds (the channel through which the stream runs) or beaches. The most famous placer deposits are gold nuggets, although silver is sometimes found as well. Placer metals must be resistant to water, or they would dissolve again. The usual way to extract the placer deposits is to scoop sediment (particles of rock, clay, or silt) from the stream and sift it, leaving the larger rock behind and making the gold easier to spot. California, Alaska, Oregon, and Idaho have all had significant placer deposits of gold.

Placer deposits and the California Gold Rush

On January 24, 1848, placer gold was discovered in Sutter's Mill, California, setting off what would become the "Gold Rush." People from all over the United States came to California to seek their fortune in gold and silver mining in stream beds. These people were known as prospectors and San Francisco was a major center to prospectors. The Gold Rush was so large, the population of California exploded almost instantly.

Where did the gold come from? To the East, in the Sierra Nevada mountain range, gold-containing rocks eroded (wore away) over tens of thousands of years. Streams transported gold dust and nuggets to northern California where the gold was lying in streams, waiting to be collected.

Panning for gold was the usual way to collect the placer deposits. Like a strainer from the kitchen, the pan let water and small particles through and did not allow larger particles to pass. In this way, mud and other sediments could be washed away, and the resulting rocks examined to see if any were gold. Shaker tables were also used. This is a slanted surface that mechanically vibrated, sending the less dense (heavy or thick per unit of volume) rocks to the bottom of the table while the more dense rocks, such as gold, stayed near the top.

Evaporite deposits form by evaporation. As waters that contain dissolved mineral species evaporate, the minerals remain in solid form. Minerals found in evaporites include potassium chloride, sodium chloride (halite or table salt), calcium sulfate (gypsum), barium sulfate (barite), and potassium nitrate (saltpeter). Most of these deposits are near the surface and are scooped from the ground with large earth-moving equipment. Gypsum is used to make sheetrock, which is used to construct the walls of homes and buildings. It is fire-retardant and easily cast into shapes. Barium sulfate is used as drilling mud in oil-producing wells because it is very dense, and prevents oil gushers from erupting as the drill is lowered. Barium itself has use in medicine. Saltpeter is used as an ingredient in gunpowder and fertilizers.

In the oceans, concentrations of dissolved mineral ingredients are very high. Evaporites of the chloride type are most common, and they occur in areas where seawater collects in shallow areas that are confined. Thus, a pool of salt-rich water forms, evaporation speeds up the process, and salt deposits result. Another widespread mineral formed in marine environments is limestone, or calcium carbonate. This mineral is formed in the same way as the chloride salts, but also includes another source, organisms whose skeletons are made from calcium carbonate. These organisms die and collect on the sea floor, where they add to the content of calcium carbonate. Limestone is used in constructing buildings and as an ingredient in concrete.

Todd Minehardt, Ph.D.

For More Information

Books

Postel, Sandra, and Brian Richter. *Rivers for Life: Managing Water for People and Nature.* Washington, DC: Island Press, 2003.

Websites

"Geoenvironmental Model of Volcanogenic Massive Sulfide Deposits." *Government of British Columbia Ministry of Energy and Mines.* http://www.em.gov.bc.ca/Mining/ Geolsurv/MetallicMinerals/metallogeny/O98_abstract_ alpers.HTM (accessed onAugust 27, 2004).

"The Gold Rush." *Oakland Museum of California.* http://www. museumca.org/goldrush (accessed on August 27, 2004).

"Manganese Nodules." *Wikipedia.* http://www.fact-index.com/ m/ma/manganese_nodule.html (accessed on August 27, 2004).

"Rivers, Dams, and Climate Change." *International Rivers Network.* http://www.irn.org/programs/greenhouse/ (accessed on August 27, 2004).

Municipal Water Use

Many people live in municipalities (cities, towns, and villages with services such as water treatment, police, and fire departments). One benefit of living in a municipality is that potable water (water safe to drink) is usually available at any time by turning on the tap. Part of the responsibility of citizens and municipal officials however, is to manage and protect the local water supply.

If municipal water becomes contaminated, the result can be far-reaching and rapid. Bacteria and viruses in water can spread throughout the underground reservoir of water (the aquifer) or throughout the miles of pipelines that carries water to houses in towns and cities. As well, non-living pollutants such as oil, gasoline and sediment can spread contaminate water.

The results of such contamination can be disastrous. In the summer of 2000, the municipal water supply of Walkerton, a town in the Canadian province of Ontario, became contaminated with a certain type of bacteria called *Escherichia coli* (or *E. coli* for short). This type of *E. coli* caused a serious illness in over a thousand people who drank the town water, and killed seven people.

In addition to protecting water for human use, water management also benefits the environment. Polluted water is bad for the many creatures that live in the water and depend on the watercourse in their lives.

◊**Escherichia coli:** Type of bacteria that is found in the intestines of warm-blooded animals including humans; some types can cause illness if ingested.

◊**Groundwater:** Freshwater that resides in rock and soil layers beneath Earth's land surface.

◊**Municipality:** A village, town, or city with its own local government that provides services for its residents.

◊**Potable:** Water that is safe to drink.

◊**Surface water:** Water that is located on the surface, naturally in the form of streams, rivers, lakes and other waterways, or in reservoirs, swimming pools and other containers that have been built.

◊**Water treatment:** A series of steps that makes water potable and removes chemicals and microoganisms that could be harmful to the natural environment.

Protecting municipal drinking water

People who live in a municipality usually have to pay money to the local government for their water. Municipal drinking water may come from wells, which pump water that is located underneath the ground (groundwater) into an underground reservoir. Groundwater is often free of contaminating chemicals and microorganisms because the contaminants are filtered out of the water as it moves downward into the ground, yet the water still must be tested to ensure the absence of contaminants. Once tested, the water is pumped through pipes that run underneath the streets of the municipality. The pipes lead to houses, fire stations, other offices, swimming pools, and the many other places where water is used.

Some municipal drinking water is obtained from streams, rivers, and lakes. This water is called surface water. Surface water must be treated before it can be used for drinking, because there is a greater chance that harmful chemicals or microorganisms could have washed into surface water. Municipalities that rely on surface water will pump the water from the river or lake to a water treatment plant. The water will be cleaned in a series of steps and tested to ensure that it is safe to drink. The treated water can then be pumped to storage tanks until it is used.

In many municipalities, one of the treatment steps is the addition of a chemical called chlorine. This chemical kills bacteria such as *E. coli*, and so is an effective and inexpensive way to keep the water free from bacteria. The amount of chlorine that is added to water needs to be monitored, since too much chlorine can create taste and odor problems. Furthermore, excess chlorine can combine with organic material in the water (like rotting leaves) to form a compound called trihalomethane that has been linked to the development of cancer in humans. Some municipalities have installed other means of killing or removing microorganisms. These include the use of ultraviolet (UV) light, which kills microorganisms by breaking apart their genetic material. Another technique is to pass the water through a series of filters (a material that has very tiny holes in it). While the water molecules can pass through these holes, the holes are too small to allow most microorganisms to pass through.

After water is used, the chemicals, sewage, and other contaminants must be removed before the water can be reused or returned to a reservoir. In order to accomplish this, wastewater

New York City Municipal Water

Supplying water to densely packed New York City requires a complex municipal water supply system. © 1996 Corbis. Reproduced by permission.

New York City has a population of over seven million people. Another one million people are connected to the drinking water pipelines that supply water throughout the city. Drinking water from lakes and storage containers (reservoirs) journeys to treatment plants through underground pipelines, tunnels cut through hillsides, and channels called aqueducts. From the treatment plants, drinking water makes its way to the huge number of people through a system of pipes that, if put together in a straight line, would stretch nearly 7,000 miles (11,265 kilometers), about the distance from New York City to Tokyo. Sewage and other used water are collected by another system of pipes that is also about 7,000 miles (11,265 kilometers) long. Each day, 14 sewage treatment plants can treat about 1.2 billion gallons of wastewater, enough to fill 2,000 Olympic size swimming pools!

The water quality of the New York City municipal water is the responsibility of the New York Department of Environmental Protection. Over 6,000 people work to make sure that the water is safe to drink.

leaves buildings through sewage pipes that lead to the treatment facility, and the treatment cycle begins again.

Other uses of municipal water

Many municipalities provide golf courses, swimming pools, sports fields, gardens and parks for their residents. All of these places require water. Fire fighters need easy access to water, which is provided by a system of pipes that lead to fire hydrants positioned throughout the municipality. The fire fighters hook their hoses up to the high-pressure hydrants to fight fires with water. Many municipalities have cleaning programs, where roads and other surfaces are cleared of dirt and other material that piles up during the winter or a dusty, dry summer. Water is sprayed from vehicles that move slowly along the road, to wash away the accumulated grime.

Safeguarding municipal water

Many municipalities have laws that restrict people from throwing garbage into streams, rivers, and lakes, and to stop the dumping of liquids such as oil and gasoline into the water. Preserving undeveloped areas of riverbanks or lakes also encourages growth of natural vegetation that benefits the water supply. By leaving grass, trees, and other vegetation alongside a stream or river, it makes it more difficult for toxic (poisonous) material to wash into the water. Along with this benefit, the natural stream or river bank often becomes an attractive spot to walk, bike ride, and picnic.

Brian Hoyle, Ph.D.

For More Information

Books

Marek, Lee, and Lynn Brunelle. *Soakin' Science.* Toronto: Somerville House, 2000.

U.S. Environmental Protection Agency. *The Water Sourcebooks: K-12.* Washington: USEPA, 2000.

Water available for fire control is an important benefit of a municipal water supply.
© *Henry Diltz/Corbis.*
Reproduced by permission.

Websites

"Drinking Water Kid's Stuff." *U.S. Environmental Protection Agency.* http://www.epa.gov/safewater/kids (accessed on August 27, 2004).

"How Urbanization Affects the Hydrologic System." *Water Science for Schools, U.S. Geological Survey* http://ga.water.usgs.gov/edu/urbaneffects.html (accessed on August 27, 2004).

"Water for People." *Water for People.* http://www.waterforpeople.com (accessed on August 27 2004).

Petroleum Exploration and Recovery

Petroleum, also called crude oil, is a thick, yellowish black substance that contains a mixture of solid, liquid, and gaseous chemicals called hydrocarbons. Since its discovery as an energy source in the mid-1800s, petroleum has become one of humans' most valuable natural resources. Petroleum is arguably the single-most important product in the modern global economy.

Hydrocarbons separated (refined) from crude oil provide fuels and products that affect every facet of life in industrialized nations like the United States. Natural gas and propane are gaseous hydrocarbons that are used to heat homes and fuel stoves. Natural gas actually exists as a gas in underground reservoirs (underground rock formations containing oil or natural gas) and is not refined from crude oil, but it is still considered a petroleum product. The liquid portion of petroleum becomes such essential products as home heating oil, automobile gasoline, lubricating oil for engines and machinery, and fuel for electrical power plants. Asphalt road surfaces, lubricating oils for machinery, and furniture wax are all composed of semi-solid hydrocarbons. Petroleum products are the building blocks of plastics. The hydrocarbon gas ethylene is even used to help ripen fruits and vegetables!

Oil and water don't mix, but these two essential natural resources do have a lot in common. Naturally occurring petroleum forms from the chemical remains of organisms that lived and died in ancient seas. Petroleum collects in deeply buried rock layers called sedimentary rock that are, more often than not, the geologic remains of water-laid deposits like beds of sand or coral reefs on the sea floor. (Sediment is particles of rock sand or silt.) Petroleum reservoirs are similar to groundwater reservoirs, the water below Earth's surface. Petroleum scientists use many of the same skills and methods to find and extract oil that groundwater scientists use to prospect for underground water. Finally, many untapped petroleum deposits are buried beneath the seafloor, and much of our present and future petroleum supply lies offshore.

Formation of petroleum deposits

Hydrocarbons are organic (part of or from living organisms) chemicals; they form by the breakdown of microscopic organisms that were once living. (Biological organisms combine the chemical elements *hydro*gen and *carbon* during their lives, thus the term hydrocarbon.) Microscopic plants and animals that collect on the seafloor provide the organic material that eventually becomes petroleum. Dark, smelly, organic-rich mud collects where a heavy rain of dead plants and animals accumulates in an oxygen-poor seafloor environment. (Oxygen-rich waters support animals and bacteria that eat or decompose the organic material.)

WORDS TO KNOW

◆**Hydrocarbon:** Chemical substance made up of carbon and hydrogen; propane, gasoline, kerosene, diesel fuel and lubricating oil are common hydrocarbons.

◆**Internal combustion engine:** An engine takes the energy in fuel and combusts (burns) it inside the engine to produce motion.

◆**Natural gas:** Naturally-occurring hydrocarbon gas.

◆**Organic:** Of or relating to or derived from living organisms.

◆**Platform:** Large buildings, attached to the sea floor or floating, that house workers and machinery needed to drill for oil or gas.

◆**Reservoir rocks:** Rocks where petroleum collelcts.

◆**Source rocks:** Mud layers rich with plant and animal material that become rocks where temperature and pressure transform the plant and animal material into petroleum.

Oil and Gas in the North Sea

An offshore platform supplies oil and gas from the North Sea. © *Lowell Georgia/Corbis. Reproduced by permission.*

Today, energy companies explore and drill for oil and natural gas in extreme offshore environments like the North Sea, a frigid, wind-blown expanse of ocean between Great Britain and Scandinavia. (Most relatively straightforward oil and gas deposits on land have long since been located and exploited. Earth's largest remaining petroleum reserves lie beneath regions that are rife with poverty, corruption, and hostility for petroleum-hungry developed nations like the United States.) Prospecting for oil and gas in the North Sea is an extreme challenge for geologists and engineers, but our ever-growing need for petroleum makes it economically worthwhile.

Geologists from companies like British Petroleum (BP) and Norsk Hydro (a Norwegian petroleum company) seek petroleum deposits in complex rock layers beneath the seafloor. The waters of the North Sea fill an ocean basin that was created by rifting (separation of continental blocks) between the British Isles and Scandinavia that began about 200 million years ago. Oil and gas deposits are the organic remains of microscopic plants and animals that lived and died in the ancient North Sea. Extractable petroleum now lies in sandstone reservoir rocks that have been folded and broken since their formation.

Weather conditions in the North Sea are severe; workers and equipment must withstand harsh cold and violent storms. Petroleum engineers have designed and built strong platforms (large buildings, attached to the sea floor or floating, that house workers and machinery needed to drill for oil or gas) and powerful drills that can extract crude oil and natural gas from hard rock deep beneath the North Sea's notorious towering waves and roaring wind. In spite of extreme weather, difficult geology, and technological challenges, the oil and gas fields of the North Sea are productive, economical sources of petroleum.

Unfortunately for petroleum users, oil doesn't simply collect in underground puddles. Organic material must undergo a series of complex changes over many thousands of years before it becomes petroleum that can be extracted for human use. First, organic-rich mud layers become source rocks like shale and mudstone when they are buried beneath thick stacks of newer sediment. Heat, pressure, and bacteria within source rocks chemically transform plant and animal parts into hydrocarbons. Next, pressure squeezes the petroleum out of the source rocks and it migrates (moves) to reservoir rocks where it fills tiny openings, fractures, and cavities.

Productive petroleum reservoir rocks, such as sandstone and some types of limestone, are like swiss cheese. They have lots of empty space between mineral grains (high porosity) and the space is interconnected so petroleum can flow easily through the rock (high permeability). Finally, exploitable petroleum reservoirs are typically contained beneath layers of relatively impermeable rock called cap rock that keeps oil from escaping onto the land surface. Geologic structures like faults (fracture or break along which rocks slip) and folds (bends in rock layers due to the stress imposed by the movement of Earth's tectonic plates) trap petroleum from the sides. Petroleum geologists use maps and rock samples from the land surface as well as images of the subsurface to search for deeply-buried oil and natural gas deposits.

Oil storage tanks line the channel from the Gulf of Mexico to the Port of Houston, Texas. © Ray Soto/Corbis. Reproduced by permission.

History of the modern petroleum industry

Petroleum has been known to mankind for thousands of years. Ancient Mesopotamians, Egyptians, Greeks, and Romans collected the sticky black substance called bitumen from tar pits and seeps (an area where groundwater or oil slowly rises to the surface) and used it to pave roads, heal wounds, waterproof buildings and, to a limited extent, for lighting. The modern quest for petroleum began in the mid-1800s when rapid industrialization and population growth prompted a search for a new type fuel that could replace coal in furnaces and whale oil in lamps. (Coal, like petroleum, is an organic fossil fuel that must be mined from underground. Coal beds are the fossilized remains of land plants that grew in ancient swamps.)

North American prospectors seeking inexpensive lamp oil first struck oil in Ontario, Canada in 1858. They made the first major petroleum discovery one year later in Titusville, Pennsylvania in 1859. John D. Rockefeller (1839–1937), a businessman who saw economic potential in Pennsylvania oil, founded the Standard Oil Company in 1865, the same year the American Civil War (1861–65) ended. (Rockefeller went on to become the world's first billionaire. Most major U.S. energy companies, including Exxon-Mobil, Chevron-Texaco, Conoco-Phillips, and the American portion of British Petroleum-AMOCO were originally part of Standard Oil.) By 1901, when a gusher (fountain of pressurized petroleum) shot up into the air above the famous Spindletop well near Beaumont Texas, the American oil industry was positioned to capitalize on an invention that has changed the face of modern civilization, the internal combustion engine. An internal combustion engine takes the energy in fuel and combusts (burns) it inside the engine to produce motion.

Petroleum releases heat energy and gaseous carbon dioxide when combusted. Like wood, coal and other organic fuels, petroleum can be used to heat homes, cook food, and power steam engines in trains, ships, and factories. However, petroleum fuels are more efficient than coal and wood, meaning that they produce more energy and less pollution per unit volume. Smoke-belching nineteenth century steam trains required a carload of coal and a full-time laborer to feed the coal into the just to leave the station. Today, automobiles powered by internal combustion engines drive hundreds of miles (kilometers) using only a few gallons of gasoline. Petroleum-fueled engines and furnaces generate electricity, heat homes, propel ships, and run industrial machinery.

Problems of petroleum use

Petroleum is presently industrial nations' most affordable, efficient, and accessible source of energy. Its use, however, presents a number of grave environmental, economic, and social problems. Petroleum that spills and leaks from oil and natural gas wells, tankers, pipelines, refineries, and storage tanks into ocean, surface, and ground water causes serious water pollution that threatens the health of plants and animals, including humans. (Hydrocarbons are carcinogenic; they cause cancer.) Explosions and fires threaten petroleum workers and people who live near petroleum facilities. Smokestacks and automobile exhaust pipes emit poisonous gases and ash particles that block sunlight, cause acid rain, and negatively affect biological health.

Strict regulations and new technologies have made petroleum extraction, processing, and use cleaner and safer in recent years. However, two more-difficult problems remain as the reliance on petroleum continues to grow. First, only a few regions, including many politically unstable countries in the Middle East, South America, and Africa produce significant amounts of petroleum. Counties that use more oil than they produce, like the United States, are at the mercy of oil producers like Saudi Arabia and Venezuela. Economic and social conflicts often arise over oil, and sometimes these oil-related disagreements escalate to armed conflict. Second, the carbon dioxide gas emitted during petroleum combustion is a greenhouse gas. Scientists have observed rising levels of carbon dioxide in Earth's atmosphere (mass of air surrounding Earth), and worry that it may lead to global climate change. Scientists, energy companies, governments, environmentalists and other groups share a common concern for meeting the needs of Earth's ever more energy-dependent human population while reducing the negative effects of petroleum use.

Laurie Duncan, Ph.D., and
Todd Minehardt, Ph.D.

For More Information

Books

Pipkin, Bernard W., and D. D. Trent. "Energy Resources." In *Geology and the Environment.* Pacific Grove, CA: Brooks/Cole, 2001.

Press, Frank, and Raymond Siever. "Energy and Mineral Resources from the Earth." In *Understanding Earth.* New York: W. H. Freeman and Company, 2003.

Yergin, Daniel. *The Prize: The Epic Quest for Oil, Money and Power.* New York: Simon and Schuster, 1992.

Websites

The Energy Institute. "Fossils into Fuels." *Schoolscience.* http://www.schoolscience.co.uk/content/4/chemistry/fossils/p1.html (accessed on August 24, 2004).

"Looking for Oil and Gas?" *San Joaquin Geological Society.* http://www.sjgs.com/exploration.html (accessed on August 24, 2004).

Residential Water Use

In the United States, approximately 408 billion gallons (1,544 billion liters) of water are used every day! While power production and irrigation (watering crops) consume the majority of water usage, public and self-supply water systems produce 47 billion gallons (178 billion liters) a day for residential users and businesses. Residential water use includes both indoor and outdoor household water usage. Water is used indoors for showering, flushing toilets, washing clothes, washing dishes, drinking, and cooking. Outdoor water usage includes washing the car, and watering the lawn, pools, and plants.

Public and private water

Nearly 85% of residential water users in the United States receive their water from public supply water systems. A public supply water system is a government facility or private company that collects water from a natural source such as a lake, river, or the ground. Through a process called purification, pollutants, mud, and salt are removed from the water, and then the clean water is delivered to residents for a fee. Public water systems also remove wastewater, all water that goes down a drain, away from homes. Sewer systems carry wastewater to treatment plants where the water is cleaned and then released. County and city water utilities are examples of public supply water systems. The remaining 15% of residential water users in the United States obtain water from a self-supplied water system. A self-supplied water system typically uses a well to obtain clean water from the ground and a septic system to purify wastewater.

Since the 1950s, the number of Americans on public supply systems has more than doubled, while the number on self supplied systems has decreased slightly. This pattern of water usage reflects the trend of Americans moving from rural areas, which often must rely on wells, to the cities.

Conserving water

In many parts of the United States, particularly in the West and Florida, the increased reliance on public water systems has put a strain on the water supply. This has led many local and state governments to ban or limit certain forms of residential water usage. State and local laws may restrict how often residents may water their lawns or wash their cars. Some cities encourage residents to use lawn and garden plants that require less water.

Water conservation is important because the average American uses 60 to 70 gallons (227 to 265 liters) of water per day. The high rate of residential water usage led Congress to promote the manufacture of low-flush toilets. The Energy Policy Act of 1992 stated that toilets must operate on 1.6 gallons (6 liters) or less per flush. While this may appear to be an unusual law, older toilets, which used 3.5–5 gallons (13 to 19 liters) per flush, accounted for almost half of indoor residential water usage. Before the Energy Policy Act, toilets used 4.8 billion gallons (18 billion liters) of water per day or 9,000 gallons (34,069 liters) per person every year.

The introduction of other water saving devices may further lessen residential water usage while also saving money on water bills. Showers account for about 20% of indoor water use. A low-flow showerhead uses 2.5 gallons (9.5 liters) per minute instead of the standard 4.5 gallons (17 liters) per minute. Studies have shown that a low-flow showerhead can save thousands of gallons (liters) of water per person every year. Even a simple and inexpensive water aerator, which mixes air with the water coming out of a kitchen or bathroom sink, can reduce faucet water usage by up to 60% a year.

Adrienne Wilmoth Lerner

For More Information

Books

Gartrell, Jack E., Jr., Jane Crowder, and Jeffrey C. Callister. *Earth: The Water Planet*. National Science Teachers Association, 2001.

Websites

"How Can I Save Water? Residential Water Use." *City of New York Department of Environmental Protection*. http://www. nyc.gov/html/dep/html/wateruse.html (accessed on August 24, 2004).

WORDS TO KNOW

◆**Aerator:** Device that screws onto the end of a faucet that mixes air into the water flow, reducing splashing and saving water.

◆**Purification:** Process by which pollutants, mud, salt, and other substances are removed from the wastewater.

◆**Sewer system:** Network of channels or pipes that carry wastewater to a treatment facility for purification.

◆**Wastewater:** Water that has been used or consumed and contains unwanted substances from homes, businesses, and industries.

Brine: Water that contains a high concentration of salt.

Compound: Substance in which two or more elements are joined together.

Element: A substance that cannot be divided by ordinary chemical means.

Halite: A mineral composed of sodium chloride, commonly known as rock salt.

Solar salt production: A process that yields sea salt by allowing the sun to evaporate saltwater.

Solution mining: Producing table salt by pumping water underground where it dissolves halite, then returning the solution to the surface where the salt is recovered through evaporation.

"How to Conserve Water and Use It Effectively." *U.S. Environmental Protection Agency.* http://www.epa.gov/watrhome/you/chap3.html (accessed on August 24, 2004).

"Water Resources of the United States." *U.S. Geological Survey.* http://water.usgs.gov (accessed on August 24, 2004).

Salt

Common table salt is a compound. A compound is a chemical substance in which two or more elements are joined together. An element is a substance that cannot be broken down into a simpler substance. Elements, either alone or joined together as compounds, make up every object. The elements sodium and chlorine join together to make table salt. Sodium is represented by the symbol "Na," and chlorine is represented by the symbol "Cl." Because one atom (smallest unit that has all the chemical and physical characteristics of an element) of sodium joins with one atom of chlorine, table salt is represented by the symbol "NaCl."

The need for salt

All animals, including humans, require salt. Salt is needed to regulate many bodily functions including maintaining a regular heart rhythm, blood pressure, and fluid balance in the body. Additionally, salt is required for nerve cells to communicate efficiently, and for regulating the electrical charges moving into and out of cells during processes such as muscle contraction. An adult human has about 9 ounces (about 250 grams) of salt in the body. As the body cannot produce salt, animals must get salt from food and water. If too much salt is consumed, the kidneys remove the salt and flush it out of the body.

Salt is also economically important. In ancient societies, salt was often traded for other valuable goods. Early cultures used salt for food preservation and Roman soldiers were paid partially in salt, probably giving rise to the word soldier from the Latin *sal dare* for "giving salt."

Today salt is used in food, on food, to de-ice highways, and in the production of industrial chemicals. Nearly 250 million tons (220 metric tons) of salt are produced worldwide every year.

Getting salt

Salt comes from a variety of sources. Salt is known as rock salt, or halite, when it is found in the ground. Rock salt can be mined from beneath the surface through drilling, blasting, and hauling it to the surface. Most mined rock salt is used to de-ice roads in the winter. Salt may also be extracted by solution mining, which involves pumping water underground. The water dissolves the salt, creating brine, which is then pumped back to the surface. The water is evaporated out of the brine, leaving behind salt deposits. Solution mining produces purer salt than rock salt mining. Solution mining is often used to produce edible (able to be eaten) salt.

Salt can also be removed from seawater through a process called solar salt production. Solar salt production involves removing seawater and allowing the water to evaporate. Salt deposits are left behind, forming sea salt. Sea salt is pure and highly sought after for cooking due to its clean taste. A single cubic foot of ocean water produces 2.2 pounds (1 kilogram) of salt.

A composite photograph of the removal of salt by weather desalination. © Jim Cummins/ Corbis. Reproduced by permission.

The oceans hold more salt than humans could ever use. Salt accounts for about 3.5% of the weight of the oceans. The oceans contain an estimated 39 quadrillion tons (39 million, billion tons, or 35 million, billion metric tons) of salt! The oceans are getting even saltier. Flowing rivers pick up dissolved salts and minerals such as chloride, sodium, sulfate, and magnesium from the rocks and soils. Once rivers flow into the ocean, these salts and minerals are deposited in the ocean. Salts and minerals do not evaporate out of the ocean. Once salts are deposited, they will remain there forever, unless humans remove them. Gradually, the ocean gets saltier as more dissolved salts are carried into it.

Joseph P. Hyder

For More Information

Books

Farndon, John. *Water (Science Experiments).* Salt Lake City, UT: Benchmark Books, 2000.

Websites

"Water Basics." *Water Science for Schools, U.S. Geological Survey.* http://ga.water.usgs.gov/edu/mwater.html (accessed on August 27, 2004).

"What You Always Wanted to Know About Salt." *Salt Institute.* http://www.saltinstitute.org/4.html (accessed on August 27, 2004).

Shipping on Freshwater Waterways

For thousands of years humans have used freshwater waterways to ship food, building materials, and goods between regions. A freshwater waterway is any low-salt body of water, such as a river, lake, or man-made canal on which ships may travel. The need for freshwater for drinking and irrigation (watering crops) led most early civilizations to develop along rivers. Shipping on freshwater waterways continues to be a reliable and important way to transport goods. Shipping goods over waterways is slower than other forms of shipping, yet it is less expensive and allows larger loads of cargo. Therefore many heavy raw materials such as coal, oil, timber, food products, and metal are often shipped over water. Many modern cities are still located along rivers and lakes.

Shipping in ancient Egypt

The ancient Egyptians (3000 B.C.E.–30 C.E.) depended upon the Nile River for their survival. The Nile River was the only source of drinking water for most Egyptians. Its yearly floods deposited silt (fine particles smaller than sand) that fertilized Egyptians crops. The Egyptians also used the Nile as their main highway, connecting Upper Egypt in the south with Lower Egypt in the north. Egyptian boats relied on wind or oars to travel on the Nile. Generally, boats traveled south by wind, as the wind usually blew from the north. Since the Nile flows from south to north, most ships would follow the flow of the river and drift with the current or row north.

The Egyptians relied on barges to transport large amounts of goods. A barge is a large, usually flat ship that can carry heavy cargo. Egypt depended on barges to move building materials such as stone from places where it was mined and cut in the south to the major cities such as Cairo and Alexandria in the north. Without transporting goods on the Nile, the Egyptians would not have been able to construct the pyramids or construct large cities.

Propulsion systems

The ancient Greeks, Romans, Phoenicians, and numerous European civilizations also relied on freshwater shipping to move goods. Like the Egyptians, all of these civilizations relied on sails or oars for propulsion. Propulsion is the means by which a ship moves through the water. Sometimes animals, such as horses or mules, walked along the shore and pulled a ship along a slow-moving river or canal using a rope.

Over the last few centuries however, humans have developed new forms of propulsion. In the early nineteenth century, the first steamships were developed. Steam propulsion ships, whose power came from boilers that provided steam under pressure to turn turbines or paddlewheels, proved useful on freshwater waterways such as rivers and lakes, which were poorly suited for sailboats. Inland waterways (water bodies away from the coast, such as rivers) often lacked enough wind, or wind blowing in the proper direction, to propel large cargo ships against the current of the river. The invention of diesel engines in the early twentieth century led to diesel-powered ships that replaced steamboats because diesel engines allowed cheaper shipping without the dangers of pressurized steam.

With these new forms of propulsion goods can be shipped on freshwater waterways faster, cheaper, and in greater quantity. For example, in the United States, over 700 million tons (635 million metric tons) of cargo are shipped on freshwater waterways every year. Most of this cargo is carried on freshwater waterways by barges. Modern barges are large, flat boats that are often joined together like railroad cars. A typical string of about fifteen barges is pulled or pushed by small, powerful tugboats, or tugs. A single barge can carry as much cargo as sixty large truck containers or fifteen railroad cars.

Types of freshwater waterways

Major river systems are the most common form of freshwater waterways used for shipping. A river system is made up of a major river and all of its tributaries, the smaller rivers or creeks that feed into the main river. Lake systems are also often used to ship goods. In the United States, for example, there are two main freshwater systems that are used for shipping, the Mississippi-Missouri river system and the Great Lakes-St. Lawrence River system. The Mississippi-Missouri river system allows shipping in the Midwest and Southeast. The Great Lakes-St. Lawrence River system serves the Midwest and northeastern United States and part of eastern Canada. Over 75% of all materials shipped over freshwater waterways in the United States are shipped on either the Mississippi-Missouri river system or the Great Lakes-St. Lawrence River system.

Freshwater Shipping in the American Frontier

Americans often think of the "frontier" as being the far western United States, but in the eighteenth century colonial period, the American frontier began in western New York, western Pennsylvania, and the Appalachian mountains. In the late eighteenth century, the Northwest Territories, which are known as the Midwest today, were the western frontier. In the early frontier days before railroads, towns and forts were usually built near rivers. The Ohio River became an important waterway for shipping for settlers in the Northwest Territory.

Settlers relied on freshwater waterways for their livelihood and for the westward transportation of needed finished goods. Settlers relied on rivers, streams, and lakes to ship raw materials such as furs, timber, or metal to the eastern United States.

After the Louisiana Purchase in 1803, the Mississippi-Missouri river system helped both people and trade move westward. The Louisiana Purchase, in which the Louisiana Territory was purchased from France, nearly doubled the size of the United States and opened up much of the West to American exploration and settlement.

While French explorers and fur traders had relied on the Mississippi and Missouri Rivers for over one hundred years, American settlers now relied on it as they moved west. The Mississippi-Missouri river system also became important to settlers in the Northwest Territories who shipped their goods to the southern United States. The Mississippi-Missouri river system also provided an outlet to the ocean at the port of New Orleans.

Settlers on the American frontier encountered one major shipping problem: river systems did not go everywhere that the settlers desired. The Great Lakes and its developing ports had no way to ship goods from the frontier to the major population centers in the East. The 363 mile (584 kilometer) long Erie Canal, which opened in 1825, solved this problem. The Erie Canal connected Buffalo, New York on Lake Erie to Albany, New York on the Hudson River. Shipping costs from Buffalo to New York City were 90% less once the canal opened. The Erie Canal helped create a strong shipping economy in the Great Lakes and Eastern United States.

Other smaller river systems are also used for shipping in the United States. The Ohio River system in the Midwest, the Tennessee River system in the Southeast, the Colorado River system in the West, and the Columbia River in the Northwest are important for shipping. There are also major river systems in other parts of the world that are used for shipping: the Danube, Rhine, and Volga river systems in Europe; the Nile in Africa; the Amazon in South America; and the Yangtze in China.

Canals

What happens when river systems do not quite reach important places? Other forms of shipping, such as trains, airplanes, or trucks may be used, but the best solution may be the con-

Barges carry freight along the Mississippi River. © *Nathan Benn/Corbis. Reproduced by permission.*

struction of a canal. A canal is a man-made deep and wide waterway through which ships may travel. A canal can connect one river or lake with another to allow ships to travel farther inland to reach major cities.

The bodies of water that a canal links may be at different elevations (heights) above sea level and therefore, not navigable for ships. Therefore the water level in a canal is usually not the same from one end of the canal to the other. To solve this problem and allow the passage of ships through the canal, a series of gates and locks must be constructed along the course of the canal. A lock is a large area with gates at each end that raises or lowers a ship to areas of the canal that have different water levels. Similar to an elevator with door on opposite sides, locks are an essential part of any canal.

When a ship is going from an area of lower water level to an area of higher water level the ship enters the lock and the gate behind it closes. Water is pumped into the lock to raise the ship. When the water level inside the lock is at the same level as the higher water level in the canal the front gate opens and the ship continues its journey on the canal. When a ship is moving from an area of higher water level in the canal to an area of lower water level, then the process works in reverse. Once the ship enters the lock, water is pumped out of the lock to lower the water level until it matches the lower level on the other side. Once the water level is the same the gate opens and the ship continues its voyage.

Shipping on the Great Lakes

The Great Lakes–St. Lawrence River waterway is one of the busiest and most important freshwater waterways in North America. The Great Lakes are a series of five large, connected lakes in the upper midwestern United States and southeastern Canada. The lakes are Huron, Ontario, Michigan, Erie, and Superior. (The word HOMES—Huron-Ontario-Michigan-Erie-Superior—is helpful to remember the names of the lakes.) The St. Lawrence River connects the Great Lakes with the Atlantic Ocean.

The Great Lakes–St. Lawrence River waterway and connecting canals serve major ports in the United States and Canada, including Chicago, Illinois; Detroit, Michigan; Duluth, Minnesota; Buffalo, New York; Cleveland, Ohio; Pittsburgh, Pennsylvania; Toronto, Ontario, Canada; and Montreal, Quebec, Canada. Each year over 100 million tons (91 million metric tons) of cargo are shipped to and from the ports on the Great Lakes–St. Lawrence River waterway. Great Lakes cargo ships, known as "lakers," can be over 1,000 (305 meters) feet long and can carry up to 70,000 tons (63, 500 metric tons).

Many improvements have been made to the Great Lakes-St. Lawrence River waterway to make it more navigable over the last two hundred years. The Great Lakes and the rivers that feed into them have different water levels and locks were constructed along the waterway to allow ships to better navigate and to replace dangerous rapids (areas of turbulent, fast-flowing water). In 1855 the opening of the Soo Locks connected the St. Mary's River and Lake Superior. The Soo Locks have undergone many improvements over the years and every ship that passes into or out of Lake Superior must pass through the Soo Locks.

In the 1950s the United States and Canadian governments began construction on the St. Lawrence Seaway, which allows ocean-going vessels to enter the Great Lakes. The St. Lawrence Seaway is a deep channel that is 450 miles (720 kilometers) long. While the seaway allowed the largest ocean-going vessels (ships) of the mid-twentieth century to enter the Great Lakes, the increased size of ships means that only today's mid-sized ocean-going vessels may enter the Great Lakes.

Problems with shipping on freshwater waterways

One disadvantage of shipping on freshwater is that it is much slower than other forms of shipping such as trucks, railroads, or airplanes. Also, freshwater waterways do not reach everywhere that goods are needed. The construction of canals can extend freshwater waterways to some, but not all areas. These locations must ship their goods to and from the nearest port (seaside) city by another means of shipping. A third disadvantage is that like roads, waterways must be maintained or they fall into disrepair. Tree limbs, trash, and soil clog waterways so that a ship cannot pass. Freshwater waterways must be dredged occasionally to remove buildup on the bottom of the waterway and around bridges and shores. Dredging is a process where a ship drags a hook or grate along the bottom of a waterway in order to remove the accumulated silt and mud. Dredging makes freshwater waterways more navigable (able for ships and barges to move through the waterway) by deepening the waterway and sometimes helping to smooth areas with strong currents.

Joseph P. Hyder and Adrienne Wilmoth Lerner

For More Information

Books

Batio, Christopher. *Super Cargo Ships.* Osceola, WI: Motorbooks International, 2001.

Bauer, K. Jack. *A Maritime History of the United States: The Role of America's Seas and Waterways.* Columbia: University of South Carolina Press, 1988.

Casson, Lionel. *The Ancient Mariners.* 2nd ed. Princeton, NJ: Princeton University Press, 1991.

Websites

Schultheiss, N. "Great Lakes and Seaway Shipping." *Boatnerd.* http://www.boatnerd.com (accessed on August 27, 2004).

"The Soo Locks." *Michigan State University.* http://www.geo.msu.edu/geo333/SooLock.html (accessed on August 27, 2004).

"Waterways and Shipping." *Michigan State University.* http://www.geo.msu.edu/geo333/waterways.html (accessed August 27, 2004, 2004).

Shipping on the Oceans

Throughout recorded history, humans have relied on the oceans to ship goods quickly and efficiently. Historically, shipping on the oceans had several advantages over shipping over land. Shipping over land required moving bulky and heavy goods over mountains, across deserts, or through forests. The location of roads often dictated where goods could be shipped. Before vehicles, land travelers also had to carry enough food and water to keep their pack animals alive, adding to the weight of their loads.

Two thousand years ago, the power of the Roman Empire was founded on the economic benefit that Rome gained from its control of trade on the Mediterranean Sea. Most of Rome's empire lay on the shores of the Mediterranean Sea, which served as a highway for the trade of wine, food, timber, spices, and other valuable materials. Rome's power stretched from Gaul (modern France) around the Mediterranean Sea to the Middle East and to North Africa. Rome also had territory in modern Britain. Rome typically imported raw materials from its faraway territory and exported finished goods back to its territory.

The expansion of European nations into lands fueled trade with their colonies over vast expanses of oceans. British trade with India and Southeast Asia under the British East India Company in the sixteenth through eighteenth centuries delivered spices and teas to Britain via ships. Britain's colonies in North America also shipped raw materials such as timber, furs, and cotton across the Atlantic Ocean to Britain, who shipped finished goods back to the United States.

In the nineteenth century, ships made of iron and steel used steam power to transport goods across the oceans faster than ever before. The rise of diesel powered vessels in the twentieth century made shipping cheaper and faster. Goods could be shipped to ports on the other side of the world in days instead of weeks and months.

Shipping today

Today, merchant ships transport more than 90% of the world's cargo. There are several reasons that ships move more cargo than any other form of shipping. First, ships are the cheapest form of transportation. Second, in a world in which many countries have poor roads, boats are often the most efficient and reliable means of shipping. Third, boats can move greater amounts of cargo than any other form of shipping.

Despite the rise of shipping cargo by aircraft, the ocean shipping industry continued to grow throughout the twentieth century. From the early 1920s through the end of the century, the worldwide number of ships in the merchant shipping fleet increased from under 30,000 to nearly 90,000. Total tonnage increased at an even greater rate. The total tonnage of merchant ships increased from 59 million gross tons (a unit of measurement to describe the size of a ship) to over 500 million gross tons during the same period.

Types of merchant ships

Modern merchant ships serve a variety of purposes. Therefore, shipping vessels come in many different shapes. Some ships, called tankers, are designed to carry liquids. The most common type of tanker is the oil tanker. Over 3,500 oil tankers carry petroleum products to ports around the world. Oil tankers are among the largest ships in the world. Some oil tankers are over 1,300 feet long, or the length of about 4.5 football fields! Similar to oil tankers, chemical tankers carry various liquids such as vegetable oil, acids, and liquid fertilizers. Many of the chemicals carried by chemical tankers are hazardous. Chemical tankers carry smaller loads than oil tankers due to the increased danger of the cargo, and because consumers require greater amounts of oil.

Most merchant ships carry dry cargo. Over the last fifty years, container ships have become one of the most important ship designs. Container ships carry sealed cargo containers that can be unloaded directly onto trains or trucks, thus becoming a railway car or a truck trailer. This allows the container to be loaded only once upon departure and unloaded once upon delivery to its final destination. New designs for cargo ships will soon carry up to 15,000 containers that are each 20 feet in length.

Large container ships carry freight across the world's oceans. © Lester Lefkowitz/Corbis. Reproduced by permission.

Bulk carriers, another type of dry cargo ship, carry large quantities of raw material such as iron ore, steel, coal, or wheat. Bulk carriers transport their goods in large cargo holds without the use of containers. A cargo hold is a section of a ship that is divided from the rest of the ship for the transport of a single type of cargo. Shipping in bulk decreases transportation cost by reducing loading and unloading costs. For example, with modern loading methods, more than 15,000 tons of iron ore can be loaded onto a bulk carrier in one hour. Bulk carriers can carry more than 250,000 tons of goods and may have over 10 individual cargo holds.

Problems with shipping

Shipping on the oceans poses a variety of possible problems, including harm to the environment, loss of cargo, and loss of lives. The major causes of shipping accidents are human mistakes, poor equipment maintenance, and natural disasters. Most accidents are avoidable, and the last 100 years have seen a dramatic decrease in the number of shipping accidents.

Increased training and safety regulations have lessened the number of accidents caused by human error and poor maintenance. Weather forecasting has improved greatly in the last century, leading to fewer accidents from natural disasters such as hurricanes.

Oil and chemical tankers pose a serious threat to the environment if they lose their cargo. Oil and chemical spills can poison fish and marine mammals. A well-known oil spill, although not the largest, was the *Exxon Valdez* accident in 1989, when the tanker *Exxon Valdez* ran aground on rocks in Prince William Sound, Alaska. Nearly 11 million gallons of oil spilled out into the natural environment, killing fish, birds, and marine mammals. The resulting cleanup of the waters and shore cost about $2 billion.

Bulk container ships are involved in more accidents than any other form of cargo ship. Bulk container ships have large hatches that stretch across most of the width of the ship. This decreases the overall strength of the ship, especially in rough seas. About thirteen bulk container ships sink each year. On average, about 70 people lose their lives every year in accidents involving bulk container ships.

Although shipping by ocean is far less expensive than shipping by aircraft, it is also slower. Because the large amount of cargo that modern merchant ships can carry means that less than one percent of the purchase price of a product goes towards ocean shipping, many merchants and consumers choose to wait the extra time for the goods.

Adrienne Wilmoth Lerner

For More Information

Books

Bone, Kevin, et al. *The New York Waterfront: Evolution and Building Culture of the Port and Harbor.* New York: Monacelli Press, 2003.

Gardiner, Robert. *The Shipping Revolution: The Modern Merchant Ship.* New York: Book Sales, 2000.

Websites

"Marine Navigation." *NOAA National Ocean Service, National Oceanic and Atmospheric Administration.* http://oceanservice. noaa.gov/topics/navops/marinenav/welcome.html (accessed on August 27, 2004).

Surface and Groundwater Use

Surface water is the water that lies on the surface naturally as streams, rivers, marshes, lagoons, ponds, and lakes. Surface water can also be collected and stored in containers that have been built especially for that purpose. These containers are called reservoirs. Fresh water also collects in areas of soil and rock underground. This is groundwater.

Rain falling from the sky and snow melting in the springtime can flow downhill to gather in stream or riverbeds. From there, the water flows to a lake or ocean. In other locations, the rain or melted snow is soaked up by the soil and makes its way further down into the ground because of gravity (the force of attraction between all masses in the universe).

Uses of surface and groundwater

Surface water tends to be used by humans more often than groundwater. This is because it is much easier to obtain surface water. Inserting a pipe or tube into the water and then pumping out the water is all that is needed. Sometimes, if the surface water source is located on a hillside, the water flows through the pipeline because of gravity. Surface water makes up almost 80% of the 410 billion gallons of water that is used in the United States every day. Groundwater makes up the remaining approximate 20% This huge amount of water is enough to fill 400,000 Olympic swimming pools, every day of the year!

Drinking water. The main use of surface and groundwater is for drinking water. Without freshwater to drink, animals such as humans die within days. Much of our drinking water is surface water, which must be treated before drinking. Soil and plant material can wash into surface water in a rainstorm or as the snow melts into the stream, river, pond, or lake. Microorganisms that live in the feces of animals can also be washed into the water. If the water is not treated to remove the material and the microorganisms, the contaminated water can make humans and animals ill. This is why campers and hikers filter their drinking water or add chemicals that kill the harmful organisms in the water. This is also why the water that comes out of the tap in towns and cities has usually come from a water treatment plant; a place where the water is put through a series of steps to make it potable (drinkable).

Groundwater may not require treatment before drinking. This is because the ground itself is a filter. As the water moves down into the soil and rocks, big objects like leaves are left on

Aquifer: A underground reservoir of water; source of wells and springs.

Groundwater: Freshwater that resides in rock and soil layers beneath Earth's land surface.

Irrigation: In agriculture, a process where dry land or crops are supplied with water.

Potable: Water that is safe to drink.

Surface water: Water that is located on the surface, naturally in the form of streams, rivers, lakes and other waterways, or in reservoirs, swimming pools, and other containers that have been built.

the surface, and smaller objects including bacteria (a million bacteria could fit on the period at the end of this sentence) either stick to the soil or cannot pass through the even tinier holes in the rock. By the time the water collects in the ground, the harmful microorganisms and chemicals have been removed by the filtering action of the soil and rock layers. This can often mean that potable water can be pumped out of the ground from wells.

However, it is wise for those who have a private well to have their water tested at regular intervals. Community wells are checked every month to ensure that no contamination of the groundwater has occurred that could be harmful to the community that the well supplies.

Recreation. Diving into the swimming pool, water-skiing, and fishing in a lake are all fun (recreational) uses of water that make use of surface water. Groundwater aquifers are sometimes the source of warm or cool springs that come to the surface and are also popular for recreational use. The need to take care of recreational water has been recognized for a long time. In the United States, laws made in the 1960s were designed to help keep surface waters healthy. These laws are known as the Federal Water Project Recreation Act and are still important in maintaining surface water for recreation.

Agriculture. Both surface and groundwater help keep crops growing. Depending on the type of crop being grown, water can be pumped or sprayed onto the field. Additionally, farm owners and their livestock such as cattle, pigs, and poultry all require drinking water to stay healthy, and water is needed to keep the farm clean.

Industry. Industry uses large amounts of water to keep machinery cool, to pump into oil fields to help force the oil up to the surface, to generate electricity, and for other purposes. Much of this water is used and then put back into the ground or onto the surface.

Colorado River

The Colorado River is a major river located in the southwestern United States. The river drains an area of over 240,000 square miles (621,597 square kilometers). From its start at over 9,000 feet (2,743 meters) above sea level in the Rocky Mountains of Colorado, the river winds over 1,000 miles (1,609 kilometers) to Mexico.

By the time the river reaches the Grand Canyon (the over one-mile-deep canyon carved out by the river over millions of years), the river has dropped about 6,000 feet (1,829 meters). In the 277-mile (446 kilometers) journey through the Grand Canyon, the river drops another 2,200 feet (671 meters) in a series of calm stretches and roaring rapids.

In 1963, the Glen Canyon Dam was built upstream of the Grand Canyon. The dam was built to generate electricity and to reduce the amount of soil particles (silt) being washed down the river. Scientists hoped that the reduced amount of silt would help keep another dam, the Hoover Dam, from clogging. The reduced amount of silt has harmed some species of fish and plant life in the Colorado River, resulting in some scientists and environmentalists to campaign for the Glen Canyon Dam to be put out of service and the return of a free-flowing river at Glen Canyon.

Surface water is used to generate electricity by building a wall (dam) across a river. The dam causes water to collect on one side. When gates in the dam are opened, water rushes through. The rushing water turns turbines, a device that converts the fluid into mechanical motion that in turn generates electricity. While dams are necessary to supply the electricity that big cities need, they can sometimes change the river in ways that are not healthy for the animals, plants, and microorganisms that live further in the river.

Brian Hoyle, Ph.D.

For More Information

Books

Marek, Lee, and Lynn Brunelle. *Soakin' Science.* Toronto: Somerville House, 2000.

U.S. Environmental Protection Agency. *The Water Sourcebooks: K-12.* Washington, DC: USEPA, 2000.

Websites

"Drinking Water for Kids." *U.S. Environmental Protection Agency.* http://www.epa.gov/safewater/kids (accessed on August 24, 2004).

Water for People. http://www.waterforpeople.com (accessed on August 27, 2004).

Tourism on the Oceans

Human interest in the sea fuels a multi-billion dollar a year ocean tourism industry. Ocean tourism refers to pleasure travel in which the sea is the primary focus of activities. Ocean tourism comes in many forms including cruises, ecotourism, and fishing expeditions.

Cruising the oceans

Cruises are one of the most popular forms of ocean tourism. In the late nineteenth and early twentieth century, cruise liners were needed to carry passengers across the oceans. Many of these cruise ships—including the ill-fated *Titanic,* which sank in 1912 killing over 1,500 people—provided passengers a luxurious way to travel. Originally powered by steam-driven engines, most modern cruise ships use diesel fuel to power their engines.

Sailboats moor off the Tahitian islands, a popular tourist destination in the South Pacific. © *Neil Rabinowitz/Corbis.* *Reproduced by permission.*

WORDS TO KNOW

Cruise ship: Large ships, once used as the primary means of transporting people across an ocean, that now serve as vacation destinations, while visiting various ports of interest.

Ecotourism: Tourism that focuses on nature and the environment without harming it.

Gross tons: Marine term equal to 100 cubic feet (about 10 cubic meters) used to describe the size of a boat, ship, or barge.

International Maritime Organization (IMO): International agency of the United Nations that is concerned with shipping regulation and safety.

Port state: Nation where a ship docks.

Scuba diving: "Scuba" is the acronym for self-contained underwater breathing apparatus, referring to the air tanks and mouthpieces used by divers.

While cruise ships were needed for Atlantic Ocean crossings, by the mid-twentieth century, air travel made ocean crossings cheaper and faster. An airplane can cross the Atlantic in several hours instead of the one week required by most cruise ships. Cruise lines could no longer promote their services as providing a means of travel to and from vacation. (A cruise line is a company that owns one or more cruise ships.) With little need for cruise ships for ocean crossings, cruise line operators had to take a different approach to their business. They began to change the concept of the cruise itself to a vacation. Ships started traveling to exotic locations and offering more services and activities.

Today's cruise ships are large ships that serve as floating hotels for vacationers. Cruise ships include restaurants, shops, swimming pools, theaters, and cinemas. Some cruise ships even offer college-level courses onboard. Cruise ships cost hundreds of millions of dollars to construct and may be over 1,000 feet (305 meters) long, over 150,000 gross tons (a term use to describe the size of a boat, ship, or barge), and stand taller than a 20-story building. The length of the largest cruise ship in 2004, the *Queen Mary 2,* is only 117 feet (36 meters) shorter than the height of the Empire State Building. The largest cruise ships can carry nearly 4,000 people, including the crew.

Tourism on the oceans provides a major boost to the economies of countries that are popular cruise destinations. In the United States, nearly 8 million people take a cruise every year. Cruises contribute an estimated $18 billion per year to the American economy. Cruise lines directly employee over 25,000

The *Titanic*

Prior to sinking on her maiden voyage, the R.M.S. *Titanic* was the largest and most luxurious vessel in the world. © *Bettmann/Corbis. Reproduced by permission.*

On April 10, 1912, the *Titanic* set sail on its maiden voyage from Southampton, England, to New York City. At the time, the *Titanic* was the largest, most expensive ship ever constructed. The *Titanic* was over 882 feet (269 meters) long and over 46,000 gross tons. The *Titanic* had 2,227 passengers and crew onboard. Only 705 passengers made it to New York City. More than 1,500 people died when the ship sank on the night of April 14 and early morning of April 15, after hitting an iceberg (large chunk of ice) in the North Atlantic Ocean.

The *Titanic* was an engineering marvel. The ship took three years to build and cost over $7.5 million, a considerable sum in 1912. It contained a swimming pool, gymnasium, library, and several dining rooms. The *Titanic* was designed to be large and luxurious, not fast. It traveled at 21 knots (24 miles per hour). This was considerably slower than the fastest ship at the time, *Mauritania,* which traveled at 26 knots (30 miles per hour).

At 11:40 P.M. on April 14, 1912, the *Titanic* struck an iceberg. The iceberg was spotted while only a few hundred yards (meters) in front of the ship, which did not allow enough time to avoid the collision. Two hours and forty minutes later, the *Titanic* slipped beneath the surface of the cold ocean waters. The *Titanic* only had sixteen lifeboats, the minimum number required by outdated British regulation. The shortage of lifeboats resulted in many unnecessary deaths. The ship *Carpathia* responded to the *Titanic's* distress signal, but did not reach the scene until after the ship had sunk.

The *Titanic* lay in its icy grave until September 1, 1985, when scientists Robert Ballard and Jean Louis Michel discovered its remains. The *Titanic* lies 12,500 feet (3,810 meters), or about 2.5 miles (4 kilometers) below the water surface.

Americans. An estimated 250,000 American jobs are supported by the cruise industry.

The ocean tourism industry is highly regulated. Every commercial ship, including cruise ships, must be registered with a country in order to sail in international waters. A country may register ships only if it is a member of the International Maritime Organization (IMO). The IMO is an agency of the United Nations. The United Nations is an organization consisting of most of the independent states of the world and is designed to promote peace and security. Any country that registers ships under the IMO must have adopted the IMO's Resolutions and Conventions on maritime safety. The cruise industry has taken a major role in promoting safety on the seas. The International Council of Cruise Lines (ICCL) is a non-governmental group that works with the IMO to promote maritime safety and environmental preservation.

In additional to ship registration, the nation where a ship docks, called the port state, may also impose restrictions on cruise ships. The United States has a reputation for strictly enforcing safety rules. The U.S. Coast Guard inspects every ocean-going ship in its ports four times per year. The United States imposes additional restrictions on ships registered in the United States, including that construction and ownership of the ship must be American. This leads many cruise ships to register in other countries, including Norway, Liberia, Panama, and the Bahamas. Over 90 cruise ships are registered in Liberia and Panama.

Ecotourism and fishing on the ocean

Cruise ships are not the only form of ocean tourism. Ecotourism of the oceans has become increasingly popular. Ecotourism involves tourism that focuses on the natural environment without harming it. One popular form of ecotourism is scuba diving. Scuba diving involves the use of a self-contained breathing system that allows a person to remain underwater for long periods. Scuba stands for "self-contained underwater breathing apparatus." Scuba divers enjoy the beauty of fish, coral reefs, and other marine features. Another form of ecotourism involves cruises to view wildlife such as humpback whales or dolphins, while impacting their environment as little as poissible.

Deep-sea fishing expeditions are another popular form of tourism on the oceans. Deep-sea fishing involves taking a boat several miles from shore in order to catch large fish, including tuna, marlin, and dolphin fish. Some species of deep-sea fish can weigh from several hundred to over 1,000 pounds (454 kilograms).

Protecting the environment

In many areas of the world, such as the Sea of Cortez off the coast of Mexico, numbers of large game fish are reduced, presumably from over-fishing. Many countries, including the United States, have laws stipulating the number, types, and sizes of game fish that may be caught and kept in order to reduce harm to the fish population.

Cruise lines have placed an increased emphasis on protecting the environment over the last two decades. Cruise ships must follow the environmental laws of a country when in that country's territorial waters. Ships must follow the Clear Air Act, the Clean Water Act, and the Oil Pollution Control Act when in American waters. These are all laws passed by Congress to control pollution in the United States.

The IMO and the ICCL also set environmental regulations for all registered ships. In 1973, IMO adopted the International Convention for the Prevention of Pollution from Ships at Sea (MARPOL), which it revised in 1978. MARPOL sets environmental standards that all ocean-going ships must meet. Cruise lines have also sought better methods to prevent pollution from the waste that cruise ships generate, including sewage and garbage.

Joseph P. Hyder

For More Information

Books

Cudahy, Brian J. *The Cruise Ship Phenomenon in North America.* New York: Cornell Maritime Press, 2001.

Websites

International Council of Cruise Lines (ICCL). http://www.iccl.org (accessed on August 27, 2004).

International Maritime Organization (IMO). http://www.imo.org (accessed on August 27, 2004).

R.M.S. Titanic, Inc. http://www.titanic-online.com (accessed on August 27, 2004).

Transportation on the Oceans

For thousands of years, oceans provided one of the fastest and most valuable forms of transportation. By 3200 B.C.E., Egyptian ships made of reeds (tall, woody grass) used sails to travel along the coast of northern Africa. Over the centuries, ocean-going ships became larger and faster. Around 1000 B.C.E. the Vikings explored the coast of Canada in sailboats. Spanish ships explored the Americas in the fifteenth and sixteenth centuries. British tall ships carried settlers to the Americas, Asia, Australia, and Africa in the sixteenth through nineteenth centuries.

Until the mid-twentieth century, ships were the only mode of transportation for ocean crossings. The rise of air transportation after 1930 reduced the role of ocean-going vessels in transportation. Airplanes provided a quicker and often cheaper way to move people great distances, which caused the types of vessels and purposes of ocean transportation to change.

Immigration to the New World

For the first 450 years after the discovery of the New World, ships provided the only form of transportation between Europe and the Americas. Nearly every citizen of the United States is descended from ancestors who traveled to the New World by ship, and immigration to the New World was a major factor in ocean transportation during this time.

Immigration patterns to the United States reflect that immigrants came from various countries in waves. The earliest settlers came from the British Isles and Africa. Before 1790, about 500,000 immigrants came to the United States from the British Isles, and 300,000 immigrants came from Africa. The middle half of the nineteenth century saw a flood of immigrants from Europe with 3 million from the German Empire, 2.8 million from Ireland, and 2 million from England.

The United States experienced its greatest influx of immigration between 1880 and 1930. During this period, nearly 20 million immigrants crossed the Atlantic Ocean on ships. These immigrants came primarily from Italy, Russia, Germany, Britain, and the Austro-Hungarian Empire. Twelve million of these immigrants entered the United States through Ellis Island, near New York City. Between 1897 and 1938, Ellis Island served as the main processing point for immigrants. Today over 100 million Americans can trace their ancestry to an immigrant who landed on Ellis Island.

Ocean transportation in America has a dark side. Slave ships transported tens of thousands of Africans to the New World every year. Between the sixteenth and nineteenth centuries, between 15 million and 20 million Africans were involuntarily brought to the Americas as slaves. About 400,000 slaves were transported to the British colonies and the United States. Scholars estimate that as many as 1 million African slaves died during ocean transit to the Americas.

Transatlantic journeys

Not all ocean crossing ships were only filled with immigrants. Travelers also used ships to cross the Atlantic Ocean to go between Europe and the Americas. In 1818, New York's Black Ball Line became the first company to offer regular travel across the Atlantic Ocean. The rise of steam ships in the mid-1800s made ocean crossings faster. While these ships focused on luxury travel for wealthy passengers, they also fueled immigration. Cruise liners offered low-cost, no frills transportation for many immigrants. The immigrants stayed in steerage class, the least expensive accommodations, and were often responsible for bringing their meals.

Following a long ocean voyage, 1920 era immigrants to America arrive at Ellis Island, New York. © Bettmann/Corbis. Reproduced by permission.

By the early twentieth century, cruise liner companies began to build larger and more luxurious ships, including *Olympic, Lusitania, Britannic,* and *Titanic.* These ships emphasized comfort and extravagance over speed. Many of these cruise liners contained swimming pools, dance halls, and tennis courts. Unfortunately, the superliners of the early nineteenth century did not stress safety. Thousands of lives were lost in the sinkings of the *Titanic* in 1912 and *Lusitania* in 1915.

The rise of the cruise ship

By 1950, airplanes replaced cruise liners as the main mode of transportation across the oceans. Many travelers did not choose to spend days crossing the ocean when it could be done in hours by plane. Cruise liner companies had to change their approach to fit the new reality of air travel. They could no longer market cruise liners as a form of transportation to take while on vacation. Instead, cruise companies began advertising cruise liners as a vacation by themselves. By focusing on exotic locales, such as the Caribbean and Mediterranean Seas, cruise companies found a willing audience. In modern day cruise ships have swimming pools, cinemas, dance clubs, theatres, and classrooms. Modern cruise ships are subject to many safety regulations.

Today nearly 8 million Americans go on cruises every year. Cruises generate about $18 billion every year for the United States' economy. A modern cruise ship carries about 2000 guests and 900 crew members. The largest cruise ship in the world as of 2004, *Queen Mary 2,* was 1,132 feet (345 meters) long and 151,400 gross tons (term describing the size of a boat, ship, or barge). *Queen Mary 2* can carry 2,620 guests and 1,253 crew members. In 2004 *Queen Mary 2* was the only passenger ship that made regular transatlantic journeys.

Ferries

Ferries are one of the most important forms of modern ocean transportation. Ferries are ships that carry people and, occasionally, cars over relative short distances. Some ferries are simple ships that transport only people. Ferries that transport people and cars are called "roll-on, roll-off" ships. Cars can quickly roll on these ferries upon departure and easily roll off upon arrival.

While some ferries are simple boats, many ferries are technologically advanced ships, including hovercrafts or hydrofoils. A hovercraft is a ship that floats above the surface of the water on a cushion of air. A rubber skirt is located between the main ship and the water. Air is pushed into the rubber skirt, creating a cushion of air. Hovercrafts offer smooth rides over rough seas. A hydrofoil is a ship that has wing-like foils (wing-like structures that raises part or all of a powerboat's hull out of the water) underneath the hull of the ship. As the boat increases speed, the foils lift the hull of the ship out of the water. Only the foils skim the top of the water. Like a hovercraft, the main body of a hydrofoil rides above the surface of the water. This reduces drag and increases speed.

Unlike most cruise ships, not all ferries are subject to strict safety regulations. Many passengers die in ferry accidents every year, mostly in the developing world. In 2002, the ferry *Joola* sank off the coast of Africa near Senegal. *Joola* was carrying over three times its capacity. Over 1,800 people died in the accident, which is more than the number of people who died on the *Titanic*.

Adrienne Wilmoth Lerner

For More Information

Books

Cudahy, Brian J. *The Cruise Ship Phenomenon in North America*. New York: Cornell Maritime Press, 2001.

Walters, Eric. *The Hydrofoil Mystery*. New York: Penguin, 2003.

Websites

American Family Immigration History Center. http://www.ellisisland.org (accessed on August 27, 2004).

Ellis Island Immigration Museum. http://www.ellisisland.com (accessed on August 27, 2004).

International Council of Cruise Lines. http://www.iccl.org (accessed on August 27, 2004).

Whaling

Whaling, which is the hunting and killing of whales, is an activity that dates back centuries. Native people like the Macah, Nootka, and Coastal Salish of the Pacific Northwest are known to have hunted whales nearly 2,000 years ago. Whaling became popular with Europeans when they colonized North America in the late 1600s. By 1672, whaling parties were organized off of Cape Cod in Massachusetts and off of Long Island in New York. However, by the early 1700s, the number of whales that close to shore had already begun to decline, so larger ships called sloops were developed that could capture whales farther off shore.

In the late 1800s, whaling had become a thriving commercial industry. Two of the most commonly hunted whales were the right whale and the sperm whale. The right whale was so named because it was the "right" whale to catch. It floated after it was killed and so it was easy to recover from the ocean. Sperm whales were highly prized for their spermaceti, an oil found in their heads and used for making candles.

Whales had a variety of commercial uses. Whale oil was used for lubrication, lighting, cosmetics, and food. Whale bones were ground and sold as fertilizer and animal feed supplements. The baleen (horn-like substance that hang from the upper jaws of some whales) from whales was once commonly used in women's corsets (an undergarment). A type of fat called ambergris was occasionally found in the intestines of whales and sold for great sums of money. It was used to make perfume. Today, there are substitutes for all of the products that whales supplied.

The decline of whales

The whaling industry quickly overwhelmed the stocks of whales in the ocean. It is estimated that 4.4 million large whales swam in the oceans in 1900. By 2004, the estimates are that only 1 million are left. Of the 11 species of whales that are commonly hunted, in 1999, 8 were commercially extinct, which means that they are too rare to justify the expense of hunting. The blue whale is in danger of becoming totally extinct (no longer in existence). When commercial blue whale hunting ended in 1964, only about 1,000 animals were left and that may be too small a number for the population to recover.

The International Whaling Commission (IWC) was established in 1946 in order to develop guidelines to maintain whale stocks and allow for a healthy whaling industry. In response to the declining numbers of whales in the oceans, the IWC

A group of whales swimming off Tomiura, Japan. *AP/Wide World Photos. Reproduced by permission.*

banned all commercial whaling in 1986. Because their countries depend on a whaling industry, Norway withdrew from the IWC in 1993 and Iceland withdrew in 1996. Japan never stopped hunting whales, even when the ban was in place. These three countries currently hunt the minke whale in Arctic waters.

Several whale sanctuaries (areas where whales may not be hunted) have been imposed by the IWC. The Indian Ocean Sanctuary, established in 1979, prevents whaling in the southern Indian Ocean, in the feeding grounds of many large whales. In 1994, the IWC voted to make the oceans around Antarctica—where many species of large whales feed—a conservation area from whalers. This sanctuary neighbors the Indian Ocean Sanctuary. Unfortunately, this sanctuary is often ignored. Both Norway and Japan have killed whales in these waters since the sanctuaries were established.

The conservation efforts of the IWC have resulted in increases in numbers of whales. Since the commercial whaling ban was put in place, estimates of blue whales off the coast of California increased from 500 in 1979 to more than 2000 in 1991. Similarly, approximately 88 humpback whales were observed off the coast of California in 1979, while more than 600 were observed in 1991. The California gray whale was nearly extinct in 1986. Since then, its numbers have rebounded dramatically to approximately 26,000 animals in 2000. In 1993, it was removed from the endangered species list.

Juli Berwald, Ph.D.

For More Information

Books

Garrison, Tom. *Oceanography.* 3rd ed. Belmont, CA: Wadsworth Publishing Company, 1999.

Gross, Grant. *Oceanography: A View of the Earth.* 5th ed. Englewood Cliffs, NJ: Prentice Hall, 1990.

Murphy, Jim. *The Journal of Brian Doyle: A Greenhorn on an Alaskan Whaling Ship (My Name Is America).* New York: Scholastic, 2004.

Websites

Bryant, Peter J. "Whaling and Fishing." *Biodiversity and Conservation: A Hypertext Book.* http://darwin.bio.uci.edu/˜sustain/bio65/lec04/b65lec04.htm#top (accessed on August 24, 2004).

International Whaling Commission. http://www.iwcoffice.org/index.htm (accessed on August 24, 2004).

"Overview of American Whaling." *The New Bedford Whaling Museum.* http://www.whalingmuseum.org/kendall/index_KI.html (accessed on August 24, 2004).

Chapter 10
Recreational Uses of Water

Dangerous Waters

Ever since humans first took to the seas thousands of years ago, sailors have faced numerous dangers. Ancient civilizations tried to explain these dangerous conditions by claiming that they were the work of angry gods or monsters. While scientific explanations have been advanced for dangerous phenomena such as high waves, hurricanes, and treacherous ocean currents (steady flows of water in a prevailing direction), many lives are still lost in the water each year, mainly due to drowning or hypothermia. Hypothermia is a condition where the core body temperature becomes too cold to function properly. Prolonged exposure to waters that may initially seem warm, between 70°–80°F (21°–27° C), can cause death from hypothermia.

Whirlpools

Some of the earliest written works make references to the dangers of the seas. In the *Odyssey*, Greek poet Homer mentions a great whirlpool that a group of Greek warriors encountered on their return home from the Trojan War. Many scholars assume that Charybdis, the whirlpool mentioned by Homer, is a whirlpool that still swirls today between mainland Italy and the island of Sicily. Viking poems refer to another famous whirlpool, the Maelstrom, which lies off the rocky coast of Norway.

Several factors, working alone or together, can create whirlpools. Ocean currents that converge (come together) can cause a whirlpool. Tides and rock formations can create a whirlpool by forcing ocean currents to flow in a circular motion, as in the Maelstrom. Also, constant winds on the ocean

WORDS TO KNOW

Atmospheric pressure: Pressure exerted upon Earth's surface by its atmosphere at a given point.

Hurricane: An organized storm with sustained winds of 74 miles per hour (119 kilometers per hour) or greater in the Atlantic Ocean, Gulf of Mexico, Caribbean Sea, or eastern Pacific Ocean.

Hypothermia: A condition where the body becomes too cold to function properly.

Iceberg: Large chunks of ice that break off from glaciers and float in the oceans.

Mines: Explosive devices that usually explode when an object makes contact with them; sea mines usually float on or just below the surface.

Signs warn swimmers of dangerous conditions off the beach at Maui, Hawaii. *Kelly A. Quin. Reproduced by permission.*

WORDS TO KNOW

◆**Navigation:** The ability to determine the correct position of a ship in the ocean and the correction direction to sail in order to reach the desired destination.

◆**Tropical storm:** A low pressure storm system formed in tropical latitudes with sustained winds between 39–74 miles per hour (63–119 kilometers per hour).

can create or contribute to a whirlpool, as in the narrow waters between Italy and Sicily.

Although movies and literature sometimes refer to people or ships being drawn down into a whirlpool, this rarely happens. Whirlpools can pose a moderate danger to small crafts, as they can experience turbulence or even capsize (turn over) in whirlpools. Modern navigation allows ships to avoid large ocean whirlpools. Today, the greatest danger posed by whirlpools is on rivers, where curious boaters often wander too close to whirlpools and quickly find themselves in their midst.

Cape Horn and the Straits of Magellan

Cape Horn and the Straits of Magellan lie at the southern tip of South America where the Atlantic and Pacific Oceans meet. The Straits of Magellan are a narrow passage between mainland South America and Tierra del Fuego, a large island to the south of the mainland. Portuguese explorer Ferdinand Magellan (1480–1521) discovered the Straits of Magellan in 1520 during his trip around the world. The Straits of Magellan are narrow and often experience rough seas due to high winds. The Atlantic and Pacific Oceans are at different levels, which cause churning currents when their waters meet in the Straits of Magellan. These powerful currents caused numerous ships to sink in the Straits of Magellan.

Isaac Le Maire (1558–1624), a Dutch merchant and explorer, discovered Cape Horn in 1615. Le Maire was looking for a different and safer route between the Atlantic and Pacific Oceans. Le Maire found a different route in what is today called Cape Horn, but it did not prove to be much safer than the Straits of Magellan. Cape Horn has violent weather patterns as a result of the meeting of the Atlantic and Pacific Oceans. Cold air moving north from Antarctica also contributes to the foul weather. Large waves, some over 65 feet (20 meters) tall, often sank ships that tried to round Cape Horn's rough seas. The opening of the Panama Canal in 1914 eliminated the need for most ships to travel through the Straits of Magellan or around Cape Horn in order to pass between the Atlantic and Pacific oceans.

Hypothermia

Hypothermia is a condition where the body becomes too cold to function properly. The human body strives to maintain a constant internal temperature at or near 98.6°F (37° Celsius). Unlike some animals that live in the cold arctic climates, humans do not have a layer of fat called blubber that surrounds the body. Humans must rely on layers of clothing to keep their bodies warm. If clothing is insufficient or becomes wet, a condition called hypothermia may occur.

Many people have experienced mild hypothermia, perhaps while playing in snow. Moderate hypothermia occurs when body temperature is between 97–95°F (36.1–35°C). Symptoms of mild hypothermia include shivering, numbness in the hands, and an inability to perform complicated tasks with the hands. A person experiencing these symptoms should go indoors or try to warm herself immediately. More severe problems may occur if body temperature continues to drop.

Severe hypothermia occurs when the body temperature drops below 90°F (32.2°C). Hypothermia causes the body to lose proper mental and physical functions. If hypothermia continues for a long period or under extremely cold temperatures then death may result. Every year about 700 Americans die from hypothermia.

One reason that hypothermia claims so many lives is because many people have the mistaken belief that hypothermia only occurs by falling into cold water. Hypothermia can occur from merely being outside in the cold without proper clothing. Hypothermia can also occur at any time of year, even during the summer. Water temperatures between 70–80°F (21.1–26.6°C) can lead to hypothermia, and even death, within a matter of hours. In water less than 32°F (0°C), death from hypothermia can occur within 15 minutes.

Hurricanes, typhoons, and cyclones

A hurricane is any organized storm with sustained winds of 74 miles per hour (119 kilometers per hour) or greater in the Atlantic Ocean, Gulf of Mexico, Caribbean Sea, or eastern Pacific Ocean. Winds gusts in the strongest hurricanes approach 200 miles per hour (322 kilometers per hour). Hurricanes include circular bands of clouds that slowly swirl around a central core of low atmospheric pressure (the pressure exerted upon Earth's surface by its atmosphere at a given point), called the eye. A hurricane may be hundreds of miles (kilometers) across, but the eye of the storm is typically only 10–30 miles (16–48 kilometers). Winds are strongest around the eye and weaken further out from the eye. A hurricane that occurs in the Indian Ocean is called a cyclone, and those in the middle and western Pacific are called typhoons.

The low pressure of the eye pushes a wall of water in front of the storm called a storm surge. The storm surge is often the

The waters off Cape Horn, some of the most dangerous in the world to navigate, require a watchful eye. © Chris Lisle/Corbis. Reproduced by permission.

most destructive part of a hurricane. Storm surges can sink ships at sea, destroy buildings on the coast, and cause flooding inland.

Hurricanes are divided into categories based on the speed their sustained winds. A category 1 hurricane produces sustained winds of 74–95 miles per hour (119–153 kilometers pr hour) and storm surges 4–5 feet (1.2–1.5 meters) above normal tide levels, enough to flood low-lying coastal roads and buildings. Category 2 storms contain winds 96–110 miles per hour (154–177 km per hour) and produce storm surges 6–8 feet (1.8–2.4 meters) above normal tide levels, enough to flood coastal escape routes (roads and bridges leading away from the coastline) and require some people to evacuate their beachside homes. A category 3 hurricane has sustained winds of 111–130 miles per hour (179–209 km per hour) and storm surges 9–12 feet (2.7–3.6 meters) above tide levels. Storm surges this high can cause major erosion (wearing away) of beaches and destruction of houses and businesses on and near the beach. A category 4 storm produces winds of 131–155 miles per hour (211–249 km per hour) and storm surges 13–17 feet (4–5.1 meters) above normal tide levels. Wave action from category 4 storms can destroy buildings constructed on land less than 2 feet above sea level, and can cause flooding up to 6 miles (10 kilometers) inland. A category 5 hurricane has sustained winds over 155 miles per hour (249 kilometers per hour) and brings a storm surge 18 feet (5.5 meters) or more above normal tidal levels. Besides massive building damage from wave action and winds, damaging floods occur more than 10 miles (16 kilometers) inland, and large-scale evacuations of coastal communities are necessary. Only three Category 5 hurricanes have ever hit the United States as of 2004.

A storm with sustained winds between 39–74 miles per hour (63–119 kilometers per hour) is called a tropical storm. Tropical storms are known for their ability to produce large amounts of rainfall over a short time. An organized storm with sustained winds below 39 miles per hour (63 km per hour) is called a tropical depression. A tropical depression can become a tropical storm and possibly a hurricane.

Nor'easters

Nor'easters, or Northeast winter storms, are large winter storms that dump snow and ice on the coastlines of America's mid-Atlantic and New England states. Nor'easters have struck as far south as Florida. Nor'easters typically occur between October and April. Unlike hurricanes, which rotate, a Nor'easter is a single storm line. A single Nor'easter may stretch for over 900 miles (1,448 kilometers). Nor'easters may pack strong winds and waves, causing beach erosion and blizzard conditions in coastal cities. Ships at sea during a Nor'easter often face waves and swells over 50 feet (15 meters) high.

Nor'easters form when warm air from the southeastern United States creates an area of low pressure just off the coast. Northeastern winds pull the warm air in the low-pressure system up the East Coast. The system picks up moisture from the Atlantic Ocean as it moves north. Cold air from Canada then mixes with this moisture-filled air. The product is a line of strong storms carrying snow and ice.

Icebergs

Icebergs are large chunks of ice that break off from glaciers or icepacks (a large expanse of floating ice) and float in the oceans. A glacier is a slow-moving solid pack of ice and snow that forms over thousands of years. Most of the world's glaciers were formed between 10,000 and 15,000 years ago during the last Ice Age. Most glaciers slowly flow toward the sea. When a large piece of a glacier pushes out into the sea, it breaks away from the glacier and becomes an iceberg.

Most icebergs break away from glaciers in Greenland or Antarctica. While the majority of icebergs remain far to the north, out of the way of most ships, every year several hundred icebergs drift into areas containing shipping routes. These icebergs pose a major risk to ships. An iceberg can create a large hole in a ship and cause major damage or even sink the ship. The most famous example of this is the *Titanic*, which hit an iceberg in the north Atlantic Ocean in 1912. The ship sank within hours, killing more than 1,500 people. Following the sinking of *Titanic*, several nations formed the International Ice Patrol to search for icebergs and record their positions. Modern technology is also capable of detecting icebergs in shipping lanes during the day and night, and in bad weather as well as clear skies.

Lost at Sea

For thousands of years one major problem plagued sailors: How to tell exactly where their ship was located in the vast ocean. On the open sea there is water as far as the eye can see in every direction. This posed the problem of how to navigate successfully. Navigation refers to the ability to determine the proper position of a ship and the proper direction to sail in order to reach the desired destination. Sailors in ancient cultures solved this problem by never losing sight of land. They would sail along the coast or hop from one island to the next.

This method proved to be impractical as ships became larger and need to move cargo over great distances. Mariners (sailors) soon began to use the stars to guide their ships. However only one's position north or south of the equator (imaginary line around Earth between the North and South Poles) could be determined by using stars. Many ships continued to get lost at sea because they could not determine their east-west position.

In 1592 a Portuguese ship laden with riches was lost on the return trip from India. Six English ships sighted the Portuguese ship and defeated her in battle. The value of the cargo on the ship was roughly half of the amount that the entire English treasury department possessed at the time. In 1707 four British ships ran aground on their return to England. The ships got lost in the fog. Assuming that they were still far from home, the ships continued on through the fog. They soon realized their mistaken when they ran aground near the English coast. Nearly two thousand men died in the ensuing shipwrecks.

In 1714 England's Parliament offered £20,000, or several million dollars in today's currency, to anyone who could figure out a way to calculate one's position east-west of the equator. English clockmaker John Harrison (1693–1776) put forth the unlikely solution: a clock. Harrison's clocks could keep accurate time at sea, allowing sailors to calculate its east-west position through mathematics based on the time in London. Harrison never received the full prize money, but fewer ships got lost at sea thanks to his discovery.

An instrument called synthetic aperture radar that orbits Earth aboard a satellite (vehicle that orbits Earth) collects and sends pulsed signals back to Earth, where a digital map of icebergs, their size and shape, and their precise location is formed.

Reefs and rocks

Like icebergs, reefs and rocks near the shore can damage the hull of ships, causing them to spill their cargo and even sink within a short time. A reef is an underwater ridge of rock or coral (tiny marine creatures with hard exterior skeletons) that lies just below the surface. Rocks can be difficult to spot with the eye, and it is nearly impossible to see a reef before a collision. Many modern ships rely on sonar (images produced by sound waves) or satellite technology (images produced by light waves) to detect rocks and reefs, but accidents still occur. In

1989 oil tanker *Exxon Valdez* ran aground on a reef in Prince William Sound, Alaska, causing an oil spill of 11 million gallons (46.5 million liters) into the Alaskan ecosystem. While the *Exxon Valdez* was not one of the largest oil spills in history, it did have a major impact on the environment and shipping regulations. The ensuing cleanup cost over $2 billion, and the Prince William Sound ecosystem continues to recover to its former level of biodiversity (range of varying plant and animal species).

Animals in the seas

Although sharks, jellyfish, and other sea animals do injure people in the ocean every year, the number of these attacks are usually sensationalized. Between 70 and 100 shark attacks on humans occur throughout all the oceans worldwide each year. On average, five to ten people die every year as a result of these attacks. Americans are over 300 times more likely to be killed by a car crash involving a deer than by a shark attack in the ocean. Many coastal states monitor shark populations in beach areas where sharks and humans mix by regularly counting and mapping shark populations according to geographic features in their habitat. Areas can use this data to issue shark advisories to beachgoers when shark populations are observed to be greater than the normal number of sharks.

Most jellyfish stings cause pain, but they rarely kill humans. One exception is the sea wasp or box jellyfish (*Chironex fleckeri*) that lives in the waters off northern Australia and Southeast Asia. This species of box jellyfish carries venom (poison) in its tentacles powerful enough that a single sting can cause death without prompt medical treatment. All jellyfish species however, are passive hunters; they do not attack prey for food, but wait until a potential food source (including humans) bump into their tentacles.

Mines

Mines are explosive devices that usually explode when an object makes contact with them. While many people are aware of the danger posed by land mines, sea mines can be equally destructive. Sea mines typically float just at or below the surface of the sea. This makes sea mines almost invisible to an approaching ship. Once the ship runs into the mine, the mine explodes.

During wartime sea mines serve a defensive purpose. They prevent enemy ships from approaching too close to shore. Mines remain a hazard in peacetime because the position of mines may be forgotten or the mines may drift way. Often a defeated nation is left with little resources to pick up sea mines laid by its military. Sea mines can also remain active for many years. In 1988 a U.S. navy ship, *Samuel B. Roberts,* ran into a sea mine in the Persian Gulf in the Middle East. The mine had been planted about 70 years earlier during World War I (1914–18). The mine caused $96 million in damage to the ship.

In order to avoid setting off mines many naval vessels scout ahead for them. This process slows down ships traveling through areas thought to contain mines. When detecting sea mines, ships use sonar or a helicopter with sonar flies in front of the ship. Divers investigate any suspicious objects found. If the object is a mine then specially trained divers disable it. The U.S. Navy is currently developing robots that can find and disable mines.

Joseph P. Hyder

For More Information

Books

Gemmell, Kathy, et al. *Storms and Hurricanes.* Tulsa, OK: E.D.C. Publishing, 1996).

Lundy, Derek. *Godforsaken Sea: The True Story of a Race Through the World's Most Dangerous Waters.* New York: Doubleday, 2000.

Morris, Neil. *Hurricanes & Tornadoes: Wonders of Our World.* New York: Crabtree, 1998.

Websites

Bruneau, Stephen E. "Icebergs of Newfoundland and Labrador: Frequently Asked Questions with Short Answers and Pointers." *Newfoundland and Labrador Tourism.* http://www.wordplay.com/tourism/icebergs/ (accessed on August 27 2004).

"Hazards: Hurricanes." *Federal Emergency Management Agency.* http://www.fema.gov/hazards/hurricanes/ (accessed on August 27, 2004).

"Hurricanes." *FEMA for Kids.* http://www.fema.gov/kids/hurr.htm (accessed on August 27, 2004).

"International Ice Patrol (IIP): Frequently Asked Questions." *United States Coast Guard: International Ice Patrol.* http://www.uscg.mil/lantarea/iip/FAQ/FAQ_Category.shtml (accessed on August 27, 2004).

"International Shark Attack File." *Florida Museum of Natural History.* http://www.flmnh.ufl.edu/fish/Sharks/ISAF/ISAF.htm (accessed on August 27, 2004).

"National Weather Service, Tropical Prediction Center." *National Hurricane Center.* http://www.nhc.noaa.gov (accessed on August 27, 2004).

"Oil Spill Facts." *Exxon Valdez Oil Spill Trustee Council.* http://www.evostc.state.ak.us/facts (accessed on August 27, 2004).

Venanzangeli, Paolo. "Cape Horn the Terrible." *NauticalWeb.* http://www.nautica.it/charter/capehorn.htm (accessed on August 27, 2004).

Winchester, Simon. "In the Eye of the Whirlpool." *Smithsonian Journeys.* http://www.smithsonianmag.si.edu/journeys/01/aug01/feature_full_page_1.html (accessed on August 27, 2004).

Recreation in and on Freshwaters

Freshwater is water that does not contain a high amount of salt or dissolved solids. Examples of freshwater include lakes, river, streams, and creeks. While many Americans do not live within driving distance of the seashore, almost everyone lives close to a freshwater river, lake, or stream, and many people are drawn to water for recreation.

Fishing and swimming

Fishing is one of the most popular freshwater activities, with over 44 million anglers (people who fish) in the United States. Fish live in almost every lake, river, and stream in the United States, which makes fishing possible for most Americans. There are two main types of freshwater fishing: fly fishing and spin fishing. The form of fishing used depends on location, the type of fish, and the body of water. Fly fishing is most popular on rivers and streams. Popular types of fish for freshwater fly fishing include trout, bass, and salmon. When fly fishing, the weight of the fishing line carries the fly, or lure, out into the stream. A series of arm motions whip the fishing line overhead like a bullwhip, simulating the movement of the prey. Fly fishers lure fish with artificial flies and other artificial water-loving insects that are the natural prey of river fish.

In spin fishing, weights called sinkers are attached to the line and carry the hook and artificial lure out into the water. The hook then sinks in the water and the lure spins as the angler reels in the line impersonating an attractive meal to the fish. Trout, salmon, bass, and pike are popular targets for spin fishers.

Swimming is another popular freshwater recreational activity. The principle of buoyancy explains how humans can swim instead of sink in the water. Buoyancy is the ability of an object to float in a liquid. Water exerts an upward force, called buoyant force, on every object that is submerged in it. An object will float if this buoyant force is greater that the downward force of gravity (attraction between all masses). The object will sink if the weight of the object is greater than the buoyant force.

A boy tends a cast while fly fishing. © *Royalty-Free/Corbis. Reproduced by permission.*

WORDS TO KNOW

Buoyancy: Ability of an object to float in a liquid.

Buoyant force: Upward force exerted by a liquid on an object; an object will float if the buoyant force of the liquid is greater that the downward force of gravity.

Canoe: Boat pointed at both ends and typically with an open top, or deck.

Swimming

Swimming is perhaps the most popular form of freshwater recreation. Every summer, millions of Americans go to a local lake or stream to swim. Proper technique is important to be a strong swimmer, as the following elements must work together: leg kick; timing; arm cycle; and breathing.

There are many different methods of swimming, involving different arm and leg motions. Each method is called a stroke. Perhaps the most common stroke is freestyle. This is usually the first stroke taught in swimming classes. Freestyle swimming involves bringing the arms out of the water and over one's head. The arms provide most of the speed in freestyle, with the legs adding only about 10% of the speed. The legs primary purpose in freestyle swimming is to keep the body balanced. Other popular strokes include the backstroke, the breaststroke, and butterfly. Good stroke technique maximizes the amount of efficient stroke area exposed to the water by the body (cupping hands with fingers together, for example), while minimizing body movements that could increase drag (friction) in the water and slow the swimmer (such as allowing the legs to sink too far into the water).

WORDS TO KNOW

●**Density:** An expression of the mass of an object within a given volume.

●**Erosion:** Wearing away by wind or water.

●**Geothermal:** Heat from Earth; energy obtained from the hot areas under the surface of the Earth.

The ancient Greek mathematician and scientist Archimedes (287 B.C.E.–212 B.C.E.) realized that the density of the object determines whether or not an object will float. Density is an expression of the mass of an object within a given volume. A piece of steel has a greater density than a piece of Styrofoam of equal size. Archimedes determined that a solid object would float if its density was less than the density of water. Swimming is possible because the human body is less dense than water.

Boating

Boating comes in several forms: sailboats; motorboats; and personal watercraft or jet skis. Buoyancy also explains how a ship made of steel can float even though steel is denser than water. The density of the overall shape of an object determines if it will float. A ship is constructed so that most of the interior is filled with air. This makes the overall density of the vessel less than the density of water. A simple experiment involving a piece of modeling clay and a glass of water demonstrate how this principle works. The clay will sink if it is rolled into a ball and placed in the water, but the clay will float if it is flattened, approximating the shape of a boat.

Sailboats harness the energy of the wind in sails and the energy in the water to propel them through the water. When wind blows along the sails it creates aerodynamic lift, much like on an airplane. Trimming (adjusting) the sails harnesses this lift in a manner that moves the boat in the water. Without a keel or centerboard (the structure that protrudes from the bottom, or hull, of a sailboat), the wind would blow the boat sideways. The keel primarily acts as a stabilizer. Water passing over the keel also provides lift that counteracts the force of the wind. Together, these forces push the boat forward.

Speedboats have large engines that propel the boat through the water at high speeds. Speedboats are also known as motorboats or powerboats. These boats are used to zip around on rivers and lakes, pulling water skiers or wakeboarders. Water skiing is where a person holds onto a rope that is attached to the boat while wearing a pair of skis. The boat then pulls the person along the water. Wakeboarding is similar to water skiing, but it involves a single, larger board rather than two skis. Many fishermen also use motorboats to travel on lakes and rivers in order to reach their favorite fishing spots.

Pontoon boats and houseboats are larger forms of motorized boats. A pontoon boat has two long, hollow tubes running the length of the boat. These tubes are called sponsons and help provide buoyancy and reduce rocking. Pontoon boats have a flat deck and have an open, boxy shape, making them stable in calm waters. Pontoon boats have motors, but move much slower than speedboats and are used for leisurely cruising and fishing on lakes and rivers. Houseboats are large, enclosed boats with wide hulls to decrease rocking motion and maximize interior space. Many people vacation on houseboats, and some people live on houseboats throughout the year.

Personal watercraft, or jet skis, are small, motorized boats that usually carry one to three people. Riders straddle a personal watercraft as if riding a horse. Personal watercraft are lightweight and can accelerate quickly. As of late 2003 however, personal watercraft were prohibited in 358 of 379 water recreation areas in the U.S. National Park system because of the noise they generate.

Rowing, canoeing, kayaking, and rafting

Rowing, canoeing, kayaking, and rafting are all forms of transportation that require rowing or paddling to move the craft through the water. A paddle, or oar, is a pole that may have a large, fairly flat end, called a blade. A canoe is a boat that is pointed at both ends and typically has a completely open top, or deck. People sit or kneel in a canoe and use a paddle with a single blade to move the canoe through the water. A canoe usually holds several people.

A kayak is a boat that is pointed at both ends and has a closed deck except for a small hole where the paddler sits. A

Water Skiing and Wakeboarding

Modern water skis are made of fiberglass or wood. A water skier starts out in a sitting position in the water. As the boat speeds up, the skier rises out of the water into a standing position. Once the boat reaches the proper speed, based on the skier's weight, the skis will skim the top of the water. This effect is called planing. Planing allows water skiers to travel faster because of decreased drag from the water. A wakeboard is similar to a snowboard. Since a wakeboard has a larger surface area than skis, a wakeboard will plane out at lower speeds. Typically, wakeboarders should ride behind a boat traveling at speeds of 25 miles per hour (40 kilometers per hour) or less.

WORDS TO KNOW

Kayak: Boat that is pointed at both ends and has a closed deck except for a small hole where the paddler sits.

Thermal spring: Natural spring of water at a temperature of 70°F (21°C) or above; commonly called a hot spring.

kayak paddle has two blades, with one on each end. A kayak usually holds only one person, but some models can carry two people. In order to steer the kayak, it is necessary to use the entire body for balancing and leaning along with the paddle.

A raft is a flat-bottomed boat, which is usually inflated with air. Several riders use paddles with single blades to move and steer rafts. Rafts are flexible, so they are often used in water that may contains rocks. If the raft hits a rock or goes over a small waterfall, the raft will bend instead of breaking.

Kayaks and rafts are often used for riding down river rapids, which are stretches of fast moving water on a river or stream. Rapids form from erosion (wearing away by wind or water), when water erodes rocks in a river at different rates. The soft rocks erode first, creating a steeper gradient (the angle of slope down which a river flows) for the river to flow down among the remaining harder rocks. Whitewater rapids are formed as the water increases speed in order to move along the steeper pathway among the harder rocks. When people travel down rapids, these sports are referred to as whitewater kayaking and white-water rafting. Specially made canoes may also be used for whitewater canoeing.

Thermal springs and spas

Thermal springs (natural flow of groundwater), also commonly called hot springs, were considered healing waters by many ancient cultures and still are by many modern cultures.

Thermal springs produce water that has been heated by the earth to a temperature of 70°F (21°C) or above. The ancient Romans constructed elaborate bathhouses, or spas, at the sites of thermal springs, and hot springs continue to be a major attraction in modern times. Modern spas often locate at the source of thermal springs, making hot springs popular destinations.

The water that flows from thermal springs becomes heated by geothermal warming in one of two ways. Geothermal means relating to heat generated from the center of the earth. The presence of underground volcanoes near the surface of the Earth can heat the water. Iceland is famous for its numerous volcanic thermal springs. Thermal springs can also be produced by rainwater seeping deep into the earth and then rising quickly. One example of this method is found in Hot Springs, Arkansas, where rainwater has seeped into the earth for thousands of years. The water seeps down to a depth of 6,000 to 8,000 feet (1,829 to 2,438 meters) below the surface and warmed by the earth's internal temperature. Cracks in rocks then allow the warmed water to return to the surface in less than a year. Because the water's return trip is quick, the water loses little heat and surfaces at about 147°F (63.8°C).

Whitewater Rafting

Rapids usually contain rough water. Most whitewater rafting in the United States occurs in the West and Southeast. Not all rapids are created equal. Some may be little more than a fast river. Others may be violent, rushing torrents of water that can kill even the most experienced whitewater rafter.

Rapids are divided into six categories, which inform rafters of the difficulty of particular rapids. A Class I river is just barely above a slow moving river. Rafting on a Class I rapid is not considered whitewater rafting. A Class II rapid has small rapids and large pools of water. Class II rapids are safe for everyone and offer gentle thrills. A Class III rapid is moderately difficult to raft. They have larger rapids and faster action. Most healthy people can raft a Class III with brief training. A Class IV rapid is difficult and has long, powerful waves. A Class V is extremely difficult and should only be attempted by experienced rafters. A Class V rapid has fast, complex rapids and sudden, steep drops. A Class VI rapid is considered unsafe, and only world-class rafters should even attempt rafting a Class VI rapid.

Tourism at Niagara Falls

Sometimes observing water is a recreational activity. Niagara Falls, on the United States-Canada border, became a popular tourist destination in the nineteenth century and has remained a popular destination. Every year, over twelve million people visit Niagara Falls.

Niagara Falls actually consists of two main waterfalls. The larger waterfall is Horseshoe Falls, or Canadian Falls. Horseshoe Falls, shaped like a horseshoe, is 167 feet (51 meters) high and 2,600 feet (792 meters) across. Over 600,000 gallons of water flow over Horseshoe Falls every second. On the opposite side of the falls, American Falls is 176 feet (54 meters) high and 1,060 feet (322 meter) across. Over 150,000 gallons flow over American Falls every second. The waterfalls at

Niagara were formed nearing the end of the last Ice Age about 12,000 years ago, when melting ice flowed into what is now the Niagara River. The river flowed over the Niagara escarpment (cliff), slowly wearing away the underlying rocks until the falls was carved upstream to its current position.

Winter sports

Many parts of the country enjoy recreational activities on frozen lakes and ponds. Ice skating and ice hockey are activities that can be enjoyed on frozen bodies of freshwater. Ice fishing is also another popular activity in some parts of the United States. Ice fishing involves cutting a hole in the ice on a lake or river and dropping a fishing line into the water below the ice. Liquid water is denser (heavier per unit) than ice. This explains why ice floats and forms on top of the lake in winter.

Joseph P. Hyder

For More Information

Books

McManners, Hugh. *Water Sports: An Outdoor Adventure Handbook.* London: Dorling Kindersley, 1997.

Websites

"About Niagara." *Niagara, USA.* http://www.niagara-usa.com/about/history.html (accessed on August 27, 2004).

"Earth's Water: Lakes and Reservoirs." *U.S.G.S. Water Science for Schools.* http://ga.water.usgs.gov/edu/earthlakes.html (accessed on August 27, 2003).

Fishing.com. http://www.fishing.com (accessed on August 27, 2004).

"Great Lakes." *U.S. Environmental Protection Agency.* http://www.epa.gov/glnpo (accessed on August 27, 2004).

"Hot Springs National Park." *National Park Service.* http://www.nps.gov/hosp (accessed on August 27, 2004).

International Sailing Federation. http://www.sailing.org (accessed on August 27, 2004).

"Office of Boating Safety." *United States Coast Guard.* http://www.uscgboating.org (accessed on August 27, 2004).

USA Swimming. http://www.usaswimming.org (accessed on August 27, 2004).

Recreation in and on the Oceans

Every year, Americans spend billions of dollars and a large amount of their spare time on recreational activities in and on the oceans. Among others, popular ocean-based activities include swimming, snorkeling, scuba diving, sailing, fishing, and surfing.

In the ocean

Swimming is one of the most popular forms of ocean recreation. Millions of Americans visit the beach every year to swim in the ocean. While swimming, beachgoers participate in snorkeling. Snorkeling, or skin diving, is a form of diving in which the diver swims at or near the surface of the water. Skin diving is simply holding one's breath underwater for as long as possible. The diver can remain underwater for long periods by breathing through a snorkel, which is a hollow tube attached to a mouthpiece. The snorkel juts out above the surface of the ocean, allowing the diver to breathe surface air through the snorkel like a straw. Snorkeling allows divers to explore ocean animals, plants, and coral reefs (tropical marine ecosystems made up of tiny coral animals and the structures they produce) that lay just below the surface of the ocean.

Scuba diving allows divers to fully immerse themselves in the ocean environment. Scuba stands for Self Contained Underwater Breathing Apparatus. Scuba equipment allows divers to go deeper than snorkeling and stay underwater longer. Scuba gear provides oxygen to divers while underwater. Modern scuba equipment is made up of small cylinders of compressed air. The diver breathes through a mouthpiece, and the air tank provides oxygen with every breath.

Recreational scuba divers can explore about 150 feet (46 meters) below the surface and with advanced training they can dive deeper. Dives deeper than 150 feet (46 meters) require gradual rising to the surface and other precautions. Rising too quickly after a deep dive can cause nitrogen to build up in the body, causing a painful, and potentially fatal condition called decompression sickness, or the bends. The world record for a scuba dive set in 2003 is over 1000 feet (313 meters). It took the diver only 12 minutes to reach this depth, but the diver had to rise to the surface of the water over 6½ hours in order to avoid the bends.

WORDS TO KNOW

Deep-sea fishing: Form of fishing that requires boating several miles out to sea in order to catch fish that live far from shore, such as marlin, tarpon, and barracuda.

Sailing: Moving across the water in a boat powered by wind energy harnessed by sails.

Scuba diving: Self Contained Underwater Breathing Apparatus; a form of diving in which pressurized air allows divers to stay underwater long enough to explore deep water.

Snorkel: A hollow tube attached to a mouthpiece that can jut out above the surface of the ocean to allow a diver to breath.

Snorkeling: Form of diving in which the diver swims at or near the surface of the water using a snorkel to breathe surface air.

Swimming the English Channel

On August 30, 1926, Gertrude Caroline Ederle becomes the first woman to successfully swim across the English Channel. It took Ederle 14 hours and 39 minutes to cross from England to France. © Bettmann/Corbis. Reproduced by permission.

The English Channel is a narrow body of water that separates England and France. The Channel is 21 miles (34 kilometers) wide at its narrowest point. On August 24, 1875, Englishman Matthew Webb (1848–1883) became the first person to swim across the English Channel. It took Webb 21 hours, 45 minutes to complete the crossing. Webb set off a craze, as swimmers from around the world attempted to duplicate his feat.

Since Webb crossed the English Channel, there have been over 6200 attempts by others. There have been over 600 completions by about 470 different swimmers. As of 2004, English long-distance swimmer Alison Streeter has crossed the English Channel more times than anyone with over 40 crossings. These swimmers face numerous difficulties on their swims across the Channel. The average water temperature of the Channel is 55–63°F (13–17°C), swells of over 20 feet (6 meters) are common, and the Channel is one of the busiest shipping lanes in the world.

Perhaps the most famous swim across the English Channel belongs to American Gertrude Caroline Ederle (1906–2003). On August 30, 1926, Ederle became the first woman to swim the English Channel. Ederle took 14 hours, 39 minutes to accomplish this feat. Ederle had attempted to swim the Channel the previous year, but fell short of her goal. The press criticized her attempt, claiming that no woman could swim across the English Channel. When Ederle completed the task in 1926, she beat the previous men's record by more than two hours. Her record stood for 24 years. Experts estimate that 20-foot (6-meter) storm swells forced Ederle to actually swim 35 miles in order to cross the 21-mile (34-kilometer) wide channel.

On the ocean

Sailing involves moving across the water in a boat powered by the wind. Sailing may be done for pleasure or sport. Sailing for sport involves serious competition. Sailboats are divided into numerous classes, or divisions, for competition based on the size and style of the boat. The America's Cup race and the Volvo Ocean Race Round the World are two of the most popular and competitive sailing races.

In the Volvo Ocean Race, formerly called the Whitbread Round the World Race, each yacht and its crew receive millions of dollars from corporate sponsors to design and build newer, faster ships. The race also tests the ability and stamina of the crew over the course of nine months. The 2001–2 Volvo Ocean Race Round the World, for instance, was 31,600-nautical-miles long. A nautical mile is longer than the statutory mile used on highways (1.15 statutory miles). The race, which ran for nine months, consisted of nine legs, or sections. Sailors traveled on the following routes: England to South Africa; South Africa to Australia; Australia to New Zealand; New Zealand to Brazil; Brazil to Miami, Florida; Miami to Baltimore, Maryland; Baltimore to France; and Sweden to Germany.

Recreational fishing on the oceans generally comes in two varieties: shore fishing and deep-sea fishing. In shore fishing, the angler (one who fishes) casts his or her bait from the shore. This form of fishing catches fish that stay close to land such as redfish, snook, and seatrout. Deep-sea fishing requires boating several miles (kilometers) out to sea in order to catch fish that live far from shore, where sonar (a device that uses sound waves to locate underwater objects) is sometimes used to spot schools of fish. Tuna, marlin, tarpon, and barracuda are examples of deep-sea fish. Some species of deep-sea fish can weigh over 1,000 pounds (454 kilograms).

Deep-sea fishing is a large business. Many tourists in popular deep-sea fishing locations pay thousands of dollars to rent boats and equipment for deep-sea fishing trips. Popular deep-sea fishing locations in the United States include Florida, the Gulf of Mexico, and New England.

Surfing is the act of riding a board, called a surfboard, on the waves. Surfing requires strength and balance. Recreational surfers typically ride on relatively small waves 3–5 feet (.9–1.5 meters), although some surfers travel worldwide in search of larger waves. Surfing competitions judge competitors on wave size, distance, and quality of performance. Some professional thrill-seeking surfers, called tow surfers, ride out on personal water crafts to ride waves up to 50 feet (15 meters) high.

Joseph P. Hyder

A scuba diver encounters a Stingray in the waters off the Cayman Islands. © *Stephen Frink/Corbis. Reproduced by permission.*

A yacht prepares for the start of a section (leg) of the Whitbread Round the World Race. © *Roger Garwood &Trish Ainslie /Corbis. Reproduced by permission.*

For More Information

Books

Graver, Denis K. *Scuba Diving*. Champaign, IL: Human Kinetics, 2003.

McManners, Hugh. *Water Sports: An Outdoor Adventure Handbook*. New York: DK Publishers, 1997.

Slater, Kelly. *Pipe Dreams: A Surfer's Journey*. New York: Regan Books, 2003.

Websites

Channel Swimming Association. http://www.channelswimming-association.com (accessed on August 27, 2004).

International Sailing Federation. http://www.sailing.org (accessed on August 27, 2004).

Volvo Ocean Race Round the World. http://www.volvoocean-race.org (accessed on August 27, 2004).

Chapter 11
History and Culture

Arid Climates

An arid climate is one that receives less than 10 inches (25.4 centimeters) of rainfall in an entire year. Deserts are areas that are arid. Although the most familiar image of a desert involves hot sand, the Arctic North and Antarctica are also deserts, as they also receive little moisture, usually in the form of snow. In contrast, the island of Fiji receives drenching rains for several months of the year, and is located in a tropical area of the world. Fiji receives an astounding 120 inches of rain each year, more than ten times the rainfall that falls in arid areas.

The rain that falls in an arid climate is sporadic and when it does fall, it is usually in the form of a thunderstorm. Flash floods are frequently a danger in arid climates after thunderstorms as the dry, compact soil cannot absorb water quickly enough to capture the rain. Streams swell with water for a few hours and then dry up again until the next cloudburst.

Plants surviving in an arid climate

Plants that survive in an arid climate have adapted to cope with the rare rainfall. Some plants can remain dormant (inactive) most of the time, only growing and reproducing when water is available. This cycle of activity and inactivity that is geared to the availability of water (and sometimes to other factors such as temperature) allows these hardy plants to survive for years.

Other desert plants that grow, bloom, and die each year (annual plants) will quickly go through the life cycle from a seed to a seed-producing plant, and then having their seeds distributed in the few wet days following a heavy rain. These plants will then

Water pipes carry water to irrigation ditches from pump stations located along the Nile River in Sudan. © *Bojan Brecelij/Corbis. Reproduced by permission.*

die and the seeds will lie in wait for the next big rainfall. Surveys of the Sonoran Desert in the southwestern United States have found 10,000 or more seeds in a square yard of soil. For plants like the Desert Sand Verbena and the Desert Paintbrush, this life cycle can be hours or days in length. The brief blooms of these plants turns the desert many beautiful colors.

Plants such as cacti have few or no leaves. This reduces the loss of moisture from the leaves into the air (transpiration) that occurs with plants such as maple trees. To avoid water loss the holes in the leaves of some plants that let moisture out (stromata) can close during the heat of the day and open at night.

Some cacti and other desert plants have long roots that reach far down into the ground to where it is saturated with water (the water table). For example, the roots of the mesquite tree can be up to 80 feet (24 meters) long, the height of an 8 story building.

Animals surviving in an arid climate

Animals and humans also face the challenge of finding water in an arid climate. Even though a streambed (the channel through which a stream runs) may appear dry, flash floods that

Las Vegas Water Use

Hoover Dam (originally named Boulder Dam) is located 34 miles (54.4 km.) from Las Vegas. Hoover Dam is 726 feet high (220 meters) and 660 feet thick at its base. The dam supplies power to Las Vegas and much of the Southwest United States. © *Royalty-free/Corbis. Reproduced by permission.*

The city of Las Vegas is located in the desert in Nevada. While Las Vegas was founded in 1855, until the 1940s the area was not heavily populated. Then Las Vegas became known as a resort for gambling and entertainment.

Hotels were built and the population began to grow. The population of Las Vegas has grown from approximately 65,000 in 1960 to over 1 million today. The city's population is estimated to double by 2015. Additionally, millions of tourists flock to the area each year.

This population growth, vacation popularity, and increased demands for electricity have put a burden on the water supply of Las Vegas. As groundwater (freshwater in layers beneath earth's surface) has been pumped out to supply the city with drinking water and water for golf course management and other needs, the land in some areas of the city has settled lower by more than 5 feet (1.5 meters). If the amount of groundwater that is being withdrawn continues to be more than the amount of water that flows back into the ground (withdrawal currently exceeds the replenishment by 2 to 3 times), then the situation could become dangerous for the stability of some buildings.

Lower water levels in Storrie Lake, a lake that Las Vegas uses as a water source, has also meant that water rationing is periodically necessary. Water levels in Storrie Lake have dropped by more than 45 feet (14 meters) from levels several decades ago. The rationing of water is necessary to protect the lake from going dry.

---

fill the bed to the brim with water may leave some water below the surface of the ground. If a hole looks damp when it is dug, then some water is present. Camels conserve water in their fatty tissues for use when sources of water are scarce in the desert, and can drink over 25 gallons (95 liters) of water at one time when a source of water is found. Humans, unable to adapt without water for more than a few days, dig wells and build reservoirs in arid climates to ensure a consistent water supply. As thirsty as a desert traveler might be, the water should not be drunk before it has been treated to kill harmful microorganisms that might be present. Even in an arid climate (microorganisms

WORDS TO KNOW

◆**Transpiration:** The process where water is absorbed by a plant through its roots and passes into the air from the leaves as water vapor.

◆**Water table:** The zone above which the spaces in the soil and rocks are not completely filled with water and below which the soil and rock spaces are completely filled with water.

ordinarily thrive in moist environments) troublesome microorganisms such as Giardia can sometimes be found in natural sources of water. If water contaminated with Giardia is drunk, the microorganisms can cause an intestinal upset.

Dew is another source of water in arid climates. Water that is present in the air as water vapor can change to liquid water on the surface of leaves. Many animals in arid climates, such as lizards, make use of the water provided by dew.

The scarcity of water in an arid climate makes managing the available water resources especially important for those living in this environment. The naturally available water is not enough to supply the needs of all the people in cities in many arid climates. Water is then brought from other regions into these locations adding an expense to the water. Transporting water is typically accomplished by constructing pipelines that funnel water from often far away locations to the arid community.

Brian Hoyle, Ph.D.

For More Information

Books

Abbey, Edward. *Desert Solitaire.* New York: Ballantine Books, 1990.

Alloway, David. *Desert Survival Skills.* Austin: University of Texas Press, 2000.

Cromwell, Cathy, and Carole Palmer. *Desert Landscaping for Beginners: Tips and Techniques for Success in an Arid Climate.* Phoenix: Arizona Master Gardener Press, 2001.

Websites

"How Plants Cope with the Desert Climate." *Arizona-Sonora Desert Museum.* http://www.desertmuseum.org/programs/ succulents_adaptation.html (accessed on August 27, 2004).

Exploration of the Oceans

For centuries, exploration of the oceans was primarily limited to exploration on the surface of the oceans. Explorers sailed or rowed ships across the seas in search of new lands or natural resources. Biological limits prevented humans from exploring beneath the surface. Three main issues prevented humans from exploring great depths of the ocean. First, humans must breathe air to survive, and humans can hold their breath for several minutes or less. This does not provide much time to dive, explore, and return to the water's surface. Second, the weight of water increases greatly as a diver descends into deep water. Finally, water temperature decreases with increasing depths. The temperature near the ocean floor is near freezing.

In the last half of the twentieth century, humans made great advancements in ocean exploration. Technological advancements greatly increased knowledge of marine biology (ocean life) and marine geology (ocean floor composition and structure). Humans and machines can now dive to great depths to explore the hidden world that lies below the surface of the ocean. Most of the vast ocean however, still remains unexplored.

Diving

Until the last several hundred years, humans had to rely solely on free diving to explore beneath the ocean's surface. When free diving, the diver simply holds their breath underwater. Ancient peoples used free diving to gather pearls, mother-of-pearl, and sponges, and some pearls are still gathered today by free diving. The depth of a free dive is limited by the diver's ability to hold his breath and the risk of hypoxia. Hypoxia is a condition in which body tissues do not receive enough oxygen to function efficiently. Hypoxia can lead to anoxia, or the absence of oxygen in tissues, and death.

The invention of the diving bell in the sixteenth century allowed divers to remain underwater for a longer period. A diving bell is a large metal bell that is placed underwater, trapping air from the surface inside the bell. This principle can be observed by turning a glass upside down and plunging it into a full sink or bathtub. A diver could explore underwater, but was required to return to the diving bell for fresh air. The diver returned to the surface before the oxygen supply in the trapped air inside the diving bell was exhausted.

By the eighteenth century scientists improved the diving bell and also created diving suits. Like diving bells, diving suits relied on air supplied from the surface to fill the helmet of the sealed suit. Often a long air hose and a series of hand pumps supplied the air to divers. These improvements allowed divers to explore underwater to depths of 60 feet (18 meters) for over one hour. By the nineteenth century scientists began to develop diving systems that did not rely on fresh air from the surface. Divers instead carried a supply of air or oxygen with them. Any diving system in which a diver does not rely on surface air is called scuba diving. Scuba stands for Self Contained

WORDS TO KNOW

◆**Atmosphere:** A unit to measure pressure; one atmosphere is 14.7 pounds per square inch, which is the standard atmospheric pressure measured at sea level.

◆**Bathyscaphe:** Small, underwater vehicle used for deep dives during underwater exploration.

◆**Chemosynthesis:** The use of chemicals, rather than sunlight, for the production of food.

◆**Coral reef:** Tropical marine ecosystem made up of tiny coral animals and the structures they produce.

◆**Diving bell:** Device used for early diving that has an open bottom and contains compressed air; later versions received a continuous supply of air from the surface through hoses.

◆**Diving suit:** Sealed suit that received a constant supply of air, usually surface air supplied by hoses; used for early ocean dives.

◆**Free diving:** Underwater swimming without the use of a breathing apparatus; also known as skin diving or breath-hold diving.

◆**Hydrothermal vents:** Volcanic-powered, hot spring openings in the ocean floor that spew out a fluid that is rich in chemicals and minerals.

◆**Hypoxia:** Condition in which the concentration of oxygen in body tissues is too low for the body to function normally.

◆**Marine biology:** Study of living organisms in the ocean.

◆**Marine geology** Study of the formation and structure of underwater land and rock formation.

◆**Photosynthesis:** Process used by plants to make food from sunlight, water, and carbon dioxide.

◆**Plate tectonics:** Theory that the crust of the Earth is composed of several large masses of land that move over, under, or collide with each other.

◆ **Scuba:** Self-Contained Underwater Breathing Apparatus; equipment that supplies a diver with compressed air from a cylinder that the diver carries underwater.

◆**Sidescan sonar:** Type of sonar that emits sound energy over a wide path, tens or hundreds of miles (kilometers) across, allowing scientists to map large areas of the ocean.

◆**Sonar:** Derived from "SOound NAvigation and Ranging," sonar uses sound waves to locate and map underwater objects.

◆**Submersible:** An underwater vehicle used to dive to extreme depths; submersibles are often used by scientists to study marine biology and marine geology.

Underwater Breathing Apparatus. As pure oxygen can be harmful to the central nervous system at depths below 25 feet (7.6 meters), modern scuba equipment contains a mixture of helium, nitrogen, and oxygen.

French ocean explorer Jacques-Yves Cousteau (1910–1997) along with Canadian engineer Emile Gagnan invented modern scuba gear in 1943. Cousteau and Gagnan's scuba equipment contained a tank of air with a tube for the diver to breath through. Cousteau and Gagnan perfected a regulator for scuba gear that allowed divers to obtain compressed air from a tank simply by breathing normally through a tube. Until this invention, divers had to turn a valve on and off to control the flow of air from a diving tank. The scuba equipment of Cousteau and Gagnan made scuba diving a popular sport for millions of people who enjoy the underwater world of coral reefs (a tropical marine ecosystem made up of tiny coral animals and the structures they produce) and aquatic animals and plants that remained hidden for most of human history.

Submersibles

Submersibles (submarines) called bathyscaphes are required to go to the deepest parts of the oceans. Deep ocean temperatures average about 39°F (3.8°C). Bathyscaphes are heated to protect humans and equipment from the cold. Bathyscaphes also carry large supplies of air that allow humans to breathe underwater for hours.

Bathyscaphes also protect humans and equipment from the pressure exerted by deep water. At sea level, air produces a pressure of 14.7 pounds per square inch. Scientists label this standard one atmosphere of pressure. The human body functions best at one atmosphere of pressure. At 33.8 feet (10.3 meters) below the water, the pressure doubles to 29.4 pounds per square inch, or two atmospheres. The pressure increases by an additional atmosphere, 14.7 pounds per square inch, for every additional 33.8 feet below water. The deepest point of the ocean is Mariana Trench, at 35,802 feet below sea level, almost 7 miles (11 kilometers) below the ocean's surface. At this depth, the water pressure is nearly 16,000 pounds per square inch.

In addition to manned vessels, scientists have invented numerous types of unmanned submersibles called autonomous underwater vehicles (AUVs) or remote-operated vehicles (ROVs). These unmanned vessels prevent lives from being placed in danger while exploring the oceans; they often enter shipwrecks and other places usually dangerous for manned

Cousteau and *Calypso*

French explorer and filmmaker, Jacques-Yves Cousteau aboard his research vessel, Calypso. © Bettmann/ Corbis. Reproduced by permission.

Jacques-Yves Cousteau was an inventor, explorer, and marine biologist who popularized marine life and exploration. Born in France, Cousteau became famous after he and Canadian engineer Emile Gagnan invented the Aqualung. The Aqualung was the first modern scuba gear. Most scuba equipment used today is based on the design of the Aqualung Aqualung. The Aqualung contained a tank of compressed helium and oxygen that the diver took underwater strapped to his back. A tube carried the air from the tank to the diver's mouth. The revolutionary design aspect of the Aqualung was the demand regulator. The Aqualung's demand regulator allowed divers to obtain air from a tank by breathing naturally while underwater. Previous scuba gear either supplied air continuously or required the diver to open and shut a valve to start and stop the flow of air.

In 1948, Cousteau purchased a boat called *Calypso* and devoted his life to underwater exploration. *Calypso* contained a laboratory that allowed Cousteau to conduct experiments in marine biology. Over the next several decades Cousteau made nearly 120 documentaries while sailing around the world on *Calypso*. In 1956 Cousteau won an Academy Award for *The Silent World*. Cousteau achieved worldwide recognition through his television series *The Undersea World of Jacques Cousteau*, which aired on American television from 1968–75. The series provided many viewers with their first glimpse of underwater creatures, including sharks, whales, exotic fish, and sea turtles.

Cousteau's explorations also revealed the negative impact that humans can have on the oceans. Cousteau witnessed the damage that pollution can cause in the seas. These experiences led Cousteau to become one of the first and most famous advocates for improving the ocean environment.

shipwrecks and other places usually dangerous for manned submersibles. Unmanned underwater vehicles are normally more economical to operate than manned submersibles.

Mapping the oceans

Below the surface of the ocean, there is an underwater world of topographic (surface) features similar to that on land. Mountain ranges, hills, volcanoes, and trenches lie on the sea

Beebe Expeditions

William Beebe and Otis Barton pose with their invention, the bathysphere. © *Ralph White/Corbis. Reproduced by permission.*

Charles William Beebe (1877–1962) was a naturalist and ocean explorer. Beebe began his career as an ornithologist (a scientist who studies birds) with the New York Zoological Society. Beebe spent most of his early career traveling the world and writing several books about his explorations and bird studies. In the late 1920s Beebe became interested in marine biology. At this time Beebe was the director of the New York Zoological Society's Department of Tropical Research. Beebe used his position to conduct studies of marine life. Beebe led several expeditions to recover marine animals using nets. Most of the animals from the deep sea were dead by the time they reached the ship's deck.

Beebe hoped to observe sea animals living in their natural habitat, as he had observed birds. Beebe began diving with a bulky helmet and soon became frustrated with his inability to observe sea creatures in deeper water. Beebe worked with inventor Otis Barton to design a vessel that could descend deep below the ocean's surface. Beebe called the vehicle that Barton designed a bathysphere. In 1932 Beebe and Barton dove 3,028 feet (923 meters) below the surface, a distance over one-half mile. This diving record stood for fourteen years. Beebe wrote many popular books about his adventures in the ocean and tropics, influencing generations of naturalists.

twentieth century. Scientists now map the features of the oceans to provide information for the military, geologists (scientists who study earth and rock formations), seismologists (scientists who study earthquakes), and other marine scientists.

In the nineteenth century, scientists and shipping companies attempted to map the ocean near the coast. They were mainly interested in discovering reefs and underwater rocks that could pose a problem to ships. A process called sounding was used to produce these early ocean maps. Sounding involved dragging a weighted rope along the sea floor. The rope would slacken when dragged up an underwater hill. The amount of rope taken up by the slack indicated the height of the hill. A crude map could then be made indicating the position of hills and valleys.

In the early twentieth century sonar allowed scientists to produce better maps of the ocean. Sonar stands for SOund NAvigation and Ranging. Sonar equipment sends out a pulse of sound energy (all energy travels in waves) that travels about 4,500 feet (1,372 meters) per second. When the sound wave hits an object, such as the sea floor, it bounces back to the source. By determining the length of time that the sound wave takes to return, scientists can calculate the distance of an object. When mapping the floor of the ocean, a sonar signal would take less time to return after striking a hill or mountain than when striking the bottom of a trench. Using these calculations scientists are able to produce maps of the ocean floor. The drawback to conventional sonar is that a sonar beam covers a very narrow area, making mapping the entire ocean with sonar impractical.

A newer form of sonar, called sidescan sonar, allows scientists to map larger areas of the ocean at once. Sidescan sonar equipment is placed in the water and towed by a boat. The equipment is usually towed several hundred yards (meters) above the ocean floor. Unlike active sonar, sidescan sonar emits signals over a wide path instead of straight down. This allows the sidescan sonar to create maps of an area tens or hundreds of miles (kilometers) across.

Jason Junior, a submersible, highly maneuverable camera, allowed from Woods Hole Oceanographic Institute to explore the wreck of the *R.M.S. Titanic.* © *Bettmann/Corbis. Reproduced by permission.*

Marine biology

Saltwater covers nearly three-quarters of Earth's surface. Animals, plants, and other organisms live throughout the oceans. Many species of marine life were only discovered in the last several decades. Numerous other marine species will undoubtedly be discovered in the future as humans continue to explore the oceans. Until the last century humans were not able to explore far below the surface of the ocean. Scientists could only study species of plants, animals, and other organisms that lived near the surface. The invention of deep-sea submersibles has exposed a world of living organisms that lay hidden for millions of years. Scientists had long assumed that all organisms depended on sunlight for life. Plants require sunlight to conduct photosynthesis, or the conversion of sunlight, water, and carbon dioxide into their food. Animals then rely on plants as the bottom of their food chain (the relationship between plants and animals where one species is eaten by another).

In the 1970s discoveries at the bottom of the ocean changed the assumption that organisms require sunlight for survival. Scientists found small communities of organisms on the ocean floor that were living without sunlight. These organisms depend on hydrothermal vents for survival. Powered by volcanic activity, hydrothermal vents are geysers (hot springs) that spew out a fluid rich in chemicals and minerals. The temperature of some of the fluids from hydrothermal vents is nearly 750°F (399°C). The animals that live near these vents rely on chemosynthesis for survival. Chemosynthesis is the use of chemicals, rather than sunlight, for the production of energy.

In addition to the discovery of new species of plants, animals, and microorganisms, recent ocean exploration has also led to new findings about animals that scientists assumed were extinct. In 1938 fishermen near South Africa caught an unusual looking fish. Scientists later determined that the fish was a coelacanth. Before this discovery scientists had believed that the coelacanth had become extinct between 65 and 80 million years ago. Unchanged for hundreds of millions of years, many scientists call the coelacanth a living fossil. The coelacanth is a fish that has a pair of lobed-fins in the front and an extra lobe on its tail. The coelacanth can use its front lobed-fins to "walk" on the ocean floor. In 1991 scientists used a submersible to record the first images of living coelacanths in their natural environment.

Marine geology

Ocean exploration has also revealed a deep sea landscape that is similar to land. Marine geology is the study of the formation and structure of underwater land and rock formation. Mountain ranges, hills, valleys, volcanoes, and trenches cover the floor of the ocean. Most of these features remained undiscovered until the twentieth century. Advancements in ocean mapping and submersibles revealed the geology of the ocean floor. The Mid-Atlantic Ridge, a mountain range that stretches the length of the Atlantic Ocean, was not discovered until 1952. Mariana Trench, the deepest point in the ocean, was not discovered until 1951.

Ocean exploration has also increased the understanding of plate tectonics. The entire surface of the earth and the ocean floor is composed of large masses of land called tectonic plates. These tectonic plates constantly move over, under, or collide with each other. The movement of these tectonic plates creates mountains. The movement of tectonic plates also causes volcanic eruptions and earthquakes. Most volcanic and seismic activity (earthquakes) occurs at the edges of tectonic plates. The area surrounding the Pacific Plate is one of the most volcanically and seismically active areas of the world. The Pacific Plate is a large tectonic plate that lies beneath the Pacific Ocean. Volcanic eruptions and earthquakes occur as the Pacific Plate moves under several other tectonic plates. About three quarters of the world's active volcanoes lie around the Pacific Ocean. For this reason, the area surrounding the Pacific Ocean is called the "Ring of Fire."

Joseph P. Hyder

For More Information

Books

Cousteau, Jacques-Yves. *Jacques Cousteau: The Ocean World.* New York: Abrams, 1985.

Cousteau, Jacques-Yves. *The Living Sea.* New York: HarperCollins, 1963.

Graves, Don. *The Oceans: A Book of Questions and Answers.* New York: Wiley, 1989.

Websites

Embley, Bob. "Sea Floor Mapping." *National Oceanographic and Atmospheric Administration.* http://oceanexplorer.noaa.gov/explorations/lewis_clark01/background/seafloormapping/seafloormapping.html (accessed on August 27, 2004).

Martin, Lawrence. "Scuba Diving Explained: Questions and Answers on Physiology and Medical Aspects of Scuba Diving." *Mt. Sinai Educational Web Portal.* http://www.mtsinai.org/pulmonary/books/scuba/sectiona.htm (accessed on August 27, 2004).

"Woods Hole Oceanographic Institute." http://www.whoi.edu (accessed on August 27, 2004).

Water and Cultures in the Ancient World

Water was the center of life in many ancient cultures. In Greek mythology, one of the most ancient and powerful gods was Neptune, the god of the sea. Ancient Greek literature, such as *The Odyssey* by Homer (about 800 B.C.E.), mentions sea mon-

Aqueduct: Man-made conduit for carrying water, usually by gravity.

Cistern: A man-made reservoir for storing water.

Deposition: Process by which dirt, silt, and sand is moved from its original place by wind or water and deposited elsewhere.

Erosion: Wearing away due to wind and water.

Irrigation: Water channeled to farmlands for growing crops.

Sedimentation: The process by which particles of dirt, sand, and silt that are heavier than water are deposited by water and settle at the bottom of a body of water.

Sediments: Gravel, sand, and silt that are deposited by water.

Silt: Sedimentary particles smaller than sand particles, but larger than clay particles.

Terra cotta: Ceramic material made from baked clay used in Ancient Rome for aqueduct pipes, dishes, and some tools.

sters, whirlpools, and harrowing voyages upon the sea. In India, the Ganges River was considered sacred from historical accounts over 3000 years old. To the ancient Egyptians, the Nile River was the political, economic, and life-sustaining center of their kingdom. Without the Nile, Egypt would be as barren as its nearby deserts. Ancient civilizations' respect for water grew from their absolute need for water. Like today, water sustained life in many ways.

Seafaring in the ancient world

Ancient cities constructed beside the sea based their economies on the nearby water. Fishing, exploration, trade, and warfare necessitated shipbuilding. Shipbuilding was one of the most important crafts of the ancient world. Most ships were wooden, but smaller boats used for fishing were sometimes made of bark or cured (dried and treated) animal skins. Making wooden ships required a good supply of timber and a means of transporting that timber to seaside shipyards. A shipyard is a place where ships are built and repaired.

Trade was a key development of the great ancient civilizations. The cultures of the Mediterranean Sea traded actively with each other. Most trade ran along the coastline, with ships sailing close to land to aid navigation. However, some open water trade routes successfully connected various parts of the Mediterranean and Asia. When the Roman Empire overtook most of the Mediterranean region in the first century B.C.E., trade continued to flourish. For example, Rome exported (sold to other countries) wine, olive oil, gold, and silver. The Romans imported (brought into the country) cotton, slaves, silk, ivory, and spices from other parts of the empire and from exotic locations such as India, the Middle East, and Africa. Many of the trade routes used by the Romans in the eastern Mediterranean region had been established by the region's first great seafaring and trading culture, the Phoenicians, beginning in 1200 B.C.E.

Sailors, soldiers, and explorers in ancient Greece and Rome returned to their homes with stories of other cultures and far away places. This sparked interest in travel. In Rome, for example, ancient tourists boarded boats to sail to Greece and Egypt. One of the most popular tourist attractions for wealthy Romans was a cruise on the Nile.

Ancient civilizations utilized different styles of boats for shipping than they did for transportation. Cargo ships, ships that carried goods, tended to be large and more broad, for example. However, most ancient boats have some similarities.

Ancient Egypt and the Nile River

Ancient pyramids dominate the landscape along the Nile River near Giza, Egypt. © *Bettman/Corbis.* *Reproduced by permission.*

Life in ancient Egypt depended on the Nile River. The banks of the Nile were lush with vegetation. Silt deposited on farm fields by yearly floods provided crops with fertile soil. Although its waters were heavy with silt, the Nile was the largest source of drinking water in the desert region. Most of Egypt's cities grew along the banks of the Nile.

The Nile was Egypt's main highway. Goods, people, and crops all moved along the Nile on boats or barges. The Nile flows from south to north, and ships heading north would simply float along with the river's current. For the journey south, barges used sails to catch the prevailing winds. Water from the Nile permitted the Egyptians to build cities, statues, and the Great Pyramids. The Northern part of Egypt did not have adequate building materials. Stone was quarried (carved out of the earth) in the south and floated on the Nile to where it was need for construction projects.

Most European and Middle Eastern boats relied on harnessing the wind with sails. When there were no winds, or when the currents were too strong for their sails, men rowed the large boats. Some ships employed over 100 rowers to propel a ship through the water. The Chinese junk, a small, flat-bottomed ship made from about the ninth century, however, was completely sail-powered. Its movable sails permitted it to adapt to changing winds. However, the junk was usually limited to coastal trade.

Many ancient ports, harbors, and coastal towns faced serious problems with deposition and erosion. Deposition is the process by which dirt, silt, and sand is moved from its original place by wind or water and deposited elsewhere. Alexandria, Egypt was located near Nile River delta, the place where the Nile flowed into the Mediterranean Sea. The slow-moving waters of the delta carried large amounts of silt (fine rock, plant, or soil sediment particles) and sand. These silt and sand deposits constantly reshaped the coastline, altering the pathways into the Nile River. Erosion is the wearing away of soil or rock by wind and water. In Greece, widespread inland defor-

Ancient Polynesians

The ancient people who became the Polynesians when they settled in the South Pacific Ocean began their journey in 500 C.E. off the coast of New Guinea. As food, lumber, and other resources diminished the islands they inhabited, the people migrated to another chain of islands. The Polynesian ship was an open, double canoe-raft with of two hulls connected by ropes and timber beams. A platform laid over the beams provided the needed working, storage, and passenger space. The immigrants took their supplies, tools, animals, and crop plants with them. At first, these journeys were limited to islands already visible from the coastline. However, as the immigrants moved further, they began to send expedition parties to scout for new islands. The trips crossed tens and then hundreds of miles of open ocean, out of sight of land.

The Polynesians developed a navigation system based on observation of the stars to help them find their way. They also carefully observed birds and the currents and tide of the ocean. Watching the environment gave told them when they were close to land. By 1000 C.E., the people who became the Polynesians had settled the Islands of Fiji, Samoa, Tonga, Easter, and parts of Hawaii and New Zealand.

In 1947, Norwegian anthropologist Thor Heyerdahl (1914–2002) recreated an ancient Polynesian canoe raft. He sailed the craft across the open water of the Pacific from Peru to Polynesia. He named the legendary raft *Kon-Tiki*. Heyerdahl devoted much of his career to the study of ancient Polynesian exploration and culture.

estation (clearing of forests) caused soil loss, leaving both inland and coastal areas vulnerable to erosion. By 500 B.C.E., many Greek costal towns were creeping further inland as mud, dirt, and silt washed from the bare land into the mouths of bays and rivers. The ruins of many ancient cities that were once ports now lie several miles inland.

Water and science: inventions and discoveries in the ancient world

Ancients civilizations developed the art and science of seafaring. Their journeys were aided by the development of sail powered craft and navigational tools. Although no one knows for sure when the sail was invented, the earliest record of ships with sails is on a piece of 5,000-year-old Egyptian pottery that features a drawing of boats. While researching a Greek shipwreck, marine archaeologists (scientists who study objects found in water from the past) discovered an early toolfor calculating the movement of certain stars and planets known as the Antikythera Mechanism, which involved a complex series of moving gears. Ancient sailors in the Mediterranean Sea probably used the movement of the Sun and stars to determine which direction they were sailing and to aid navigation .

The Greek mathematician Archimedes (circa 287 B.C.E.–211 B.C.E.) discovered the principle of water buoyancy, which explains why objects float in water. The principle of buoyancy states that an object put in water (or any fluid) will displace the same volume of water as the volume of the object. Archimedes also invented the water screw, a spiral shaft within a cylinder used for drawing water out of ships, cisterns (tank used to collect water), or pools. He also invented a clock powered by a flow of water. Similar water clocks were also invented and used in ancient China.

Frieze depicting ancient Egyptians (circa 2000 B.C.) using water for irrigation. *Hulton/Archive. Reproduced by permission.*

Although most large cities and town in the ancient world were built near the sea, humans cannot drink salt water. Thus, sources of freshwater still had to be found to provide people with water suitable for drinking. Water from underground sources was the cleanest water, but it was sometimes difficult to locate. Ancient civilizations discovered several methods for finding underground water sources. Several cultures observed plant life, noticing that certain types of plants grew only where there was abundant underground water. Others observed changes in soil and rock types. The presence of porous limestone, through which water could seep, indicated that an area could contain underground water sources. A common practice among Roman water engineers was to observe patterns of fog, steam, and mist in the early morning. They noted that mist appeared low to the ground near natural springs or underground water sources.

Ancient water supply systems

In the ancient world, most people relied on wells, rivers, lakes, and streams as a source of water. As ancient cities grew, they required large amounts of clean water for their citizens. However, rivers and lakes were also sometimes used as places to dispose of wastewater, sewage, and trash. Waste disposal from one town affected the cleanliness of water downstream. Water taken from rivers that flowed though several towns sometimes carried diseases. Often, towns and cities were abandoned when a water source dried up or became too polluted to use.

Southwestern Native Americans

The ancient Native American cultures in the desert western United States thrived in places where water was scarce. Since rain was infrequent, and small streams often dried out, they devised ways to store and conserve water.

The Anasazi (100 B.C.E.–1600 C.E.) and the Hohokam (200 B.C.E. –1450 C.E.) cultures occupied lands in similar hot and dry climates, however their approach to water use and conservation was very different. The Anasazi built their towns in to the side of mesa cliffs. They used a network of ladder to reach the top of the flat mesa where they grew crops.

The Anasazi depended on seasonal rains for their crops and supply of drinking water. They would collect rainwater for drinking and store it in cool, stone cisterns constructed in their towns. They also collected rainwater that spilled out of the rocks in the cliff walls. Water was a public resource. It was conserved, and was shared among the community.

The Hohokam lived closer to larger sources of water. They diverted seasonal streams and creeks to flow into their farmland and irrigate their crops. Around 300 B.C.E., they had become skillful irrigation farmers. The Hohokam conserved water for personal use, but often took such water from their irrigation canals.

The importance of water to the ancient desert cultures is also seen in the names later people gave to the ancient inhabitants of the area. One group of ancient Native Americans thrived for nearly a thousand years before the eruption of a major volcano devastated their farmlands. The civilization became known as the Sinagua, or "those without water.'

The most successful ancient cities discovered ways to provide their citizens with ample clean water. Even cities built next to sources of water required a means to move the water to locations within walking distance of people's homes. Canals, ditches, and channels (passages for water) were employed to move water for irrigation (watering crops) and drinking. Over several centuries, this water supply system improved. In the 3rd century B.C.E. the Romans began constructing a completely enclosed water supply system that mostly ran underground. The system involved aqueducts, which are channels constructed above the ground to carry water by gravity (force of attraction between all masses) from one place to another. Aqueducts brought ample fresh, clean spring water from the hills outside of Rome into the city for public use. The Romans built thousands of miles of aqueducts throughout the Roman Empire. Remains of these aqueducts are still visible today. Some are still used today to deliver water to public fountains in the modern city of Rome!

Aqueducts were used in ancient India, Persia, Assyria, and Egypt as early as 700 B.C.E. As drinking water for people had to remain clean, covered channels or pipes were necessary to protect the water as it flowed several miles (kilometers) from its source. The first such stone structure was built by the Assyrians around 690 B.C.E. Ancient Rome's aqueducts used tunnels, pipes, and covered channels to protect the water.

In ancient aqueducts, water flowed through the channels by the force of gravity alone. Aqueduct channels were constructed along a gradual slope, allowing water from the source to flow downhill to its destination. Constructing aqueducts through hilly terrain required advanced knowledge of mathematics, architecture, and geology. Although there were no modern machines or pumps that could move water up a hill or slope, resourceful ancient engineers designed tunnels, inverted siphons, and aqueduct spans (bridges) to move water. Tunnels were constructed through hills by carving through rock. An inverted siphon is a U-shaped pipe that relies on the force of water flowing down to push the water on the other side of the U-shaped pipe. Pipes made of stone or a type of baked clay called terra cotta carried water through carved out tunnels. Inverted siphons moved water uphill for short distances. Finally, the Romans constructed aqueduct bridges (or elevated spans) from stone. To withstand the heavy weight of water, aqueduct bridges employed several stories (or tiers) of strong arches.

Cleaning water of mud, dirt, silt, and some minerals such as lead was common in the ancient world. It improved the taste and clarity of drinking water. Water from rivers, lakes, and aqueducts was often placed in large cisterns. The lack of movement in the cistern permitted sedimentation, a process in which heavier dirt, silt, and mineral particles sink to the bottom of the cistern. Water was then drawn from the upper levels of the cistern as from a well. In many parts of the Roman Empire, pipes carried water from cisterns to public fountains or into private homes. In Greece, water was sometimes strained through cloth to remove solids before being used.

Another innovation of ancient waterworks was the sewer. Sewers carried wastewater away from the city and prevented people from dumping waste into the streets. Sewer systems also

Todadzischini Navajo Medicine Man (ca. 1904) displays full mask and ceremonial decorations. *Edward S. Curtis. The Library of Congress. Reproduced by permission.*

helped drain city areas and prevent flooding. Ancient sewer systems used a network of underground channels and a flow of water to remove wastes. Sewers helped cities stay clean and aided disease prevention. However, even Rome's most advanced ancient sewer system eventually discharged wastewater into rivers or the sea.

Water supply systems also carried water to popular places such as public baths and pools. Both the ancient Romans and the ancient Chinese civilizations built spas and pools using water from naturally hot springs. The Greeks built swimming pools near their public baths. The first known swimming races were held in Japan in 36 *B.C.E.*

Ancient civilizations shaped how humans think about water today. Water is still used for the same tasks today that it was in the ancient world: drinking, cooking, cleaning, irrigation, shipping, and powering machines. Ships continue to move most of the world's goods. Even though trains, trucks, and canals permit goods and crops to be moved further inland today, many of the world great cities are still built near harbors and along the coast. Some modern cities, such as Alexandria, Egypt; Rome, Italy; and Athens, Greece are built upon their ancient foundations.

Adrienne Wilmoth Lerner

For More Information

Books

Casson, Lionel. *Ships and Seamanship in the Ancient World.* Princeton, NJ: Princeton University Press, 1995.

Culver, Henry B., and Gordon Grant. *The Book of Old Ships: From Egyptian Galleys to Clipper Ships.* New York: Dover, 1992.

Heyerdahl, Thor. *Kon-Tiki: Across the Pacific by Raft.* New York: Pocket, 1990.

Homer. *The Odyssey.* Translated by Robert Fagels. New York: Penguin, 1999.

Websites

"Aqueducts Move Water. (Water Science for Schools)." *United States Geological Survey.* http://ga.water.usgs.gov/edu/aqueduct1.html (accessed on August 27, 2004).

"A Brief History of Drinking Water." *American Water Works Association.* http://www.awwa.org/Advocacy/learn/info/HistoryofDrinkingWater.cfm (accessed on August 27, 2004).

Water and Cultures in the Modern World

Water plays an important role in shaping the modern world. Cities are built on water. Humans rely on water for cooking, drinking, washing, transportation, trade, energy, irrigation (watering crops), and recreation. The use of water in the modern world has also created problems. Population growth and advancements in technology threaten the world's water supply. Overfishing and pollution stress many of the world's seas, and shortages of water stress human populations in arid (extremely dry) lands.

Cities and ports

Most cities are located beside water, Coastal areas in particular boast large cities. Eight out of the top ten most populous cities in the world lie on the coast. Nearly 44% of the world's population lives within 100 miles (161 kilometers) of a coast. Coastal cities grow because ports are an integral part of modern life. A port is place where people and merchandise can enter or leave a country by boat. Ports are essential for trade, or the movement of materials in exchange for money.

Cities that are not located on the coast are usually located on some other body of water, such as a lake or a river. Cities need large supplies of freshwater for drinking or irrigation. Cities get most of their freshwater from the nearest river or lake. Even most coastal cities are located where rivers flow into the ocean. These rivers provide coastal cities with a supply of freshwater. Goods delivered to a coastal city's port may also be shipped further inland on the river.

Modern cities have factories that make goods required in today's world. These factories often produce pollution that makes its way into the water supply, whether through inadequate storage or treatment facilities, or as a direct source of pollution through dumping industrial wastewater. Cities must also dispose of raw sewage. In most developed countries, sewage is treated and returned to the water supply. This has minimal effect on the environment. In most developing countries though, raw sewage is pumped back into rivers, lakes, and the ocean. Both pollution and sewage can kill animals, plants, and microorganisms living in the water.

Exploration

In past centuries ocean exploration meant sailing the open seas in search of new lands. Today ocean exploration usually involves exploring below the surface of the ocean. Although

WORDS TO KNOW

Bathyscaphe: A submersible vehicle that is capable of going to the deepest parts of the ocean and withstanding extreme pressure.

Chemosynthesis: The use of chemicals, rather than sunlight, for the production of food.

Ecosystem: Community of plants and animals that interact with each other and with their physical environment.

Effluent: Wastewater that has been treated to remove most impurities.

Hydrothermal vents: Volcanic-powered openings in the ocean floor that spew out a fluid that is rich in chemicals and minerals.

Photosynthesis: Process that plants use to turn sunlight, water, and carbon dioxide into food.

Port: Place where people and merchandise can enter or leave a country by boat.

Potable: Water that is suitable for drinking.

Sanitation: Maintaining clean, hygienic conditions that help prevent disease through the use of clean water and wastewater disposal.

Turbine: Device that converts the flow of a fluid (air, steam, water, or hot gases) into mechanical motion for generating electricity.

Water treatment: Purification process that makes water suitable for drinking and sanitation.

Life Below Sea Level in the Netherlands

Much of the Netherlands lies below sea level. The Netherlands is a country in northwestern Europe, which is sometimes incorrectly called Holland. For over 2000 years, the Dutch (people of the Netherlands) have fought to reclaim land from the sea. Nearly 30% of the land area of the Netherlands actually lies below sea level. The Netherlands three largest cities, Amsterdam, Rotterdam, and The Hague, all lie below sea level.

For centuries, the Dutch have constructed dikes and levees to hold back the sea. Dikes and levees are walls or embankments that hold back water. Traditionally, dykes and levees were made of earth and stone, but concrete is often used today. Once the dykes and levees were in place, the seawater evaporated or is pumped out. Fertile, flat plains are left behind. Lands that have been reclaimed from the sea are called polders. Beginning in the thirteenth century, the Dutch started using windmills to pump water back out to sea. Today, an elaborate system of electric and diesel pumps keeps much of the Netherlands dry.

In 1287 the Dutch dikes collapsed, flooding much of the country. The Dutch began constructing new dikes and levees to reclaim land that had once been dry. The Dutch continue this process today. In 1986 the Dutch created a new province, called Flevoland, by pumping water out of a large lake in the middle of the country.

The Dutch even used their system of dikes and levees to gain their independence. The Dutch were ruled by the Spanish crown for many years. Once the Dutch started to rebel, Spain sent troops to bring the area back under control. In 1574 the Dutch, led by William of Orange, intentionally flooded their country to destroy the Spanish army. Several battles later, the Dutch managed to force out the Spanish and gain their independence.

oceans cover nearly two thirds of Earth's surface, little was known about what lay below the surface until the twentieth century. The Mid-Atlantic Ridge, a mountain range that stretches the length of the Atlantic Ocean, was not discovered until 1952. The Marianas Trench, the deepest point in the Atlantic Ocean, was not discovered until 1951.

Several technological advances made underwater exploration possible. Humans cannot dive far underwater because of a lack of air, cold temperature, and the extreme pressure underwater. Submarines called bathyscaphes are required to go the deepest parts of the oceans. Bathyscaphes protect humans and equipment from the cold temperatures and extreme pressure of the ocean depths. The deepest point of the ocean is the Mariana Trench, at 35,802 feet (10,912 meters) below sea level, and almost 7 miles (11 kilometers) below the ocean's surface. At this depth, the water pressure is nearly 16,000 pounds (7,257 kilometers) per square inch.

Discoveries at the bottom of the ocean surprised scientists. Scientist had long assumed that all living organisms depended on sunlight for life. Plants require sunlight for photosynthesis, the process where light, water, and carbon dioxide are converted into food. Many animals then rely on plants as basis of their food chain (the relationship between plants and animals where one species is eaten by another). In the 1970s scientists found small communities of organisms living in complete darkness. These organisms depend on hydrothermal vents for survival. Powered by volcanic activity, hydrothermal vents are ocean-floor geysers (hot springs) that spew out a fluid rich in chemicals and minerals. Some of the fluids from hydrothermal vents are nearly 750°F (399°C). The animals that live near these vents rely on chemosynthesis for survival. Chemosynthesis is the use of chemicals, rather than sunlight, for the production of energy.

Irrigation

More freshwater is used for irrigation than for any other purpose. Irrigation usually involves pumping or diverting water from a river or lake that may lie far away. The water is then sprayed over crops.

More than half of all freshwater usage worldwide goes toward irrigation. In the United States, 40% of freshwater usage is for irrigating over 51 million acres of cropland. Over 130 million gallons of water are used for irrigation in the United States every day, enough to fill 144 Olympic-sized swimming pools. Farms in the western United States use most of this water.

Over the last century methods of irrigation have improved. As a result humans are growing more crops than ever before. This is a useful advancement given the world's growing population and increasing need for food. Irrigation is a necessity but the process has some negative impacts on the environment. First, only about half of all water used for irrigation is returned to the water supply. The rest evaporates. Second, irrigation can carry pesticides into the water supply. Pesticides are chemicals that are used to kill or repel insects, rodents, and other pests. These pesticides can build up in the water supply and harm ecosystems (communities of organisms and their environ-

A large flood control dike in Zeeland, the Netherlands, stands ready to hold back a surging sea. © *Dave Bartruff/Corbis. Reproduced by permission.*

ment). Third, areas that use seawater for irrigation run the risk of depositing too much salt onto the land. Salt is usually removed from water through a process called desalinization, yet some salt may remain in the water. Soil with accumulated salt prevents crops from growing. About 10% of soil in the world's irrigated land now contains too much salt. Fourth, irrigation can place heavy demands on a freshwater source, such as a river, and deny the river's resources to those downstream of the point where water is removed for irrigation. Because of irrigation and other overuse, the Colorado River in the western United States and Mexico no longer flows into the Gulf of California.

Water systems

Freshwater has two primary household uses: drinking and sanitation. Sanitation uses include showering, washing clothes, flushing the toilet, and washing dishes. These are important activities to control the spread of diseases. Clean drinking water is also important for preventing disease. Freshwater that comes directly from a river or lake is not usually clean enough to drink or use for sanitation. Water from a river or lake can contains disease-causing microorganisms. Water must be treated to remove these microorganisms. The treatment process occurs at a water treatment facility. The treatment process purifies water by removing microorganisms, dirt, and sediment (particles of sand, soil, and silt) from water. This process improves the purity of drinking water.

Once water has been used in the home the water then goes to a wastewater treatment facility. Wastewater treatment facilities remove most of the waste from water. Wastewater facilities usually do not purify the water well enough for it to be used as drinking water. Treated wastewater, called effluent, is often used for irrigating crops or cooling power plants. Effluent that is not used is returned to a lake or river.

Most people in the United States are accustomed to having clean water whenever it is needed. In many countries however, clean water is not available. Over 1 billion people do not have access to potable water (water safe to drink). About 2.4 billion people lack proper sanitation facilities. This lack of drinking water and poor hygiene causes the deaths of millions of people every year from cholera, the disease responsible for more deaths than any other worldwide. This problem could become worse as the population in developing countries increases.

Joining Waters: The Impact of Canals

Often there is a need to connect different bodies of water as a shortcut for ocean transportation. The construction of a canal is often the best solution. A canal is a man-made, deep, wide waterway through which ships may travel.

Canals are not simply trenches filled with water. Canal builders face challenges of linking water bodies that are at differing elevations, or of creating canals through land that is at differing elevations. In order to solve this problem, a series of gates and locks must be constructed along the course of the canal. A lock is an elevator for ships that raise or lower a ship to areas of the canal that have different water levels. Locks are an essential part of any canal.

A canal lock is not an elevator in the traditional sense however. A canal lock is basically a large area with gates at each end. At one end, the water level of the canal is at a higher level than it is at the other end. If a ship is going from an area of lower water level to an area of higher water level, then when the ship enters the lock, the gate behind it closes. Water is then pumped into the lock to raise the ship. When the water level inside the lock is at the same level as the higher water level in the canal, then the front gate opens and the ship continues its journey on the canal. If a ship is going from an area of higher water level in the canal to an area of lower water level, then the process works in reverse. Once the ship enters the lock, water is pumped out to lower the water level inside the lock to match the lower level on the other side. Once the water level is the same, the gate opens and the ship continues.

One of the greatest engineering marvels of human history was the construction of the Panama Canal that links the Atlantic and Pacific Oceans. The canal through Central America saves ships going between the Atlantic and Pacific Oceans 8,000 miles (12,875 kilometers) in each direction. The construction project proved to be immense and began in 1880 with the canal opening 34 years later in 1914. France and the United States spent nearly $640 million on the project, and 30,000 lives were lost during its construction, mostly to mosquito-borne diseases and construction accidents.

Trade and transportation

Ships began to replace their steam engines with diesel in the twentieth century. A diesel engine burns oil products to create the energy needed to turn a ship's propellers. In the 1950s scientists developed nuclear powered ships and submarines that could remain at sea for months without refueling. Due to environmental concerns and cost, nuclear power is only used on military vessels. The ability of a submarine to remain underwater for months at a time is a great military advantage.

For centuries shipping cargo over the oceans was cheaper than shipping over land. Shipping by boat has become even cheaper in the modern world. Large ships that could travel faster and carry more cargo led to an expansion of trade. As shipping costs decreased, the cost of products went down. Today, nearly 90% of the weight of all cargo is shipped by boat.

Travel

During the nineteenth century steam-powered ships made travel more popular. A steamship could cross an ocean in a matter of days compared to weeks for a sailboat. Passenger ships carried tourists and immigrants from continent to continent. By the 1950s and 1960s air travel had replaced ships as the primary form of ocean transportation. The passenger ship industry responded by making their ships a vacation instead of simply transportation. Millions of people take cruises to exotic locales every year.

Around the world, many people visit bodies of water. The shores of rivers, lakes, and oceans are favorite places for vacations. Venice, Italy, a city built upon canals, is one of the world's most popular tourist destinations. In Venice, the canals are the city's roadways. Instead of cars, busses, and taxis, and ambulances, people use boats for transportation.

Sometimes water makes travel more difficult. To cross the English Channel, a narrow body of water between England and France, people used to rely on ferries. Ferries are large boats that transport people, cars, and trucks. Frequent storms often delayed ferry travel. In 1994 a tunnel opened that runs beneath the channel seafloor. The Channel Tunnel (or Chunnel) allows trains to rapidly transport cars and people between France and England in any weather.

Hydroelectric power

Humans have learned to harness the energy of river water and use it to generate electricity, called hydroelectric power. Hydroelectric power is electricity generated by an electric power plant whose turbines (devices that converts the flow of a fluid into mechanical motion) are driven by falling water. About 10% of the electric power generated in the United States comes from hydroelectric power.

Hydroelectric power production requires the construction of a dam. A dam is a barrier that holds back the water on a river, forming a lake called a reservoir. The water from the reservoir is released through gates in the dam. The water turns turbines as it flows rapidly through the dam. The turbine turns generators, or machines that produce electricity. The water then comes out the other side of the dam and flows downriver.

Religion and popular culture

Because water is necessary for life, many of the world's religions use water in their rituals. Hindus believe the waters of the Ganges River in India are sacred. Christians use water for baptisms. Muslims bathe their feet before entering a mosque. In Japan Shinto shrines feature a tsukubai, a large bowl of water for followers to wash their mouths and hands before entering.

Water is also part of popular culture. The main ingredient in all popular soft drinks is water. Drinks brewed in water, such as coffee and tea, are favored around the world. The Japanese, Chinese, and several indigenous cultures developed special ceremonies for drinking tea. In Europe and the United States coffee shops and cafes are popular gathering places. Many gathering places and public parks feature fountains as works of art and areas for reflection. Beaches and other waterways are popular settings for educational and entertaining books, movies, and television programs. The "Jaws" series of books and movies in the 1970s and 1980s created intense public interest and misconceptions about sharks, most notably the myth that sharks seek out people to kill for food.

Joseph Hyder

For More Information

Books

Sorrenti, Francesca, and Shibuya, Marisha, eds. *Water Culture.* New York: Trolley, 2003.

Websites

"Drinking Water for Kids: Water Treatment Cycle." *EPA for Kids.* http://www.epa.gov/OGWDW/kids/treat.html (accessed on August 27, 2004).

"Human Settlements on the Coast: The Ever More Popular Coasts." *United Nations Atlas of the Oceans.* http://www.oceansatlas.org/servlet/CDSServlet?status=ND0xODc3Jjc9ZW4mNjE9KiY2NT1rb3M¯ (accessed on August 27, 2004).

"Introduction to Hydroelectric Power." *National Renewable Energy Laboratory.* http://www.nrel.gov/clean_energy/hydroelectric_power.html (accessed on August 27, 2004).

"NRCS Irrigation." *United States Department of Agriculture: National Resources Conservation Service.* http://www.wcc.nrcs.usda.gov/nrcsirrig/ (accessed on August 27, 2004).

"Transportation and Telecommunications." *United Nations Atlas of the Oceans.* http://www.oceansatlas.org/servlet/CDSServlet?status=ND0xODU1Jjc9ZW4mNjE9KiY2NT1rb3M⁻ (accessed on August 27, 2004).

"U.N. Says Water, Sanitation Still Sorely Lacking in Developing World." *U.S. Water News Online* (January 2001). http://www.uswaternews.com/archives/arcglobal/1unsay1.html (accessed on August 27, 2004).

"Wastewater Management." *Environmental Protection Agency.* http://www.epa.gov/owm/ (accessed on August 27, 2004).

"Water Library-Culture. 2003-The International Year of Freshwater."*UNESCO* http://www.wateryear2003.org/en/ev.php-URL_ID=5095&URL_DO=DO_TOPIC&URL_SECTION=201.html (accessed on August 27, 2004).

Where to Learn More

Books

Barry, Roger, et. al. *Atmosphere, Weather, and Climate.* 8th ed. New York: Routledge, 2003.

Bauer, K. Jack. *A Maritime History of the United States: The Role of America's Seas and Waterways.* Columbia: University of South Carolina Press, 1988.

Berger, Melvin, and Berger, Gilda. *What Makes an Ocean Wave?: Questions and Answers About Oceans and Ocean Life.* New York: Scholastic Reference, 2001.

Birnie, Patricia W., and Alan E. Boyle. *International Law and the Environment.* New York: Oxford University Press, 2002.

Burroughs, William, ed. *Climate: Into the 21st Century.* New York: Cambridge University Press, 2003.

Bush, Mark B. *Ecology of a Changing Planet.* Upper Saddle River, NJ: Prentice Hall, 1997.

Byatt, Andrew, et al. *Blue Planet.* London: DK Publishing, 2002.

Cousteau, Jacques. *Jacques Cousteau: The Ocean World.* New York: Harry N. Abrams, 1985.

Cousteau, Jacques-Yves. *The Living Sea.* New York: HarperCollins, 1963.

Cronkite, Walter. *Around America: A Tour of Our Magnificent Coastline.* New York: W. W. Norton, 2001.

Cunningham, William P., and Barbara Woodworth Saigo. *Environmental Science: A Global Concern.* Boston: WCB/McGraw-Hill, 1999.

Davenport, John, et al. *Aquaculture: The Ecological Issues.* Malden, MA: Blackwell Publishers, 2003.

Day, John A., et al. *Peterson First Guide to Clouds and Weather.* Boston: Houghton Mifflin, 1999.

Doris, Helen. *Marine Biology (Real Kids, Real Science).* New York: Thames & Hudson, 1999.

Earle, Sylvia. *Atlas of the Ocean: The Deep Frontier (National Geographic).* Washington, DC: National Geographic, 2001.

Farndon, John. *Water (Science Experiments).* Salt Lake City, UT: Benchmark Books, 2000.

Garrison, Tom. *Oceanography.* 3rd ed. New York: Wadsworth, 1999.

Gemmell, Kathy, et al. *Storms and Hurricanes.* Tulsa, OK: E.D.C. Publishing, 1996.

Gleick, Peter H. *The World's Water 2002–2003: The Biennial Report on Freshwater Resources.* Washington, DC: Island Press, 2003.

Graham, Ian. *Water: A Resource Our World Depends On.* Burlington, MA: Heinemann, 2004.

Graves, Don. *The Oceans: A Book of Questions and Answers.* New York: Wiley, 1989.

Gross, Grant M. *Oceanography: A View of the Earth.* 5th ed. Englewood Cliffs, NJ: Prentice-Hall, 1990.

Haslett, Simon K. *Coastal Systems.* New York: Routledge, 2000.

Josephs, David. *Lakes, Ponds, and Temporary Pools.* New York: Franklin Watts, 2000.

Kennett, James. *Marine Geology.* Upper Saddle River, NJ: Prentice-Hall, 1981.

Kozloff, Eugene. *Invertebrates.* Philadelphia: Saunders College Publishing, 1990.

Levinton, Jeffrey S. *Marine Biology: Function, Biodiversity, Ecology.* 2nd ed. New York: Oxford University Press, 2001.

Marek, Lee, and Lynn Brunelle. *Soakin' Science.* Toronto: Somerville House, 2000.

Marx, Robert F. *The Underwater Dig: An Introduction to Marine Archaeology.* 2nd ed. Oakland, CA: Pisces Books, 1990.

McLeish, Ewan. *Wetlands.* New York: Thomson Learning, 1996.

McManners, Hugh. *Water Sports: An Outdoor Adventure Handbook.* New York: DK Publishers, 1997.

McPhee, John. *The Control of Nature.* New York: Farrar, Straus and Giroux, 1989.

Morgan, Sally, and Pauline Lalor. *Ocean Life.* New York: PRC Publishing Ltd., 2000.

National Audubon Society. *National Audubon Society Pocket Guide to Clouds and Storms.* New York: Knopf, 1995.

Pielou, E.C. *A Naturalist's Guide to the Arctic.* Chicago: University of Chicago Press, 1995.

Pipkin, Bernard W. *Geology and the Environment.* St. Paul, MN: West Publishing Company, 1994.

Postel, Sandra, and Brian Richter. *Rivers for Life: Managing Water for People and Nature.* Washington, DC: Island Press, 2003.

Raven, Peter H., Linda R. Berg, and George B. Johnson. *Environment.* 2nd ed. Fort Worth, TX: Saunders College Publishing, 1998.

Rowland-Entwistle, Theodore. *Rivers and Lakes.* Morristown, NJ: Silver Burdett Press, 1987.

Sayre, April Pulley. *Lake and Pond.* New York: Twenty-First Century Books, 1996.

Sayre, April Pulley. *River and Stream.* New York: Twenty-First Century Books, 1996.

Sayre, April Pulley. *Wetland.* New York: Twenty-First Century Books, 1996.

Steele, Philip W. *Changing Coastlines (Earth's Changing Landscape).* Minneapolis: Smart Apple Media, 2004.

Sunk! Exploring Underwater Archaeology. Minneapolis: Runestone Press, 1994.

Taylor, Leighton. *Aquariums: Windows to Nature.* New York: Prentice Hall, 1993.

U.S. Department of the Interior. *Wetlands and Groundwater in the U.S.* Washington, DC: Library of Congress, 1994.

U.S. Environmental Protection Agency. *The Water Sourcebooks: K-12.* Washington, DC: USEPA, 2000.

Vasquez, Tim. *Weather Forecasting Handbook.* 5th ed. Austin, TX: Weather Graphics Technologies, 2002.

Websites

"About Ecology." *Ecology.com.* http://www.ecology.com (accessed on October 7, 2004).

"About Water Levels, Tides and Currents." *NOAA/NOS Center for Operational Oceanographic Products and Services* http://www.co-ops.nos.noaa.gov/about2.html (accessed on October 7, 2004).

"Boston Museum of Science. Water on the Move." *Oceans Alive.* http://www.mos.org/oceans/motion/index.html (accessed on October 7, 2004).

"Chapter 8a. Physical Properties of Water." *Physical-Geography.net.* http://www.physicalgeography.net/fundamentals/8a.html (accessed on October 7, 2004).

"Chemistry Tutorial. The Chemistry of Water." *Biology Project. University of Arizona.* http://www.biology.arizona.edu/biochemistry/tutorials/chemistry/page3.html (accessed on October 7, 2004).

"Conservation: Fresh Water." *National Geographic.com.* http://magma.nationalgeographic.com/education/gaw/frwater (accessed on October 7, 2004).

"The Hydrologic Cycle: Online Meteorology Guide." *WW2010 Department of Atmospheric Sciences. University of Illinois at Urbana-Champagne.* http://ww2010.atmos.uiuc.edu/(Gh)/guides/mtr/hyd/home.rxml (accessed on October 7, 2004).

"Meteorology, the Online Guides." *Weather World 2010, University of Illinois at Urbana-Champagne Department of Atmospheric Sciences.*http://ww2010.atmos.uiuc.edu/(Gh)/guides/mtr/home.rxml (accessed on October 7, 2004).

"National Weather Service Climate Prediction Center." National Oceanic and Atmospheric Administration. http://www.cpc.ncep.noaa.gov/ (accessed on October 7, 2004).

"National Weather Service." *National Oceanic and Atmospheric Administration.* http://www.nws.noaa.gov/ (accessed on October 7, 2004).

"National Weather Service, Tropical Prediction Center." *National Hurricane Center.* http://www.nhc.noaa.gov (accessed on October 7, 2004).

"NOAA National Ocean Service. Marine Navigation." *National Oceanic and Atmospheric Administration.* http://oceanservice.noaa.gov/topics/navops/marinenav/welcome.html (accessed on October 7, 2004).

"An Ocean of Sound." *Oceanlink.* http://oceanlink.island.net/oinfo/acoustics/acoustics.html (accessed on October 7, 2004).

Shaner, Stephen W. "A Brief History of Marine Biology and Oceanography." *University of California Extension Center for*

Media and Independent Learning. http://www.meer.org/mbhist.htm (accessed on October 7, 2004).

"This Dynamic Earth: The Story of Plate Tectonics." *U.S. Geological Survey (USGS).* http://pubs.usgs.gov/publications/text/dynamic.html (accessed on October 7, 2004).

U.S. Environmental Protection Agency. "How to Conserve Water and Use It Effectively." *Cleaner Water Through Conservation.* http://www.epa.gov/watrhome/you/chap3.html (accessed on October 7, 2004).

U.S. Geological Survey. "Water Basics." *Water Science for Schools.* http://ga.water.usgs.gov/edu/mwater.html (accessed on October 7, 2004).

"Water Resources of the United States." *U.S. Geological Survey.* http://water.usgs.gov (accessed on October 7, 2004).

Index

Italic type indicates volume number; **boldface** *indicates main entries and their page numbers; illustrations are marked by (ill.).*

Amoeba, *1:* 84
Amsterdam, *2:* 370
Amundsen, Roald, *1:* 170
Amur River, *1:* 129
Anadromous fish, *1:* 103
Anasazi people, *2:* 366; *3:* 448
Ancient world, inventions and discoveries in, *2:* 364–65
Andes Mountains, *1:* 52
Aneroid barometer, *1:* 195 (ill.)
Angel Falls, *1:* 138
Angler fish, *1:* 47
Animal Feeding Operations (AFOS), *2:* 228
Animals
    in arid climates, *2:* 352–54
    in estuaries, *1:* 143–44
    impact of sound on marine, *2:* 273
    in lakes and ponds, *1:* 107–8, 124
    in rivers and streams, *1:* 103–4
    in the seas, *2:* 339
    on the tundra, *1:* 156–57
Annapolis Royal (Nova Scotia), *2:* 223
Annelida (segmented worms), *1:* 69
Anoxia, *2:* 355
Antarctic Circumpolar Current (ACC), *1:* 37
Antarctic ice sheet, *1:* 160, 169
Antarctic melting, *3:* 406
Antarctica, *1:* 159, 168, 169–70
Anticyclones, *1:* 196
Antikythera Mechanism, *2:* 364
Appalachian Mountains, acid deposition in, *3:* 380
Aquaculture, *2:* **279–83**
    drawbacks to, *2:* 280, 282–83
    economics of, *2:* 282–83
Aquaculture center, *2:* 282 (ill.)
Aqualung, *2:* 357
Aquarists, *2:* 234
Aquariums, *2:* **233–37**
    development of modern, *2:* 234–36

in the home, *2:* 235, 235 (ill.)
Aquatic life, *1:* 100
Aqueducts, *1:* 98; *2:* **199–203,** 202 (ill.), 205, 299, 366–67
    ancient, *2:* 199–200
    innovations in technology, *2:* 200–202
    Roman, *2:* 201, 201 (ill.)
    today, *2:* 203
Aquifers, *2:* 243, 287–88, 289; *3:* 422
    confined, *1:* 112
    defined, *1:* 1, 109–12, 113
    fossil, *3:* 457
    as source of freshwater, *3:* 457
Arabian Desert, *1:* 175
Arabian Sea, *1:* 183
Aral Sea, *1:* 116, 117–18
Arbitration, *3:* 492
Arch dams, *2:* 204
Archaeology
    exploring underwater sites in, *2:* 251–54
    marine, *2:* 251–54
Archimedes, *1:* 18, 19; *2:* 342, 365
Arctic Circle, *1:* 155
Arctic ice, *1:* 155, 156
Arctic ice caps, *1:* 38, 155, 156
Arctic Islands, *1:* 156
Arctic melting, *3:* 406, 406 (ill.)
Arctic Ocean, *1:* 156
Arctic region, *1:* **155–58**
    geography of, *1:* 156
    humans in, *1:* 157–58
Arid climates, *2:* **351–54**
    animals in, *2:* 352–54
    defined, *2:* 351
    plants surviving in, *2:* 351–52
Arid deserts, *1:* 176
Aristotle, *1:* 87; *2:* 256
Arkansas River, *1:* 129, 132, 133
Arno River, flooding of, *3:* 398
Arsenic, *3:* 387, 460
Arsenic antimony, *3:* 459

Art, acid rain and, *3:* 378, 379 (ill.)
Artesian Basin, *3:* 457
Artesian flow, *1:* 112
Artesian wells, *2:* 288
Arthropods, *1:* 69, 72–73
Artificial reefs, *1:* 32, 32 (ill.)
Asia
    rivers in, *1:* 128–29
    steppe in, *1:* 175
Asian monsoon, *1:* 183, 185–86
Aswan High Dam, *2:* 208, 208 (ill.), 209
Atacama Desert, water shortage in, *3:* 484
Athens, Greece, *2:* 368
Atlantic bottlenose dolphins, *1:* 75
Atlantic City, New Jersey, *3:* 385
Atlantic salmon, survival of, *3:* 472
Atmosphere, *1:* 173
Atmospheric chemistry, *1:* 8
Atmospheric pressure, *1:* 193, 194, 196
Atoms, *1:* 2, 8, 9
Australia
    Outback in, *1:* 175
    rivers in, *1:* 129
Autecology, *2:* 239
Autonomous underwater vehicles (AUVs), *2:* 262, 263, 356
Autotrophs, *2:* 240, 241
Avalanche forecasting, *1:* 161
Aviation meteorologists, *1:* 180

B

Backstroke, *2:* 342
Bacteria, *2:* 297
Bahamas, *1:* 58, 59
Bahamian platform, *1:* 59
Baikal epischura crustacean, *2:* 249
Bald maples, *1:* 148
Baleen, *1:* 76; *2:* 329
Baleen whales, *1:* 75, 76
Bali, *1:* 58
Ballast water, *3:* 443–44

Cumuliform clouds, 1: 178
Cumulonimbus clouds, 1: 179, 182, 188
Cumulus clouds, 1: 179, 182
Curation, 2: 254
Currents. See Air currents; Ocean currents
Cuttle fish, 1: 72
Cuyahoga River, 1: 121
Cyanide, 3: 417
Cyanobacteria, 1: 106
Cyclones, 1: 97, 189, 196; 2: 335
    mid-latitude, 1: 192
    tropical, 1: 189–92

D

Daldsterben, 3: 382
Dams and reservoirs, 1: 13, 16, 113, 127; 2: **203–9,** 218, 243, 321, 374. *See also* specific dams and reservoirs
    arch, 2: 204
    buttress, 2: 204
    to control flood waters, 3: 403
    embankment, 2: 204
    gravity, 2: 204
    in history, 2: 204–5
    modern, 2: 206
    petroleum, 2: 301
Dangerous waters, 2: **333–40**
Danube River, 1: 129
Daphnia, 1: 84
Darling River, 1: 129
Darwin, Charles, 1: 57, 60; 2: 256
DDT, 3: 441
De Orellana, Francisco, 1: 130
De Soto, Hernando, 1: 133
Dead Sea, 1: 10, 116, 119
Decomposers, 2: 240
Decompression sickness, 2: 347
Deep ocean currents, 1: 38
Deep ocean drilling, 2: 262
Deep ocean sampling device, 2: 267 (ill.)
Deep Sea Drilling Project (DSDP), 2: 262

Deep-sea fishing, 2: 324, 349
Deep-sea submersibles, 2: 359
Deforestation, 1: 130; 3: 393, 468
Delaware River, 1: 131
Deltas, 1: 16, **95–100,** 96 (ill.)
    Brahmaputra, 1: 97
    defined, 1: 13, 29
    formation of, 1: 95–96
    Ganges, 1: 97, 185
    humans and, 1: 98–99
    life in, 1: 99–100
    Mississippi, 1: 56, 93, 96 (ill.), 97, 133
    Nile, 1: 98; 2: 271 (ill.)
    structure of, 1: 96
    types of, 1: 96–98
Density, 1: 2
Dentricles, 1: 45
Denver, Colorado, 2: 244
Deposition, 1: 136–38; 2: 363. *See also* Acid deposition
    dry, 3: 377
    wet, 3: 377
Depositional coastlines, 1: 30–32
Desalination, 2: **210–12,** 211 (ill.), 309 (ill.), 372; 3: 496, 504
    manipulated, 2: 210
    natural, 2: 210
Desert oases, 1: 116
Desert Paintbrush, 2: 352
Desert Sand Verbena, 2: 352
Desertification, 3: **390–94**
    causes of, 3: 393
    halting, 3: 393–94
    impact of, on environment, 3: 392 (ill.), 392–93
Deserts
    arid, 1: 176
    defined, 3: 390
    rainshadow, 3: 393
Developed nations, water use in, 3: 455
Dew, 2: 354
Diadromous fish, 1: 103
Diamonds, 2: 292
Diatoms, 1: 24, 102

Dichlorodiphenyl trichloroethane (DDT), 3: 441
Diesel-powered ships, 2: 311
Dikes, 2: 370, 371 (ill.)
Dimethyl mercury in water pollution, 3: 460
Dinoflagellates, 1: 83, 106; 2: 258
Dipolar molecule, 1: 8
Dipolarity, 1: 9
Discharge zones, 1: 109; 2: 245
Dissolution, 1: 137
Distillation
    multistage, 2: 212
    solar, 2: 211
Distributaries, 1: 96
Divergent plates, 1: 50
Diversion hydropower facilities, 2: 216
Diving, 2: 355–56
Diving bell, 2: 355
Diving suits, 2: 355
Doctors Without Borders, 3: 487
Doctrines, 3: 499
Dodo, 3: 472
Dolphins, 1: 75, 76 (ill.); 2: 257
    Atlantic bottlenose, 1: 75
    Pacific white-sided, 1: 75
Downdrafts, 1: 188
Downwellings, 1: 38–39
Dowsing, 2: 289
Drag, 1: 102
Dragonflies, 1: 107, 148
Drainage divides, 1: 132
Drainage patterns, 1: 133–34
Dredges, 2: 261
Dredging, 2: 221, 254, 314–15
Drilled wells, 2: 289
Drinking water, 2: 319–20
Drip irrigation, 2: 276–77
Driven wells, 2: 289
Drogues, 2: 268
Droughts, 1: 193; 3: 445
Dry deposition, 3: 377
Dry season, 1: 185
Ducks, 1: 148
Duckweed, 1: 106, 148

Dugongs, *1:* 78
Dustbowl, *3:* 391, 391 (ill.)
Dwarf seahorse, *3:* 418
Dwarf treefrog, *1:* 124 (ill.)
Dynamic equilibrium, *1:* 13, 15–16
Dynamite fishing, *3:* 481
Dysentery, *3:* 448

E

Earth
   highest point on, *1:* 49
   lowest point on, *1:* 49
   water budget of, *1:* 12–13, 163–64
   water on, *1:* 1, 5, 8, 17; *3:* 446–47
Earthworm, *1:* 71
East Antarctica, *1:* 169
East Australian Current, *1:* 36, 64
Easterlies, *1:* 192
Easterly jet streams, *2:* 231
Ebro River, *1:* 129
Echinoderms, *1:* 68, 69–70, 73–74, 84; *2:* 256
Echolocation, *1:* 75, 76
Echosounders, *1:* 50, 51
Ecological damages of oil spills, *3:* 434
Ecological pyramid, *2:* 241
Ecological system, *2:* 238
Ecologist
   community, *2:* 238
   ecosystem, *2:* 238
   population, *2:* 238
Ecology, *1:* 80, 113, 149; *2:* **237–42,** 255; *3:* 449
   important concepts in, *2:* 239–40
   as part of biological sciences, *2:* 237–38
   subdivisions of, *2:* 239
Economic uses of groundwater, *2:* **287–91**
Ecosystem ecologist, *2:* 238
Ecosystems, *1:* 55; *2:* 238, 239–40
   coastal, *1:* 31, 31 (ill.)
   energy in, *2:* 241

Ecotourism on the ocean, *2:* 324
Ectotherms, *1:* 24, 25–26, 43
Eddies, *1:* 137
Ederle, Gertrude Caroline, *2:* 348, 348 (ill.)
Edwards Aquifer, *1:* 110
Eelgrass, *1:* 143, 144
Eels, *1:* 47
Effluent, *2:* 372
Egrets, *1:* 150
Egypt
   ancient, *2:* 363, 363 (ill.)
   Aswan High Dam in, *2:* 208, 208 (ill.), 209
   shipping in ancient, *2:* 310
Ekofisk blowout, *3:* 432
El Niño, *1:* **39–43,** 41 (ill.); *2:* 268
   discovery of, *1:* 40–41
   effects of, *1:* 41–42
El Niño Southern Oscillation (ENSO), *1:* 39, 42
Elbe River, *1:* 129
Electromagnetic spectrum, *1:* 18
Electron shells, *1:* 2
Electrons, *1:* 2, 8–9
Elements, *1:* 8
Elephant Island, *1:* 170
Embankment dams, *2:* 204
Emissions allowances, *3:* 382
Endangered species
   heightened need for protection of, *3:* 473–75
   laws on, *3:* **471–76**
   whales as, *2:* 331
Endangered Species Act (1973), *1:* 78; *3:* 474, 506
Endangered Species Conservation Act (1969), *3:* 472, 473
Endangered Species Protection Act (1966), *3:* 472–73
Endothermic process, *1:* 18
Endotherms, *1:* 25–26
Endurance (ship), *1:* 170, 171 (ill.)
Energy Policy Act (1992), *2:* 307

English Channel, *2:* 348, 348 (ill.), 374
Environment, protecting, *2:* 324
Environmental Protection Agency, U.S. (EPA), *3:* 439, 505, 505 (ill.)
   acid rain and, *3:* 379, 382
   landfills and, *3:* 422
   pesticide contamination and, *3:* 413
   survey of acid deposition, *3:* 380
   water pollution and, *3:* 462
   water quality monitoring, *3:* 418
Epilimnion, *1:* 104
Epipelagic zone, *1:* 66–67, 68
Equator, *1:* 20
Equatorial current, *1:* 40
Erie Canal, *1:* 121; *2:* 312
Erosion, *1:* 56, 136–38
   beach, *3:* 383–87, 384 (ill.)
   coastal, *2:* 209
   development and, *3:* 385–86
   problems caused by, *3:* 384–85
Erosional coastlines, *1:* 32–33
Erosional features, *1:* 161
Escherichia coli, *2:* 297; *3:* 464
Eskimo, *1:* 157–58
Estuaries, *1:* 29, 31, **141–47;** *2:* 229
   animal life in, *1:* 143–44
   danger to, *1:* 145–46
   general structure of, *1:* 141–42
   importance of, *1:* 145
   plant life in, *1:* 143, 143 (ill.)
Estuaries Environmental Studies Lab, *1:* 146 (ill.)
Euphausids, *1:* 69, 82, 84, 85
Euphotic zone, *1:* 118
Euphrates River, *1:* 127, 129; *2:* 205
Europe, rivers in, *1:* 129
European Union, Kyoto Treaty and, *3:* 408

Groundwater discharge, *1:* 109

Groundwater discharge lakes, *1:* 122

Groundwater flow, *1:* 15

Groundwater formation, *1:* 108–12

Groundwater rights, *3:* 498–501

Grouper, *1:* 144

Groynes, *3:* 385, 386

Guam, *1:* 54, 60

Gulf eutrophication, *3:* 396

Gulf of Ababa, *1:* 119

Gulf of Mexico, *1:* 93; *3:* 396

Gulf Stream, *1:* 35–36, 38, 55, 191–92

Gulf War (1991), oil spill during, *3:* 432

Gullies, *1:* 132

Guyots, *1:* 57

Gymnodinium breve, *1:* 83

Gypsum, *1:* 138; *2:* 296; *3:* 484

Gyres, *1:* 37– 38

H

Habitat loss and species extinction, *3:* 414–18

Hadley cells, *1:* 174

Haeckel, Ernst, *2:* 237

Hagfish, *1:* 44–45

The Hague, *2:* 370

Hail, *1:* 182

Halibut, *1:* 144

Halite, *2:* 308–9

Halocarbons as greenhouse gas, *3:* 407

Halocline, *1:* 142

Halogens as greenhouse gas, *3:* 407

Hand-dug wells, *2:* 288, 290

Hanging valley, *1:* 161

Harbors. *See* Ports and harbors

Hares, *1:* 157

Harrison, John, *2:* 338

Hawaiian Islands, *1:* 56, 57, 59, 60

Hawaiian monk seal, *1:* 78

Hawaiian-Emperor seamount chain, *1:* 57

Hawaiian-Emperor volcanoes, *1:* 57

Headwater streams, *1:* 126

Heart of Darkness (Conrad), *1:* 128

Heavy metals, *3:* 421
  bioaccumulation of, *3:* 387–90
  as non-source pollutants, *3:* 426
  in sediment contamination, *3:* 441

Heezen, Bruce, *1:* 51

Henley, Don, *1:* 125

Herbivores, *2:* 241

Herodotus, *1:* 95; *2:* 208, 265

Herons, *1:* 107, 144, 148, 150

Hetch-Hetchy reservoir, debate over, *3:* 451, 451 (ill.)

Heterotrophs, *2:* 240

Heyerdahl, Thor, *2:* 364

High seas, *3:* 476

High-pressure systems, *1:* 196

Himalayan Mountains, *1:* 50, 97, 126, 129, 183, 185

Hindus, *1:* 129; *2:* 375

Hispanola, *1:* 55

Historical groundwater use, *2:* 289–90

Hohokam, *2:* 366

Holdfasts, *1:* 62, 64, 102

Holoplankton, *1:* 84

Homeostasis, *2:* 240

Homer, *2:* 333, 361–62

Hong Kong, ports of, *2:* 221, 221 (ill.)

Honolulu, Hawaii, *3:* 385

Hooker Chemical Company, *3:* 420

Hoover Dam, *2:* 209, 214, 217, 217 (ill.), 218, 353 (ill.); *3:* 450

Horseshoe Falls, *2:* 345

Hot spot, *1:* 56, 57

Hot springs, *2:* 344, 368

Hot Springs, Arkansas, *2:* 345

Houseboats, *2:* 343

Hovercraft, *2:* 328

Hualalai, *1:* 57

Huang He River, *1:* 128

Hudson River, *1:* 130

Human body, water in, *1:* 1, 16

Humans, in Arctic, *1:* 157–58

Humboldt, Alexander von, *2:* 256

Hurricanes, *1:* 38, 89, 186, 189; *2:* 335–37
  Andrew, *1:* 191
  categories, *2:* 336
  eye of, *1:* 191; *2:* 335
  Isabel, *1:* 36, 36 (ill.)
  Mitch, *1:* 190 (ill.)
  names of, *1:* 192
  storm surge from, *3:* 398
  strength of, *1:* 191

Hutchinson, George Evelyn, *2:* 247

Hydrocarbons, *2:* 261, 300–301, 305; *3:* 430

Hydroelectric technology, *2:* 214–15, 374

Hydroelectricity, *1:* 113

Hydrofoil, *2:* 328

Hydrogen atoms, *1:* 2

Hydrogen bonds, *1:* 4, 5, 9, 10, 20

Hydrogeologic maps, *2:* 245

Hydrogeologists, *1:* 113; *2:* 242

Hydrogeology, *2:* 242–46

Hydrologic cycle, *1:* 12–17, 14 (ill.), 126, 136, 173; *2:* 210; *3:* 446

Hydrologic potential, *2:* 205

Hydrologists, *1:* 113, 136; *2:* 242

Hydrology, *2:* 242–46

Hydrophilic molecules, *1:* 2, 4

Hydrophobic molecules, *1:* 2, 4

Hydropower, *2:* 205, 206, 212–19
  benefits and drawbacks of, *2:* 218
  future of, *2:* 218
  in history, *2:* 213–14
  sizes of facilities, *2:* 217–18
  types of facilities, *2:* 215

Hydrosphere, *1:* 8; *2:* 238

Hydrothermal deposits, *2:* 293–94

moon, *1:* 71 (ill.)
water in, *1:* 1, 16
Jet skis, *2:* 342, 343
Jet stream, *1:* 196
Jetties, *1:* 30; *2:* 222
John, Abbot of Wallingford, *1:* 86
Johnstown (PA), flood damage in, *3:* 400
Joint Oceanographic Institution for Deep Earth Sampling (JOIDES), *2:* 262
Joola (ferry), *2:* 328
Jurassic Period, *1:* 12

K

Kahoolawe, *1:* 57
Kalahari Desert, *1:* 175; *3:* 457
Karst, *1:* 110, 122; *3:* 484
Kauai, *1:* 15, 57
Kayaking, *2:* 343–44
Kazakhstan, *1:* 117
Keel, *2:* 342
Keiko, the killer whale, *1:* 77, 78 (ill.)
Kelp, *1:* **61–65,** 65 (ill.); *2:* 257, 280
Kelp forests, *2:* 240
Kelvin, Lord, *1:* 87
Kerguelan Islands, *1:* 56
Kesterson National Wildlife Refuge, *3:* 417, 418
Kettle pond, *1:* 163
Khartoum, *1:* 128
Kilauea, *1:* 57, 58 (ill.)
Kilimanjaro, *1:* 159
Kitty Hawk, North Carolina, *3:* 385
Klettvik Bay, *1:* 77
Koi, *2:* 233
Kon-Tiki (raft), *2:* 364
Krill, *1:* 25 (ill.), 84
Kudzu plant, *3:* 467
Kuroshio, *1:* 36, 38
Kyoto Treaty, *3:* 408

L

La Grande Dams, *2:* 207
La Rance (Brittany, France), *2:* 223

La Niña, *1:* **39–43;** *2:* 268
discovery of, *1:* 40–41
effects of, *1:* 41–42
Lagoons, *1:* 29, 56–57, 93, 141; *2:* 228
Lake Baikal, *1:* 119, 174 (ill.); *2:* 247, 249
Lake basins, *1:* 119–20, 122
Lake Erie, eutrophication of, *3:* 396
Lake Nasser, *2:* 208
Lake Okeechobee, *1:* 122
Lake Powell, *1:* 120 (ill.)
Lake St. Clair, *3:* 444
Lake systems, *2:* 311
Lake Tahoe, *1:* 120
Lakes, *1:* **113–23**
acid deposition and, *3:* 379–80
biology of, *1:* 116, 118–19
chemistry of, *1:* 115–16
difference between pond and, *1:* 123
dying, *1:* 117–18
eutrophic, *1:* 118–19
freshwater, *1:* 113
glacial, *1:* 120–21
groundwater discharge, *1:* 122
life cycle of, *1:* 113–14
life in, *1:* 104–8
monomictic/dimictic/poly- mictic, *1:* 115
saline, *1:* 115–16
volcanic, *1:* 120
Lampreys, *1:* 44–45, 45
Lanai, *1:* 57
Land bridges, *1:* 166
Land crabs, *1:* 149
Land reclamation, *1:* 99
Land snails, *1:* 149
Landfills, *3:* **422–25**
construction of, *3:* 423–24
defined, *3:* 423
monitoring of, *3:* 424–25
Laplace, Pierre Simon, *1:* 87
Larsen B ice shelf, *1:* 165, 166 (ill.)
Larval fish, *1:* 82

Las Vegas, Nevada
demand for water in, *3:* 412
water use in, *2:* 353; *3:* 437–38, 452
Layers of the ocean, *1:* **66–69**
Le Maire, Isaac, *2:* 334
Leachate, *3:* 422, 423
Lead, *2:* 292; *3:* 387, 459
effects of, *3:* 389
in sediment contamination, *3:* 441
Leatherneck turtles, *3:* 416 (ill.)
Lemmings, *1:* 157
Lena River, *1:* 129
Lentic waters, *1:* 101
Lenticels, *1:* 150
Lenticular altocumulus cloud, *1:* 181
Leopold, Aldo, *3:* 450
Lesser Antilles, *1:* 55
Levees, *1:* 96, 127, 133; *2:* 243, 370; 403
Lewis, Meriwether, *1:* 131
Light, *1:* 23–24
regulating sun, *1:* 173–74
ultraviolet, *1:* 8–9
Lighthouses, *3:* 385
Lightning, *1:* 186
Limestone, *1:* 58, 138; *2:* 296, 303; *3:* 484
Limnetic zone, *1:* 104, 118
Limnologists, *1:* 115, 118
Limnology, *1:* 113; *2:* **246–51**
biological, *2:* 249–50
chemical, *2:* 248–49
geological, *2:* 247
history of, *2:* 246–47
physical, *2:* 247–48
Limpets, *1:* 71, 103
Limpopo River, *1:* 128
Lindisfarne (Holy Island), *2:* 223
Liquids, *1:* 5, 18
Lithosphere, *1:* 119; *2:* 238
Lithospheric plates, *1:* 50
Littoral zone, *1:* 104
Liverworts, *1:* 102
Livestock industry, use of groundwater by, *2:* 291

Livingstone, David, *1:* 138
Lizards, *2:* 354
Lobsters, *1:* 83, 84
Lock, *2:* 313
Logging, *3:* 416–17
    clearcutting in, *3:* 417, 468
    impact on watersheds, *3:* 467
Loihi, *1:* 57
Long Island, New York, *1:* 58
Longshore currents, *1:* 93
Loons, *1:* 107
Los Angeles, California, water needs of, *3:* 452
Lost at sea, *2:* 338
Lotic waters, *1:* 101
Louisiana Purchase (1803), *2:* 312
Love Canal, *3:* 420, 420 (ill.)
Love, William, *3:* 420
Low-pressure centers, *1:* 196
Low-pressure systems, *1:* 196

M

Mackenzie River, *1:* 129
Macroalgae, *1:* 62
Macrocystis, *1:* 64
Macroplankton, *1:* 81–82
Madagascar, *1:* 58
Maelstrom, *2:* 333
Magellan, Ferdinand, *2:* 334
Magnesium, *1:* 24
Magnetometers, *2:* 253
Malacostracans, *1:* 72–73
Mammals, marine, *1:* 74–79
Mammatus clouds, *1:* 189
Manatees, *1:* 78, 150; *3:* 418, 473 (ill.)
Manganese, *2:* 261, 293
Manganese nodules, *2:* 293
Mangrove forests, *1:* 97, 99, 150
Mangrove swamps, *1:* 149–50
Mangroves, *2:* 280
Mantle, *1:* 71
Mapping the oceans, *2:* 357–59
Mariana Trench, *1:* 49; *2:* 356, 360, 370
Mariculture, *2:* 258, 279–80, 282–83

Marine animals, impact of sound on, *2:* 273
Marine archaeology, *2:* 251–55
Marine Biological Laboratory, *2:* 266
Marine biology, *2:* 255–59, 359–60
    history of, *2:* 256–57
    research areas in, *2:* 258
    types of organisms studied, *2:* 257
Marine geology, *1:* 48–49; *2:* 265, 268–69, 360–61
    geophysics and, *2:* 259–64
Marine geoscientists, *2:* 260
Marine invertebrates, *1:* 69–74
    Annelida, *1:* 70–71
    Arthropoda, *1:* 72–73
    Cnidaria, *1:* 70
    Echinodermata, *1:* 73–74
    Molluska, *1:* 71–72
    Porifera, *1:* 70
Marine Mammal Protection Act (1972), *3:* 473
Marine mammals, *1:* 74–79
    Carnivora, *1:* 76–77
    Cetacea, *1:* 75
    endangered, *1:* 78–79
    in military, *1:* 75
    Odontoceti, *1:* 75–76
Marine protection areas, *3:* 482
Marine science, *2:* 264
Marine sea otter, *1:* 78
Marine snails, *1:* 149
Marlin, *2:* 349
MARPOL 73/78, *3:* 483
Mars, water on, *1:* 3, 3 (ill.)
Marsh, *1:* 141
    freshwater, *1:* 147–49
    salt, *1:* 149
Marsh, George Perkins, *3:* 449
Marsh grasses, *1:* 149
Maryland crabs, effect of eutrophication on, *3:* 397
Maui, Hawaii, *1:* 57; *2:* 334 (ill.)
Mauna Loa, *1:* 57
Mayflies, *1:* 103, 107
Meandering streams, *1:* 134
Meanders, *1:* 134, 135

Meat processing industry, water uses by, *2:* 285–86
Mediterranean Sea, *1:* 119; *2:* 362
Medusa, *1:* 70
Mekong River, *1:* 129
Melting, *1:* 15, 18
Meniscus, *1:* 10
Merchant ships, types of, *2:* 316–17
Mercury, *2:* 249; *3:* 387
    effects of, *3:* 389
    in sediment contamination, *3:* 441
    in water pollution, *3:* 458, 459–60, 502
Meromictic lake, *1:* 115
Meroplankton, *1:* 84
Mesopelagic zone, *1:* 67–68
Mesoplankton, *1:* 82
Mesopotamia, *1:* 129
Mesotrophic lakes, *1:* 119
Metabolic rate, *1:* 24–25
Metabolism, *1:* 47
Metals, bioaccumulation of heavy, *3:* 387–90
Meteorologists, *1:* 180, 189, 193
Methane, *3:* 409
    as greenhouse gas, *3:* 407, 422
    landfills and, *3:* 424
Methylmercury, *3:* 388–89
Metula (ship), oil spills from, *3:* 431
Mexican monsoon, *1:* 183
Miami Beach, Florida, *3:* 385
Micro-hydropower plants, *2:* 217
Microplankton, *1:* 82
Microwaves, *2:* 270, 271–72
Mid-Atlantic Ridge, *1:* 50, 52; *2:* 360, 370
Middle East, rivers in, *1:* 129
Mid-latitude cyclones, *1:* 192
Mid-oceanic ridge, *1:* 52; *2:* 260
Mid-oceanic ridge volcanoes, *1:* 53
Milankovitch cycles, *1:* 164

Roman aqueducts, *2:* 201, 201
(ill.)
Roman Empire, power of, *2:*
315–16
Romans, *2:* 362
Rome, Italy, *2:* 368
Roosevelt, Franklin Delano, *2:*
213, 216; *3:* 449
Roosevelt, Theodore, *3:* 449
Roseate spoonbills, *1:* 150
Ross Ice Shelf, *1:* 165
Ross Sea, *1:* 165, 171
Rotifer, *1:* 107
Rotterdam, *2:* 370
Rowing, *2:* 343–44
Royal Bengal tigers, *1:* 97
Royal shroud bird, *3:* 461 (ill.)
Runoff, *1:* 15; *3:* 397–98
agricultural, *2:* 228; *3:* 429
urban, *2:* 229
Run-of-river systems, *2:* 216
Rural areas
as source of non-source pol-
lution, *3:* 427–28
watersheds in, *3:* 465
Rushes, *1:* 106

S

Safety, ships and, *2:* 328
Sahara Desert, *1:* 175; *3:* 391,
457
Sailboats, *2:* 342, 348, 374
Sailing, *2:* 348
St. Lawrence River, *1:* 129
St. Lawrence Seaway, *2:* 314
St. Mary's River, *2:* 314
St. Paul's Cathedral, *3:* 378
Saline lakes, *1:* 115–16; *2:* 246
Saline water, *3:* 456
Salinity, *1:* 26–27, 33, 34, 38,
142; *3:* 464–65
Salinization, *3:* 392
Salmon, *1:* 107, 144; *2:* 280
farming in raising, *2:* 281,
281 (ill.)
survival of Atlantic, *3:* 472
Salt, *1:* 138; *2:* **308–10**
getting, *2:* 308–9
making, *1:* 11 (ill.)
need for, *2:* 308

table, *2:* 308
Salt marsh, *1:* 141, 149
Salt marshgrass, *1:* 143
Salt wedge, *1:* 96
Salter Duck, *2:* 231–32
Salter, Steven, *2:* 231–32
Saltpeter, *2:* 296
Samuel B. Roberts (ship), *2:* 339
San Joaquin Valley, California,
agriculture in, *2:* 276
Sand bars, *1:* 30, 93, 97, 141,
142
Sand dunes, *3:* 385–86, 392,
415
Sandstone, *2:* 303
Sanitary sewers, *2:* 225
Santa Ana fires, *1:* 176
Santa Ana winds, *1:* 176
Sao Francisco River, *1:* 131
Saprotrophs, *2:* 240
Sargassum, 1: 82
Scaling, *2:* 212
Scallops, *1:* 69, 71, 72
Scuba diving, *2:* 234, 257, 324,
347, 349 (ill.), 355–56
Scurvy grass, *1:* 143
Sea anemones, *1:* 69, 70, 143;
2: 257
Sea cows, *1:* 78
Sea cucumbers, *1:* 68–70, 73,
74, 143; *2:* 257
Sea grasses, *2:* 257
Sea gulls, *3:* 415
Sea ice, *1:* 156, 168, 171
Sea Island Terminal, 3: 432
Sea lamprey infestation, *3:* 443
(ill.)
Sea lions, *1:* 75, 76, 157
Sea mines, *2:* 339
Sea of Cortez, *3:* 504
Sea of Galilee, *1:* 119
Sea otters, *1:* 77; *2:* 240; *3:* 475
(ill.)
Sea pigs, *1:* 68
Sea salt, *2:* 309
Sea slugs, *1:* 84
Sea stars, *1:* 69–70, 73; *2:* 257
Sea urchins, *1:* 64, 68, 69–70,
73, 77, 82, 84; *2:* 240
Sea-aster, *1:* 143

Seabed, oil and natural gas
exploration on, *3:* 477
Seafaring in ancient world, *2:*
362–64
Seafloor
depth and shape of, *1:*
49–51
features of, *1:* 51–52
reasons for studying, *2:*
260–61
studying, *2:* 261–64
Sea-lavender, *1:* 143
Seal furs, *3:* 473
Seals, *1:* 76, 157
fur, *1:* 76
Hawaiian monk, *1:* 78
Seamount, *1:* 56
Seatrout, *2:* 349
Seawalls, *3:* 386
Seawater, *1:* 11
Seaweed, *1:* **61–65,** 63 (ill.),
82
categories of, *1:* 62–64
characteristics of, *1:* 62
Secondary consumers, *1:* 25
Secondary water treatment, *2:*
226
Sedges, *1:* 106, 145
Sediment, *2:* 301; *3:* 426
Sediment contamination, *3:*
438–42
consequences of, *3:* 439,
439 (ill.)
examples of, *3:* 440–41
historical, *3:* 441
Sedimentary rock, *2:* 301
Sedimentation, *1:* 146; *2:* 367;
3: 438
Seeps, *2:* 287
Segmented worms, *1:* 69
Seine River, *1:* 129
Seismologists, *2:* 358
Seismology, *2:* 264
Selenium, *3:* 417, 418
Self-Contained Underwater
Breathing Apparatus
(SCUBA), *2:* 356
Self-supplied water system, *2:*
306
Semiarid grasslands, *1:* 176

Tornadoes, *1:* 186, 188–89

Toronto, Ontario, Canada, landfills in, *3:* 424

Torrey Canyon (ship) spill, *3:* 434

Torricelli, Evangelista, *1:* 194

Tourism
at Niagara Falls, *2:* 345–46
on oceans, *2:* 321–25

Tow surfers, *2:* 349

Toxic chemicals as nonsource pollutants, *3:* 426

Toxins, *3:* 411

Trade, *2:* 220, 373–74

Trade winds, *1:* 40, 174, 196

Trans-Antarctic mountains, *1:* 169

Transatlantic journeys, *2:* 326–27

Transform plates, *1:* 50

Transformers, *2:* 215

Transit zone, *3:* 491

Transpiration, *1:* 13–14; *2:* 276

Transportation on oceans, *2:* 325–28

Travel, *2:* 374

Treaties, *3:* 488

Tree death, *3:* 382

Triangle trade, *1:* 38

Tributary glaciers, *1:* 161

Trickling filter, *2:* 226

Trocadero Fountains in Paris, *2:* 284 (ill.)

Tropical cyclones, *1:* 189–92

Tropical depression, *1:* 190; *2:* 337

Tropical storm, *2:* 336–37

Trough, *1:* 90

Trout, *1:* 103

Truman, Harry S., *3:* 477

Tsukubai, *2:* 375

Tsunamis, *1:* 53, 53 (ill.)

Tube feet, *1:* 73

Tuna, *2:* 349
hazards of eating, *3:* 389
safety of, in diet, *3:* 439

Tundra, *1:* 156–57

Tuolumne River, damming of, *3:* 451

Tupelos, *1:* 148

Turbidite flows, *1:* 52

Turbine, *2:* 214, 374

Twilight zone, *1:* 67–68

Typhoid, *3:* 448

Typhoons, *1:* 189; *2:* 335

Typhus, *3:* 448

U

Ubangi River, *1:* 128

Ultraviolet light, *1:* 8–9

Ultraviolet rays, *2:* 270–71

UN Educational Scientific and Cultural Organization (UNESCO), *3:* 496

Underground storage tanks, groundwater contamination and, *3:* 414

Undersea World of Jacques Cousteau, *2:* 357

Undertow, *1:* 92

UNESCO-IHE Institute for Water Education, *3:* 488

United Nations, *2:* 323
Agreement on Straddling Fish Stocks and Highly Migratory Fish Stocks, *3:* 482–83
Children's Fund (UNICEF), *3:* 495 (ill.)
Convention on the Law of the Sea, *2:* 293
Development Program, *3:* 485
Environment Program (UNEP), *3:* 453, 492
Environment Program— Fresh Water Branch, *3:* 487
Environment Program— Fresh Water Unit, *3:* 485
environmental policies of, *1:* 118
Food and Agricultural Organization, *2:* 279
Framework Convention on Climate Change, *3:* 408, 496
Intergovernmental Panel on Climate Change (IPCC), *3:* 409
International Children's Fund, *3:* 485
Law of the Seas, *3:* 477–78, 489–92
Marine Protection Area, *3:* 482
role in Sub-Saharan Africa, *3:* 496
spread of species in ballast water and, *3:* 444
UNESCO, *3:* 496

Universal solvents, *1:* 10–11; *3:* 411

Updrafts, *1:* 188

Upwellings, *1:* 38–39, 40, 67

Urban areas as source of nonsource pollution, *3:* 426–27

Urban runoff, *2:* 229

Uruguay River, *1:* 131

U.S. agencies and water issues, *3:* 502–6

U.S. Army Corps of Engineers, *3:* 450

U.S. Centers for Disease Control, *3:* 487

U.S. Coast Guard, *2:* 324; *3:* 491, 491 (ill.)

U.S. Fish and Wildlife Service, *3:* 474, 506

U.S. Geological Survey, *3:* 503

U-shaped valley, *1:* 161

Uzbekistan, *1:* 117

V

Vanadium, *2:* 293

Vegetation, riparian, *3:* 468

Venice, Italy, *2:* 374; *3:* 401

Vent clams, *1:* 26

Venus flytraps, *1:* 151

Vertebrates, *1:* 43

Vibrio cholera, *3:* 444

Victoria, Australia, *1:* 129

Victoria Falls, *1:* 138, 138 (ill.)

Viruses, *2:* 297

Viscosity of water, *1:* 5

Volcanic arcs, *1:* 55

Volcanic islands, *1:* 55–56, 56 (ill.), 59, 60

Volcanic lakes, *1:* 120